NITYANANDA
is the Divine Presence

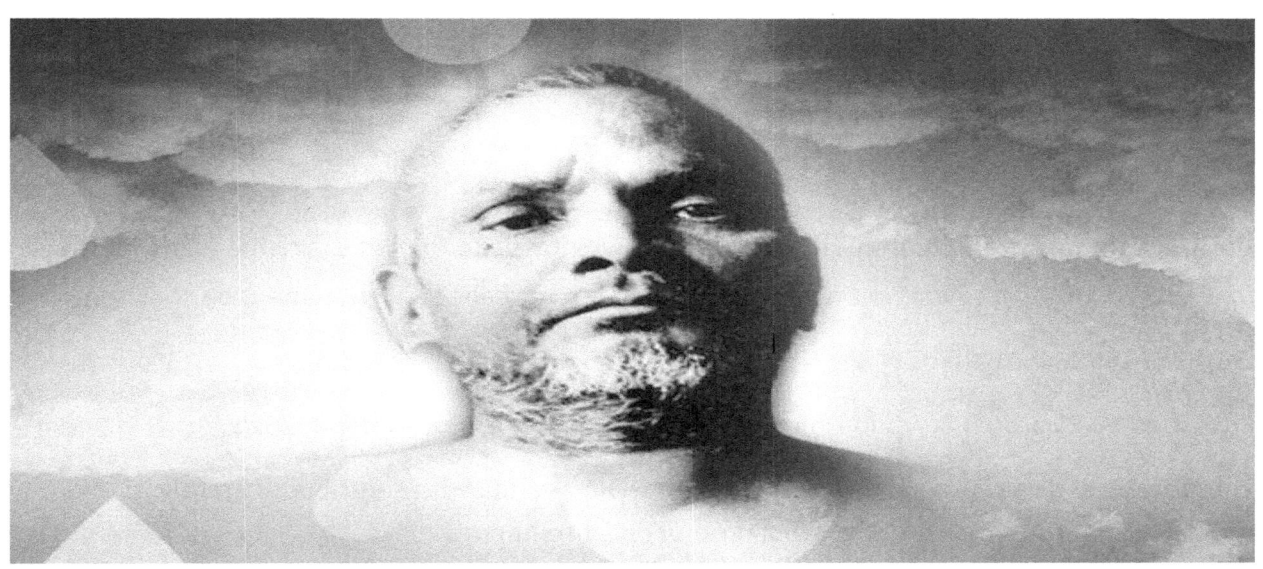

The guru is the means. – Shiva Sutra 2.6

by M. U. Hatengdi and Ricardo B Serrano, Dipl.Ac.

Bhagavan Nityananda

Nityananda is the Divine Presence

By M.U. Hatengdi and Ricardo B Serrano, Dipl.Ac.

No copyright infringement is intended. I do not own nor claim to own the rights to any of the *M.U. Hatengdi Nityananda: In Divine Presence* shared to realize enlightenment by shaktipat.

ISBN 978-0-9880502-9-7

Published by Ricardo B Serrano Holisticwebs.com Copyright, November 4, 2025

This book is dedicated to my Sadguru Bhagawan Nityananda who contributed greatly to my experience of joy and bliss upon reaching soul enlightenment.

I have included grounding with meditation, Qigong and Liu He Ba Fa with Wuji Quan to resolve health challenges.

Mantras with Heart Sutra and Vajrayana practices are included together with Wuji Quan, Liu He Ba Fa, 5 Tibetan rites to reach oneness with the Tao (emptiness). - Ricardo B Serrano, Dipl.Ac.

The predominant sign of such a yogi is joy-filled amazement. – Shiva Sutra 1.12

Shen manifests only when the heart is open. Love melts all blockages. - Master Sha

We are all buddhas. We just don't recognize it. - Mingyur Rinpoche

I practice daily Vajrayogini mantra as Guru (Deity) Yoga with Chod Damaru and Bell for efficacious healing and transformation. – Ricardo B Serrano

This book is for educational and reference purposes only. Its contents are not intended as, nor are they a substitute for, personal one-on-one diagnosis or treatment by, or consultation with, a licensed health care practitioner.

TABLE OF CONTENTS

Preface 4

Introduction 5

The Early Years 1900-1915 8

South Kanara. 1915-1936 11

Discovery in Udipi: Part 2 17

The Mangalore Days of Rail Travel 21

Kanhangad's Rock Ashram 25

Ganeshpuri--The Beginning 1936 30

The Old Ashram: Part I 32

The Old Ashram: Part II 36 The Old Ashram: Part III 41 Old Ashram 45 Old Ashram 49

The New Ashram at Kailas 52 The New Ashram at Kailas 57

Nityananda's Passing 61 Nityananda's Passing: Part II 67 Afterword Shrines of Ganeshpuri 73

Nityananda's Photographer 76 Shri Nityananda Arogyashram Hospital at Ganeshpuri 78

So Say The Stars 79 Remembering The Master 81 Remembering The Master Part II 85

Epilogue on Shaktipat 88 Distance healing and Soul Healing 90 Psoas and 5 Tibetan Rites 92

Qigong, the grandparent of Chinese Medicine 94 Kundalini syndrome and Treatment 97

TCM and Sexual Dysfunction 98 What is Kundalini Shakti? 100 Sri Yantra, Mantras, Chakras 102

Names of 32 Liu He Ba Fa movements 104 Opening and Closing the Gates of Heaven 105

Chen Tuan 115 Hara & Energetic Pathways 117 Movement as Medicine 118 Caring for Spirit 119

Three Treasures 120 Three Dantiens 123 Soul Healing 125 Wei Qi Field 130 Grounding 132

Buteyko Breathing Method 136 Love Peace Harmony 137 Mantras 138 Conclusion 139

Heart Sutra in Sanskrit 140 Neuroscience of chanting Sanskrit mantras 143 Herbs for Eyes 144

Mantra of Avalokiteshvara 145 Om Mani Padme Hum 146 Tara 148 Namo Amituofo 150

Vajra Guru Mantra 151 Guru Yoga 156 Buddha nature 158 Vajra, Bell, Damaru and Mantras 162

Books with Tibetan Book of the Dead 164 Quotes 165 Vajrayogini Mantra 167 About Author 170

Preface

As a certified Soul communicator from the Tao Academy and certified Qigong healer/teacher, I have realized after four decades of research and practice on healing and transformation, the importance of of Guru Nityananda's Shakti in my Shaktipat initiation (diksha) of others and mine to reach soul enlightenment, and Taichi Qigong's importance to prevent Kundalini syndrome.

Whenever I practice meditation and Qigong, I call upon the Soul power blessings of the Tao Source, sun, moon, planets, Mother Mary, Kuan Yin, Amituofo, 87 Buddhas and saints Father Pio, and the grace bestowing power of the *Mother Shakti Primal Guru* Bhagawan Nityananda.

I practice Six Power Techniques to purify Jing Qi Shen. They are Body Power, Soul Power, Mind Power, Sound Power, Breath Power and Tao Calligraphy Power. Body Power means that when you meditate, you use special hand and body position, like a mudra, for healing and purification. Soul Power is to say hello. You say hello to the inner souls of your systems, organs, cells, or parts of the body. You also say hello to outer souls, including Heaven, Mother Earth, the Divine, Tao, and all kinds of saints. Breath Power adds Qi to clear the Shen Qi Jing blockages. Mind Power is to visualize light. Simply visualizing golden and rainbow light is a vital technique. Sound Power is to chant healing mantras for healing and purification. Tao Calligraphy Power is to apply the healing calligraphies that Master Sha wrote. Tao Calligraphy has the Source Jing Qi Shen.

According to Master Sha, "Soul Power teaches about how the power of soul can align our soul, heart, mind and body to maintain good health, vitality, renewal, longevity, intelligence, and more." *Shen (spirit) manifests only when the heart is open. When spirit resides, Qi flows.*

What makes Bhagawan Nityananda special in the Soul Power technique? Who and what you meditate on, you become. When you meditate on the Self as the Self, you become one with Shiva, the Self of all. "Form is emptiness, emptiness is form," states the Heart Sutra. The essence of all things is emptiness. To become aware of So'ham, "I am That," is to attain oneness with the Higher Self. *May Nityananda's story by M.U. Hatengdi assist you to realize His divine presence.*

The subtle path to the Self is most easily attained through the Guru. Kabir said that the Guru makes one perfect; he unites the individual soul with Shiva. To feel the love of one's soul is the goal of yoga, according to the Bhagavad Gita.

The supreme state, which may be attained on some paths after extreme hardship, can be attained without great difficulty on the Siddha path." - Yogashikha Upanishad 1.3

Grounding, Tai chi Qigong forms like *Liu He Ba Fa, Wuji Quan* are added to Taoist / Vajrayana practices like *Guru yoga* to recognize *buddha nature*, balance the Shakti Qi flow in the body, be happy, build the Lightbody for psychic self-defense, samadhi, avoid post-kundalini syndromes.

 Ricardo B Serrano, Dipl.Ac., Tao Hands practitioner, Qigong master and Nityananda devotee

Introduction

In Nityananda's awe-inspiring presence was the heart of a compassionate mother. Already a full-fledged master in his teens and twenties, he may have been speaking of himself when he compared sadhus, or seekers of truth, to the jackfruit, whose forbidding exterior yields a honeyed sweetness when opened. From his earliest known days to the final ones in Ganeshpuri, his presence provided a sense of security for the poor and those in distress. It also gave hope to spiritual aspirants. People from all walks of life came for his blessing--yogis and renunciates, scholars and artists, politicians and civil servants, other saints and spiritual teachers. They were rich and poor, strong and sick; they came from all over India and the rest of the world.

Much about Nityananda's life remains unclear. Stories abound that put him in different places at the same time, resulting in considerable confusion about his true age or background. Not unexpectedly, his devotees listened carefully for clues or details because occasionally in casual conversation Nityananda would touch upon some incident from his past. However, he always cut short attempts to obtain details and admonished those who persisted. Some recall him making passing references to visiting Ceylon and Singapore while others say he displayed an intimate knowledge of the Himalayan region. It is said he spoke of being in Madras in 1902 when Swami Vivekananda attained samadhi.

Even his name holds a mystery. Stories of his childhood relate that his adoptive mother called him Ram. "*Nityananda*" means "*eternal bliss*" and was used to describe the state of mind he inspired. To a devotee who sat before him ecstatically repeating "**nityanand, nityanand**" as a mantra, he said, "*It is not a name--it is a state!*" In fact, early devotees called him swami, master, or sadhu while the name Nityananda was attached to him only in later years.

Clearly, a literary portrait of one such as Nityananda requires both an enormous canvas and an adept artist. Such a painting has yet to appear. Of the hundreds of thousands of people who came for his blessing, few recorded their experiences. Furthermore, Nityananda had no gospel and promoted no particular readings or spiritual practice (sadhana). The advice he gave to one person was not necessarily what he gave to another. he simply urged all devotees to *cultivate a pure mind and an intense desire for liberation* (*shuddha bhavana and shraddha*).

Nityananda's self-abnegation was complete. he wore nothing but a loincloth, and sometimes not even that. During his time in South Kanara, he only ate if food was brought to him. He had a total disregard for the physical elements including his nightly resting place. Unusual phenomena surrounded him naturally, including instances of actual healing. Yet he was never motivated by a desire for publicity and frowned on devotees who attributed to him experiences that we might describe as miracles. When pressed, he would call it the greatness of the location or the faith of the devout. "**Everything that happens, happens automatically by the will of God**," he would say.

A spiritual powerhouse, he desired only that people develop their powers to receive what he was capable of transmitting. "**While the ocean has plenty of water, it is the size of the container you bring to it that determines how much you collect**." Embodying what is ideal and pure, he would say, "**One who sees this one once will not forget**," implying that the seed of spiritual consciousness sown by his darshan would sprout in due course when correctly cultivated. He denied having an earthly guru or a particular spiritual practice. He adopted no disciples and never intended to establish an organization--although his devotees, most of them common householders, were legion. His silent, unseen mission was to offer relief to suffering humanity, whether people came or not, and to transmit a greater consciousness to those who sought higher values. **Grace emanated from his being and from his silent companionship**. A lone glimpse of his personality could shatter the ego of the proud and evoke the hope and aspirations of the genuine seeker.

Those who sought him out for material success benefited while the few who came out of pure devotion found their spiritual evolution accelerated with little or no effort on their parts. Nityananda accomplished this by becoming an obsession, if I can express it that way--a divine obsession. While living in the everyday world, devotees imbibed the spirit of the Bhagavad Gita and were gradually processed from within. They had to do very little. *Seekers and other pilgrims benefited both through the arousal of their spiritual consciousness and by capably meeting life's challenges with his help*. He converted their very breath into consciousness, bringing a gradual inner ripening, which in turn led to a restless longing for the Divine and a dispassion for worldly things. All this occurred without affecting the day-to-day efficiency in their chosen fields of endeavor. *This is how Nityananda's grace silently worked*.

His mighty spiritual force filled the South Kanara district for a few years and then moved on the Kanhangad, Gokarn, and Vajreshwari. Later he settled at Ganeshpuri, nestled at the foot of the majestic Mandakini Mountain amidst blue hills, green fields, hot springs, and the Bhimeshwar shrine. *Perhaps Nityananda chose this spot to revive the holiness of this ancient spiritual center*.

Nityananda used to say that the true reward for genuine devotion (bhakti) was a still greater dose of pure desireless devotion--not material prosperity or social success. He played and still plays the role of the eternal Krishna as Gopala, tending his allegorical herd of devotees. He guides and watches them at pasture during their earthly sojourn, helps them onward, then brings them home safely as the evening closes on their lives, either to rest permanently in *liberation (mukti)* if they have advanced enough or to start afresh by leading them to another morning of birth in a continual process of evolution. Nityananda was capable of granting all kinds of wishes but said only one thing was really worth the effort. "**One must seek the shortest route and fastest means to get back home--to turn one's inner spark into a blaze and then to merge and identify with that greater fire which ignited the spark.**"

The Early Years 1900-1915

Nityananda said it didn't matter how or where his human form came into being, that only idle curiosity prompted such useless enquiries. Nevertheless, stories gathered over the years by his devotees present a plausible picture about his birth and boyhood--even though facts often vie for veracity.

At the turn of the century, perhaps late November or early December, light from the setting sun slanted through an area of the dense jungle. On a cashew tree two crows cawed loudly to attract an elderly matriarch of the untouchable caste collecting firewood.

Curious, she followed the ruckus--and under a bush discovered a baby boy with skin the color of ripe wheat carefully wrapped in a white cloth. Now, the old woman already had a large family but remembered that Unniamma'a mother wanted to adopt a child for her barren daughter. So she dutifully picked up the infant and took him home.

The following morning she proceeded straight to the village of Uniamma's mother, who accepted the baby with great joy. To seal the bargain, Unniamma's mother gave the old woman ten pounds of rice and then hurried to Pantalayini near Calicut, in an area known as Koilande. There her daughter worked in the neighboring temples as well as in the household of Ishwar Iyer, a respected lawyer. Unniamma gratefully adopted the baby and named him Ram.

At about eighteen months of age, Ram developed liver troubles. And even though Mr. Iyer hired for him the best ayurvedic practitioner, the baby's condition worsened. He grew thin and his stomach became distended. Because he often cried through the night, Unniamma's landlord finally demanded that she get rid of him. Too agitated to go to work the next day, she instead took her ailing son out for some fresh air. As she walked, she suddenly saw a tall dark-skinned stranger carrying a large satchel. The distraught mother, thinking he was a physician, approached and begged him to help her child. As if expecting her, he removed a packet from his bag and instructed her to mix its contents with the flesh of a freshly killed crow fried in clarified butter (ghee). She should then administer a small dose to Ram each morning before he had eaten. Also, she should rub Ram's skin with the crow's blood. At this very moment, a toddy tapper* walked by and handed her the crow he carried in his right hand. Astonished, she looked up to thank the two men--but they had vanished.

Sap from the toddy palm is collected by toddy tappers for making a fermented beverage called arrack.

Unniamma started the prescribed treatment at once, and the child recovered in a short time. The crow's blood, however, permanently turned his skin a dark blue hue. Years later when questioned about any aspect of his background, Nityananda often quipped that a crow came and a crow left. He also said that his skin was not black but blue-black (Krishnavarna).

A devout man, Mr. Iyer worshipped the Sun deity Bharga--and he loved Ram, for whom he felt a strong mystical attraction. When Unniamma died, the kindly man brought the six-year-old into his household and proceeded to take him everywhere. This included the famous Krishna temple at Guruvayur where, alone together, Ram revealed an esoteric understanding that both astounded the older man and satisfied his spiritual hunger. A famous astrologer told him the child was an incarnate personality and that he was blessed to have him as ward and companion. This caused talk among colleagues and friends who were shocked to see the respected Brahmin's attachment to the lower caste boy.

The young Ram was mischievous and loved to pull pranks, and his foster father asked friends and servants to keep an eye on him. For instance, he would dive into a neighboring temple's water tank, stay under water for a long time, and then run off dripping water everywhere. He would also get up by four in the morning and insist that other household members do likewise, taking their baths and applying sacred ash to their foreheads. He refused to attend school but agreed to learn subjects like Malayalam, English, Sanskrit, and arithmetic from Mr. Iyer.

One story tells of Ram tricking a local snake-charmer who ran a dishonest money-making operation. Under cover of darkness his cohorts would release several cobras into the compound of a selected household. The snake-charmer would then appear the following morning to offer his assistance. Calling the snakes, he would depart with both the reptiles and his fee. However, trying the scheme one day on Mr. Iyer--the snakes would not heed their call. The baffled snake-charmer soon noticed Ram in the background giggling. He had rendered the trickster's mantra ineffective. The boy then let him collect his snakes with the warning never to bother the Iyer household again.

When Ram was around ten years old, Mr. Iyer decided to take him on a pilgrimage to the city of Benares and other holy places. As usual the two traveled alone together. On this trip the boy reportedly granted to his companion many divine visions. Along the way Ram took leave of his tearful foster father, promising to see him again. Exactly where the young Master went, nobody knows. However, it is thought that he traveled the northern regions, for some sources indicate his renown in the Himalayas as a great kundalini yogi. Six years later Ram returned. Having had the boy in thoughts for days and realizing that he had really come, Mr. Iyer ecstatically repeat *nityananda, nityananda*! Eternal bliss! And this, of course, became the Master's popular name.

Note that Nityananda was away from Ishwar Iyer from the ages of 10 to 16 years of age. By the time he returned at 16, he was known in the entire Himilayan region as a kundalini Mahayogi.

Shortly thereafter Mr. Iyer performed his youngest daughter's marriage ceremony at the temple in Guruvayur. There, the entire family felt the deity's presence in Nityananda. The youth then took his foster father to receive the darshan of Ananteshwar and Lord Krishna in Udipi. (Later Nityananda would indicate to devotees his previous association with the ancient Ananteshwar temple by remarking that he had been present when it was built some 400 years earlier). Mr. Iyer soon fell gravely ill and, resting in Nityananda's lap, asked to see Bharga, the divine object of his lifelong worship. The young Master granted his wish and Mr. Iyer died. To express his love and gratitude before he died, the man bequeathed some assets to his adopted son. The young Nityananda refused the gift.

So ends the chapter entitled "The Early Years."

South Kanara 1915-1936

After performing last rites for his foster father, the young Nityananda took off again, this time to wander South India and beyond. Over the years devotees heard him mention stowing away on a cargo ship, probably boarding in Madras, to work as a stoker boy and sailing to Ceylon, Rangoon, and Singapore. He spoke of being a laborer on a Burmese rubber plantation and some people think he visited Japan.

He once laughingly recounted an incident during the First World War when, as an army conscript, he was declared medically unfit because the doctor could not find his heartbeat or pulse. He is said to have been in Madras when Swami Vivekananda left India in 1896 and again when he died in 1902. In the mid-1950s, when asked if he would travel abroad like certain other Indian swamis, he answered, "**One only has to go if unable to see places or deal with people from here.**"

The following is one of the few authenticated stories from this time period. The scene is Palani Temple where Lord Subramanya, a brother of Lord Ganesh in Hindu mythology, is the presiding deity. We must visualize Nityananda in those days looking like an eccentric wanderer, his wire-thin body healthy and glowing. Late one morning he was ascending the last few steps to the shrine when the attendant priest, having just locked the doors after morning worship, was descending. Nityananda asked him to re-open the doors and wave a ritual light and incense (arati) before the deity. Astonished that a vagrant would dare make such a request, the priest curtly told Nityananda that the time for morning worship was over.

Nityananda continued on. The priest, expecting him to walk around the shrine and worship at the Muslim altar in the back, was not concerned until he heard the temple bells ringing.

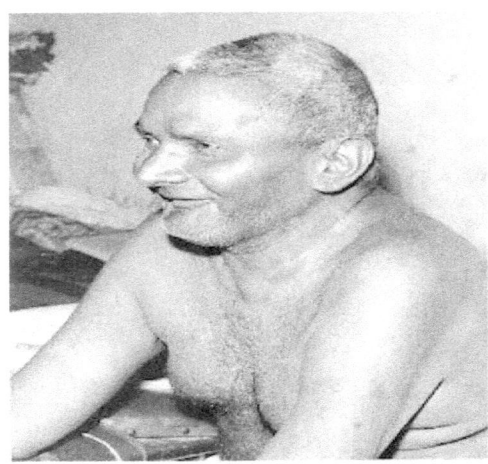

Turning, he was astonished to see the doors open, Nityananda sitting in the deity's place, and arati being waved before him by invisible hands. The vision vanished at once and Nityananda left the shrine to stand on one leg for some time, steadily gazing upward. Coins poured at his feet, offered, some say, by pilgrims, while others say by an unseen source. In any case, he was accorded all the honors of a Master. When the surrounding pilgrims begged him to stay, he refused and instructed them to use the money to provide a daily meal of rice porridge to visiting renunciates. It was later learned that local sanyasis had been praying for this very thing.

Leaving the Pantalayani area, the young master encountered an errant gang of youths in Cannanore. One of them wrapped a kerosene-soaked rag on the Master's left hand and set it ablaze. Nityananda didn't resist physically but instead transferred the burning sensation to the one who had attacked him. Crying out in pain, the unexpected victim begged for mercy. As Nityananda extinguished the fire on his own hand, the sensation in the other's subsided. Years later, he explained to devotees:

"Those with inner wisdom (jnanis) do not go in for miracles. However, this does not mean that a burning rag tied to their hands does not hurt. They suffer like anyone else but have the capacity to detach their minds completely from the nerve centers. In this way they might remember the pain only once or twice a day."

At some point the young Nityananda began appearing regularly around Mangalore and other parts of South Kanara. Again, extant stories make a clear chronology impossible.

Now approaching his early twenties and wearing only a loincloth and often not even that, he lived a life of great simplicity in the region's rocks, caves, and forests. It was a familiar sight to see him standing stiffly in a tree before the local Mahakali temple at Kaup. People would gather below his tree, mingling without regard for caste or creed, and the Master would shower them with leaves that recipients prized for their healing power. One day, after the crowd dispersed, a blind man stayed behind and begged for help, explaining the burden he was to his family. After a while, saying nothing, Nityananda climbed down and rubbed the man's eyes with leaves from the tree. The man arose next morning to find his sight restored.

Another time, in Manjeshwar, there was a man whose mother suffered from a painful lump in her leg. When medicines brought no relief, he went to Nityananda, who was standing as usual in a tree. He said, "This one knows and is there." The son, however, did not understand. He went home and returned with his mother in a carriage--but the Master had vanished. After searching in vain, they went home to find him descending from their attic. He silently massaged the astonished woman's leg for several minutes and then departed. The mother recovered completely.

Yet another story tells of a widow who brought her six-year old daughter. Nityananda said, "But the child has been blind from birth. Why do you insist I change this? Let the child say what she wants." The child then said, "I would like to see my mother once." The Master said nothing. After a while he asked them to leave. It was the mother's custom to first bathe the child, put her in a safe spot, and them perform her own ablutions. That day, as she returned, her daughter jumped up and shouted that she saw her. Their joy lasted only minutes before the blindness returned. It seems Nityananda chose not to interfere with the child's destiny.

One morning on a busy road near a village that some say was Panambur, the Master strode along at his usual rapid pace. Coming upon a pregnant woman, he stopped suddenly and squeezed her breasts. The woman did not resist but when outraged people began rushing toward him, Nityananda continued walking. he quickly outdistanced them, shouting that this time the child would live. The woman hurriedly told onlookers that her three previous children had died after their first breast feeding. Shortly thereafter, her baby was born and survived. A village delegation was organized to thank him and the story spread.

This time Nityananda's unconventional behavior became clarified after the fact, but it was not always the case. For example, prior to 1920 he was often seen in the early morning hours waiting for a cow to pass. Following it, he would catch the droppings and swallow them before they touched the ground. Another story says he came to the flooded Pavanje River during the monsoon season. When the boatman refused to ferry him, the Master simply walked across. When in 1953 someone asked him to explain the river incident, he said: "True, the Pavanje River was in flood when this one walked across and the boatman would not venture out. But there was no motive-- it was just the mood of the moment. The only meaning was that the boatman was deprived of his half anna.

One must live in the world like common men. Once established in infinite Consciousness, one becomes silent and, knowing all, goes about as if knowing nothing. Although he may be doing many things in several places, he outwardly appears as if he is simply a witness of life—like a spectator at the cinema. He is unaffected by events, whether pleasant or unpleasant. The ability to forget everything and remain detached is the highest state possible."*

*Never forget this second paragraph: It is read here every day; it is not just a statement, it is the way to live life.

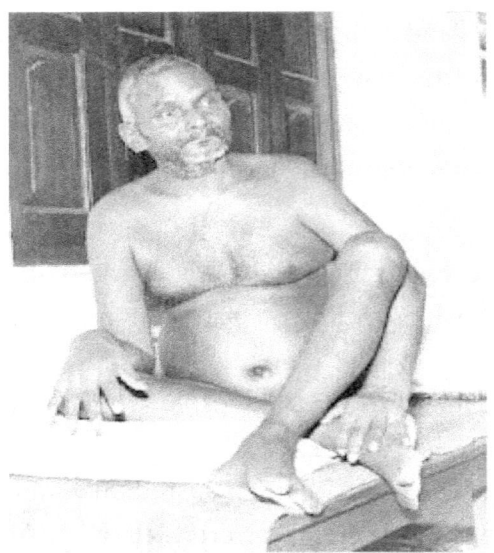

Nityananda was indifferent to social conventions, often going naked in the early days. When some people objected and reported the matter, he was taken before a local magistrate. As always, a crowd followed. When ordered to wear a loincloth, the Master reportedly replied, "To cover which with what?" The magistrate then instructed a policeman to tie a loincloth around him--but it wouldn't stay tied. Finally, in exasperation the magistrate ordered a tailor to secure it with needle and thread. The tailor was also a devotee and pleaded with Nityananda to let it stay in place. He complied, it remained, and thereafter a loincloth was his usual article of clothing.

Nityananda passed most of the time around 1915 on the beach at Kanhangad, lying on the hot sand and gazing at the sun. A devotee who as a boy often accompanied his father to the town said, years later, that it was impossible to approach Nityananda in the afternoons. The intense heat discouraged everybody from walking on the sand. Sometimes he sat from morning until evening on the blazing hot rock where his first temple would be built in 1963.*

*This was the first temple built in his honor after his mahasamadhi in 1961.

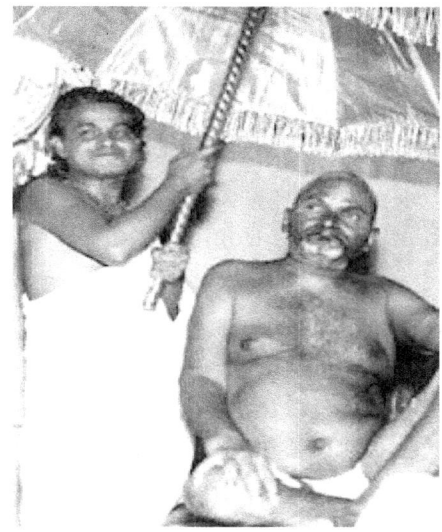

By 1918, the tiny village of Udipi was already a well-known center of pilgrimage. Here people could visit the Krishna temple, the birthplace of the third great teacher Madhvacharya, at the ancient Ananteshwar temple, and the area called Ajjara Kadu (or "Grandfather's Wood").

Two friends strolled together here every evening, always ending their walk by circling the two temples. Once, passing the Krishna temple, they were drawn to a thin young man who stood among the sanyasis in the outer corridor. At that moment the youth turned to face the wall and refused to be acknowledged. The friends both agreed that this was an uncommon holy man. Several days later they came upon him, this time at an entrance to the temple. Seeing them, Nityananda began to laugh uncontrollably. He did so for a prolonged period, and in a way that Mr. Bhat later said seemed to come from the depths of his being.

Weeks passed before they saw him again, this time sitting by himself outside the ancient Ananteshwar temple. Dr. Kombarbail caught hold of both his hands and asked him who he was and where he came from. He addressed him in Hindi, Kanarese, and English in quick succession. Nityananda had apparently been observing silence for some time because it took great effort for him to speak--but he did so in fluent English, Hindi, and Konkani, which was the local language. He ended by repeating, "*Nityananda, Nityananda*!" The two men realized he referred to his blissful state and this is why devotees from those early days called him "Sadhu" (holy man) or "Swami."

Mr. Bhat, having performed his father's anniversary ceremony that morning, invited the sadhu to his house for a special meal. To his delight, the Master readily accepted and ate his food from a plantain leaf and discarded the leaf himself. This was the last time he was observed to eat with his own hands. Subsequently, he ate only when fed by devotees. Even water he allowed devotees to pour into his mouth, indicating after a few swallows that he was satisfied. [Mr. Bhat and Dr. Kombarbail became life-long devotees.]

Nityananda stayed in Udipi for a time, often visiting Mangalore and Kaup, but he stayed nowhere for long. Mrs. T. Sitabai, Captain Hatengdi's primary source concerning these days, felt the young Master was pulled mystically by devotees thinking of him or experiencing some stress. She said Nityananda would often leave Udipi abruptly without indicating his destination and then reappear some time later. For instance, one afternoon at half past three, he suddenly stood up and said he would return soon. And in fact, by five o'clock he was back. No one inquired nor did he indicate where he had been. Two days later a devotee arrived from Mangalore to say how in the early afternoon of that particular day his fellow devotees were longing to see him. Within minutes, he appeared. As on other occasions, no one asked how he covered the fifty-odd miles to the seaport town. They were content knowing that, when needed, Nityananda often came.

Mrs. Krishnabai, an early devotee, describes a similar incident. It was to be Nityananda's first visit to her house in Mangalore--but when he arrived, he immediately turned and walked away with his usual speed. A crowd watched as Mrs. Krishnabai's husband and a friend tried to stop him physically. However, the sadhu easily swept both men along with him for a quarter mile before suddenly saying "She stopped me," and agreeing to return. it seemed that Mrs. Krishnabai's anguish was too great for him to ignore.

In the beginning, to keep him from the Krishna temple, street urchins in Udipi pelted the young Nityananda with stones. Oddly, those finding their mark were transformed into jewels (or sweets, according to similar stories from Kanhangad). But those who scrambled to retrieve such treasures found only stones. When, after several days of this phenomenon, a pile of stones appeared at the feet of Krishna's temple statue, the matter was reported to the elderly swami in charge. Recognizing that Nityananda was no ordinary sadhu, he at once ordered everyone to treat him with respect.

Throughout his life, Nityananda was a friend of beggars, the lowest castes, and the poor. He would let the money left at his feet by devotees accumulate and then order a feast for the poor, insisting on the best ingredients. Even when resources were scarce, food was still miraculously abundant. This became a regular event wherever he wandered, and in later years he only accepted invitations from hosts willing to feed the needy. The Master himself liked to dish up regional specialties for his guests with his two huge hands-like Mangalore's iddlies cooked in jackfruit leaves. To this day in Ganeshpuri, feeding the local poor children (known as Bal Bhojan in India) still occurs in Nityananda's name.

Among those who sought his company in Udipi was a wealthy landlord's only son. The father, however, considered the Master to be a dangerous eccentric and became alarmed when the schoolboy began giving money to help feed the poor. He decided to hire two assassins to kill Nityananda, a practice not uncommon for people of means in those days. In this instance, because of his intended victim's frequent disappearances, the father thought the abduction would go unnoticed.

One afternoon, while sitting on a veranda, the Master suddenly smiled, stood up, and disappeared down the lane. His devotees quickly followed--and found him held by one man and about to be stabbed by another. They overpowered the assassins, attracted the police, and only then noticed that the man who had wielded the knife was in excruciating pain, his arm frozen in its attack position. At Nityananda's touch, the man's arm dropped painlessly to his side.

As the assailants were taken to jail, the protesting Nityananda followed and requested their release. The police refused. He then sat down and remained there for three days without food or water while his devotees negotiated with officials. Eventually, the prisoners were released. It is said that they became devotees of the Master and that even the local officials developed a high regard for the eccentric sadhu.

Discovery in Udipi: Part 2

Late one night, a devotee was told by alarmed women of his household that Nityananda was running a high temperature. However, the sadhu refused to leave his refuge, the filthy cattle shed, repeating, "The medicine is here." Thinking him delirious, the host pleaded with his guest until he finally agreed to move to the veranda.

Hurrying to the only chemist in Udipi, the devotee returned with a bottle of reddish-brown mixture for his fever. Nityananda shook the bottle, handed it back, and said, "What is this? Look at it." Removing the cork, the devotee found to his consternation that the liquid had changed color and now smelled like urine. The Master laughed and said it was no better than what was in the cattle shed.

This was the monsoon season when people customarily collected rainwater in drums placed below the eaves of their houses. The night of his fever, Nityananda suddenly began to gulp down the rainwater in his host's drum. Witnesses could not believe the amount of water he drank. When he finished, he turned and said, "The fever is gone." And it was.

Indian families used to perform a special ceremony six days after a birth to honor the goddess of destiny, who was thought to write the newborn's future that night. On one occasion, and six days after a devotee's wife had given birth, Nityananda entered her room, swallowed the dried umbilical cord, and left. When questioned about his behavior, he replied that this particular family had lost many children in infancy but that the new baby would survive.

Sometimes Nityananda humorously acted out a charade to describe an upcoming visitor. One morning he slung an empty shopping bag over his left shoulder, bending slightly from the weight; in his right hand he pretended to carry something light. He then walked up and down the room before suddenly taking off for a neighbor's house. Following, perplexed devotees saw a man pacing the street looking for someone. He carried a heavy bag on his left shoulder and a water container in his right hand. By now the Master was sitting on his neighbor's veranda. Approaching the steps, the stranger stopped and they gazed silently at one another for a long time. Finally, the Master stood up and the man walked away.

The man remained in the area for a while. When devotees asked about the encounter, he described himself as a Krishna devotee from Uttar Pradesh. Having had a vision that Krishna was present in living form in Udipi, he traveled to the village, where he felt drawn vibrationally to that particular neighborhood. Unsure of the exact house, he had wandered around for some time before Nityananda appeared. He added, "I said nothing to him because with one look I knew why I was there. Tomorrow I will leave blissfully happy having received darshan of Krishna."

Wistfully, Mrs. Sitabai related an event that happened when she was both a new devotee and newly married. One day Nityananda picked up a coconut and offered it to her. Now, it is rare and auspicious to receive a coconut from a holy person. Moreover, it is thought to keep widowhood at bay, and a married woman would traditionally extend the skirt of her sari with both hands to receive it. But the young Mrs. Sitabai hesitated. She considered her high-caste birth and whether it was acceptable for her to receive such a thing from a casteless sadhu. He waited patiently for several minutes and when she did not accept the offering, she threw it away-- perhaps deciding that her fate held too strong a pull on her. Three months later, her husband died. And she would always wonder whether she might have been spared widowhood had her faith been stronger.

In the early twenties, Nityananda frequently visited Mrs. Krishnabai's Mangalore residence, which included several small rental houses. In those days residents used a row of simple lavatories situated at the edge of the compound. Each morning municipal workers would arrive with a cart to collect the night soil and take it away.

We know that Nityananda's eating habits were as unpredictable as his movements. Only partaking of food and water that was fed to him, he would appear unexpectedly at Mrs. Krishnabai's door looking hopeful. Sometimes the family had already eaten and there might only be a few morsels of rice to put in his mouth. But this always seemed to satisfy him.

One morning, however, compound residents were horrified to see the Master by the lavatories sitting among piles of night soil. Always an early riser, he appeared to have collected the matter with his own hands and formed the mounds, covering himself from head to toe in the process. He held a bamboo scale in his hand and when anyone passed, he said, "Bombay halwa [Halwa is an Indian sweet confection]. Very tasty! Would you like some?" Then he would raise the scale as if to weigh out the desired quantity. He sat there all day, embarrassing everyone, even taking his afternoon nap there. When Mrs. Krisnabai finally approached, he said, "You feed me, don't you? But would you also feed me this?" Abashed, she turned away.

That evening Mrs. Krishnabai was afraid he would drop by the hose without washing. She asked two of the assembled devotees to wait at the door to prevent him from bringing the filth inside. And promptly at seven o'clock, he appeared at the back door. In those days he could be prevailed upon, at least in some matters, and the two devotees ended up taking him to the baths for a thorough scrubbing. Later, sitting with his devotees, Nityananda held out his palm and asked if they could smell the "fine Parisian perfume." He never explained the meaning of the day's events--and they never asked.

The next morning Mrs. Krishnabai found all the compound's residents lined up before the Master asking his pardon. Drawing one of them aside, she inquired what had happened. The man explained: Earlier that week while discussing how Nityananda only at food fed to him, someone had joked about offering him night soil. He went on, "We now realize how wrong we were and that such a Master can find nourishment in anything--even filth. Therefore, we seek his forgiveness."

The Mangalore Days of Rail Travel

1923-1933

Nityananda loved trains. He traveled frequently by rail and even established his Kanhangad ashram beside the tracks in 1925. When he was in Mangalore he would settle into one of the empty boxcars shunted aside at the station, and here devotees could find him.

One afternoon Mrs. Krishnabai, learning of his arrival, hurried off to receive darshan. She quickly returned home to greet a relative who had come for a visit. A sanyasi, he asked her to take him to see Nityananda the next day. Later, as they stepped down from the boxcar, Mrs. Krishnabai turned to the Master and said, "I came yesterday in such a hurry, never dreaming that I would also be able to return today." But Nityananda replied, "Who are you to decide?"

He often rode the trains between Mangalore and Kanhangad. Once a railroad official who was new to the route ordered him to disembark for not having a ticket. As he made no sign to obey, the official forcibly removed him at Manjeshwar. Submitting to the rough handling, Nityananda proceeded to make himself comfortable on a station bench. But when its departure time came-- the train didn't move. Minutes ticked by and people waited expectantly. Finally, come passengers told the official that it was unwise to treat this particular sadhu so harshly. Devotees then took Nityananda on board and the train began moving. When it reached Kanhangad, however, it went past the station and stopped where his ashram currently stands. The Master descended wearing around his neck a garland made of hundreds of tickets. He handed the garland to the same official, asking him to take as many as he wanted.

Shamefaced, the man said it would not happen again. Nityananda then jumped the small ditch and strode off toward the jungle. Again, the train would not move, and devotees ran after him for help. He retraced his steps, slapped the engine, and told it to get going. And the train did, going in reverse back to the station it had bypassed earlier.

Probably due to such incidents, Nityananda had free run of the trains. Engineers welcomed him into their engine cars and even blew a saluting whistle when passing his ashram, a custom still followed today. It is said that throughout the late 1920's the Master always had a punched ticket attached to the string of his loincloth.

Swami Chidananda of Rishikesh recalled that, as a child traveling south by train from Mangalore, he once noticed a commotion at a wayside station. Peering out the window, he watched a reed-thin Nityananda toss biscuits and sweets from a vendor's tray to a crowd of delighted children. Then, giving the pleased vendor a currency note from his loincloth, he climbed into the engine car as the departing whistle blew.

Udipi residents watched him catch cow droppings to put on his head. Then, whistling like a locomotive, he would chug away down the road like a child.

And he used a railroad analogy in his last public talk. This was on Guru Purnima, July 27, 1961, twelve days before his passing. He addressed the assembled devotees at some length, talking about the energy required to pull a train up a hill and of a spiritual seeker's need to stay firmly on the proverbial tracks.

Nityananda traveled constantly between Mangalore, Kanhangad, Udipi, Akroli and other villages. His appearances, generally unexpected, seemed magical. One day, thinking him in Mangolore, six or seven Udipi devotees decided to pay a social call on a neighboring village. Approaching a wooded area along the way, they were astonished to see the Master sitting under a tree. The devotees immediately changed their plans and decided to spend the evening there with him. When Nityananda shouted at them to keep their distance, they sat down some twenty feet away. They could hear him talking and, as their eyes adjusted to the gloom, they saw a cobra coiled at his side. It was to the snake that the Master spoke in Konkani, and it seemed to nod in the affirmative. The only words the devotees could clearly distinguish were, "Are you three comfortable?" and they inferred that there were two other snakes nearby. After a while, Nityananda patted the cobra on its hood and watched it disappear.

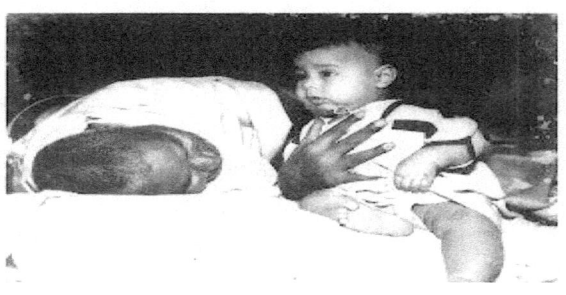

As witnessed, Nityananda's behavior could be difficult to interpret. While a person might think that he or she had been forced to undergo a minor difficulty, later reflection would indicate that something more serious had been miraculously averted. Many devotees experienced this as we see in the following story.

The young Master often visited the home of a devoted Mangalore woman. Once he told her married daughter, "She is this one's mother; yours is here," indicating himself. One evening Nityananda walked into the kitchen as the devotee was cooking over the mud hearth. He pulled out a burning piece of firewood, hit her over the head with it, and quickly left. Her children were outraged but the mother advised patience, and an explanation was neither sought nor provided. Twelve months later, while casting the family's horoscope, an astrologer from Kerala expressed his astonishment at finding the lady of the house alive. He said his calculations showed that she should have died the previous year. That was when her family realized that the Master's blow had changed his devotee's destiny.

Mrs. Lakshmibai was a young, widowed domestic in the employ of Tulsiamma, a well-known devotee. The young servant was devoted to Nityananda as well. One day she was asked to prepare the evening meal early because Tulsiamma hoped to bring Nityananda home to dinner. Now, Mrs. Lakshmibai had always nursed an intense desire to feed him with her own hands, having watched other devotees do so. Overcoming her shyness, she asked if she might accompany her mistress in case the Master refused their offer. But like Cinderella, she was told to stay home and make the house ready. So saying, Tulsiamma left.

Finishing her preparations, Mrs. Lakshmibai went outside to gather fresh plantain leaves for serving the food. Still musing over her disappointment, she slowly cut a leaf and heard an unexpected rustle in the tree above. Nityananda climbed down, asked if the meal was ready, and proceeded her to the house. The overjoyed servant ran to wash her hands and began to feed the Master. At that moment Tulsiamma returned. Her words "I couldn't find him" were rapidly followed by her amazed laughter at finding the Master already enjoying dinner at her house.

Appayya Alva was a prosperous South Kanara landlord renowned and sometimes feared for his ability to materialize objects through the strength of mantra. This powerful mantravadi, with a wave of his hands, could produce foreign cigarettes, exotic fruits, or flowers by the armful. However, when they materialized in one place, they disappeared elsewhere--often from the Car Street flower market in Mangalore where attendants would suddenly wail, "my flowers are gone!" And so it was that many people suffered from his exhibitions. Alva was also a vain and arrogant man. One time, when his presence at a concert went unrecognized, he caused the singer to temporarily lose his voice.

Eventually Alva encountered Nityananda. One May day in 1923 Mr. M.A.K. Rao, an esteemed Manjeshwar citizen, was celebrating a niece's wedding. At Mr. Rao's insistence, Nityananda was invited and seated in a place of honor. It was while the soon-to-marry couple placed garlands around the Master's neck that Alva made his entrance. He immediately belittled the host for honoring the young sadhu as if he were a divine being and boasted that he would prove his point. Reciting a mantra, he then rolled a tobacco leaf between his hands and forced it into the Master's mouth. Nityananda chewed and swallowed the leaf as if it had been offered by a devotee. As people watched, he perspired slightly--but Alva suddenly sank to the ground mortally ill. He died three days later in the Government Wenlock Hospital.

Twenty years later Nityananda was asked about this incident. he played down the connection between the tobacco leaf and Alva's death, saying that the man had misused his considerable mantric powers to bring suffering to the poor and misery to the weak. He said that divine forces had stopped the abuse and he called the tobacco leaf insignificant. He then revealed that, before dying, Alva asked to see Nityananda but his family refused to send for him.

In 1923, at the height of the monsoon season, Nityananda walked through the marketplace in Bantwal. By this time he was a known figure in the district, recognized by devotees and skeptics alike. As it was raining heavily, he entered a shop and stood in the corner with the servants and porters. The shopkeepers ordered him to leave, taunting him about his great powers. When Nityananda asked to stay, they laughed and splashed him with water. Only then did he walk away, sadly saying, "It seems God has decided that only Mother Ganga [Nityananda's reference to Mother Ganga was the Ganges river]. can wash away the sins here." The shopkeepers retorted, "Let her come. That way we can perform our ablutions without going to her banks!"

Even as they spoke, the swollen Netravati River rumbled and began to swallow the village. It was one of the worst floods in South Kanara, and Bantwal was destroyed. A span of the Ullal railroad bridge was damaged so badly that train service was disrupted for months. People still talk about Nityananda pulling many poor victims from the swirling waters.

Perhaps the most extraordinary incident of this period occurred in a devotee's house in Falnir just before sunset. While they sat before him in meditation, those present were suddenly disturbed by a blinding flash of light on the wall behind Nityananda. They opened their eyes to find him motionless on his knees in a yoga posture (veera- padmasana) with his eyes closed. Afraid to touch him, they lit lamps and tried to see if he still breathed. Finding no signs of life, they decided that he had taken mahasamadhi and invited people to come for their last darshan. Most devotees soon returned to their homes, some sad and disappointed that the young sadhu left them, some hopeful that he would return, and some thinking that he had overdone his breathing exercise. Mrs. Krisnabai was one of the few who stayed behind, maintaining a vigil throughout the night and following day. That afternoon Nityananda suddenly moved. He stretched his limbs and was immediately helped to a bed. He wore a strange look and recognized no one for quite some time. After questioning, he admitted that he had gone for good--but five divine beings persuaded him to return, saying that it was too soon. During his remaining years, the Master never spoke of it again.

Kanhangad's Rock Ashram

1925-1936

Before leaving South Kanara, around 1925 Nityananda began spending long periods in Kanhangad. Initially he chose the jungle area called Guruvana for his rock ashram. [Devotees believe Nityananda was found abandoned here as an infant. Guruvana lies several miles from a second temple that was dedicated to Nityananda in 1966.] Evidence indicates that he inhabited a certain jungle cave where he had discovered a skeleton seated in a lotus position, surrounded by pots and other personal effects.

Nityananda is said to have disposed of it in an unknown manner. This story came from an elderly woman in Kerala who fed Nityananda during this time. She also said that at the rear of the cave was once an entrance, now blocked off, to a hall that could seat several hundred people. Nityananda often said that beyond the hill in Guruvana were many saints in samadhi. Some people believe he was associated with this particular spot in a previous incarnation and the skeleton was either his own or of someone he knew.

Regardless, it was here that Nityananda struck a rock from which spring water has flowed ever since. Nearby he placed eight stone balls thought to represent the occult powers achieved through yogic discipline (siddhis) and a tank to collect the spring water. When B.H. Mehta built the temple in 1966 he added a spout, called Papanashini Ganga, for the water to pass through. For many years Swami Janananda tended the area, converting the jungle into a spiritual paradise. He rebuilt the tank as a well, constructed a road to the temple, and replaced the stone balls with eight stone linga-like structures. he also made a small shrine for Malbir, the area's protecting spirit.

Nityananda's work on the Kanhangad fort started around 1927. First he built a road, still used, from the traveler's bungalow up to the rock temple and ashram. he then began clearing the jungle growth that overran the dilapidated compound. Historically the site belonged to a long lineage of chieftains. At one time it was in the hands of the Tulu dynasty who ruled from Mangalore to Kanhangad. Nityananda began the project to the consternation of local authorities who pestered him with questions about his activities and whether he had permission. The Master always responded that he was clearing the jungle for their future offices, a prediction that eventually came to pass.

Once the fort was cleared of overgrowth, Nityananda turned his attention to the rock itself, which is where the temple erected to him in 1963 now stands. he wanted caves hewn from the rock and, without engineers or blueprints, directed everything down to the most minute detail. The task was formidable. Using no equipment, workers carved out the caves by hand. Within three years some forty caves stood ready, properly cemented and plastered inside and out. Most were large enough for a person to sit and rest. There were six entrances; three faced east and three faced west, resulting in continuous light in the passages from sunrise to sunset.

With work proceeding on the interior of the compound, Nityananda often worked on the exterior. He made the steps and lingas with his own hands. Following a visit to the caves in 1945, Captain Hatengdi asked him about their symbolism. He replied that they represented the brain and its six passages. At one point a well was dug within the cave complex, but Nityananda later ordered it closed. Today an outside well is the current ashram's main water source.

Local laborers received their pay at the end of each day. Swami Janananda recalled that the foreman usually collected the money from beneath a tree. But sometimes the workers filed past Nityananda. Opening and then closing his empty fist, he would drop the exact wages into each recipient's hand.

One day a delegation of local authorities arrived and asked him about the source of these wages. Without a word, Nityananda led them to the waterlogged field beside the rock, dived in, and emerged with a bagful of currency. He told the astonished men that a crocodile in the depths always supplied the amount he needed. He then added that they were free to find it themselves; otherwise, he offered to bring up the beast for them to see.

Feeling that they had been ridiculed by this yogi in a loincloth, the angry delegates immediately reported the unauthorized construction. They told Mr. Gawne, the British tax official in South Kanara, that a crazy sanyasi was paying workers with money from unknown and mysterious sources. It seemed that Mr. Gawne had heard of Nityananda's remarkable activities in Mangalore and decided to see for himself. Arriving at the Kanhangad railway station, he proceeded on horseback accompanied by his dog along the road built by the Master. Reaching the rock compound, he stopped and looked around. Nityananda was in a cave below the ruins on the fort's south side. here, the dog soon discovered him and started to bark.

He emerged from the cave and Mr. Gawne, still on horseback, asked him why he was doing all this work and for whom. Nityananda replied in English, "Not for this one (meaning himself). If you want it, you may have it." As the words were uttered, a change came over the British official. Turning, he ordered the local authorities to leave Nityananda alone and allow him free rein of the site. He added that the source of funds was of no concern as long as no one complained of being swindled or robbed. Imagine his surprise when, riding his horse back to the station, he saw the words "Gawne Road" on the newly erected road sign.

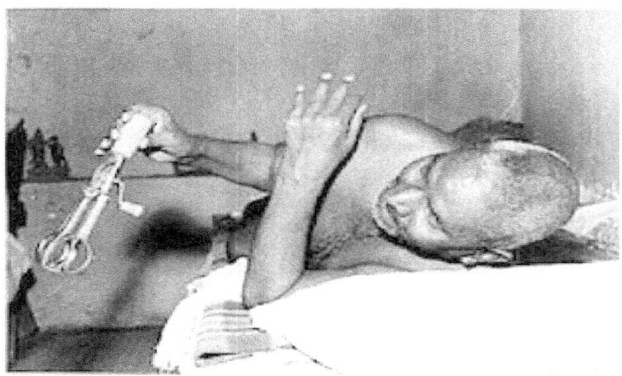

One cloudy day in the monsoon season, Nityananda was stretched out on the rock. Suddenly, a man approached and demanded to have God revealed to him. The Master told him to go away. When the man became more bombastic, Nityananda grabbed his umbrella and pointed it at the man's toe. Devotees said that the man's dormant kundalini energy, rendered active, must have suddenly risen up his spine to the brahmarandra chakra at the top of his head. Anyway, the man screamed and fainted. Reviving, he stumbled to the government hospital for treatment. The doctor in charge reported Nityananda to the police as crazy and possibly dangerous. The police promptly took him before the local magistrate. When Nityananda declared that "This one did nothing," the magistrate asked whether there were witnesses. The Master pointed at the four pillars in the hall and was ordered to jail for insolence.

Soon the prisoner announced his need to urinate. Given a receptacle, he rapidly filled it. Another was supplied, which he again filled to the brim. A water jug was offered next. When it overflowed, the constable hurried off the find the magistrate, who agreed to release this mysterious person.

Meanwhile, the interfering doctor from the hospital went home to discover his wife dancing naked around the house in an apparent state of insanity. The alarmed man rushed first to the police station where, hearing of Nityananda's release, he proceeded to the rock ashram. Begging forgiveness, he was waved away by the Master and returned home to find his wife in her normal state.

In these early days Swami Janananda noted other unusual occurrences around Nityananda. Often, for instance, he would emerge from the water tank following his morning bath with his body and loincloth completely dry. He was also seen waking in the rain without getting wet.

One evening the Master asked for a bottle of arrack, the local fermented beverage. Drinking it, he asked for seven more bottles and finished them in quick succession. Mr. Veera from Kumbla, a heavy drinker himself, could not believe his eyes and asked Nityananda why he did this. He relied that is was for the spirit haunting the rock who, now satisfied, would harm no one in the future.

Visitors to the temple today can still see a small stone in front. During worship, the arathi is waved before this stone as well as before Nityananda's statue, it is said that a powerful spirit once inhabited the site. Older Kanhangad residents remember being told as children that those passing the stone without pouring arrack on it would suffer some illness.

About a kilometer north of the rock ashram is an area called Kushalnagar. Here in 1931 the Master built a round table out of stone and called it the "Round Table Conference." He would sit at his table and speak of various world issues, relating first the views of other world leaders and then those of Gandhi. Now, at this very time there happened to be an international conference taking place in London. Skeptics among the Master's listeners who checked the newspaper accounts of the "real" Round Table Conference were amazed to find that they coincided exactly with Nityananda's words.

As work on the Kanhangad caves neared completion in 1933, Nityananda once again embarked on a period of frequent and often unpredictable travel. Sallying forth from Kanhangad and Ganeshpuri, he might appear in Vajreshwari, Gokarn, Kanheri, Bombay, or anywhere.

One day as he sat under a tree near the rock caves, three local Muslims arrived to stand reverently before him. As he had many Muslim devotees, this was not surprising. Having just returned from their Haj pilgrimage to Mecca, they were asked by the Master what they had seen there. They replied, "We saw you there, Swamiji, and have come to pay homage." Nityananda turned his face with a faint smile on his lips.

Similarly, he was seen in many places around Bombay. Achutamama, a devotee from Udipi, tells how the Master asked him to dig a small grave-like pit in the sands of Chowpati and bury him in it. Alarmed, the man then watched as people unwittingly walked over the spot. After about thirty minutes, Nityananda sprang from the sand and asked his companion to take him home. This happened several times until one day he requested a much deeper pit. When he did not crawl out at the usual time, Achutamama grew anxious but continued to wait. Finally, three hours later Nityananda emerged and casually explained that he had had business in Delhi.

He was a regular visitor to Mrs. Muktabai's Bombay home at this time. Once she and her mother went to the town of Nasik along the Godavari River for a change of climate. While they were away, Nityananda insisted on managing the house for his devotee's husband and attending to the household chores himself.

In 1934 or 1935 he reportedly moved to Akroli near Vajreshwari. Here he repaired the hot spring tanks and the nearby Nath temple. He also built a charity hostel across from the Vajreshwari temple and supervised the construction of a well that is still the site's primary water source. As usual, his followers discovered his whereabouts. One of these faithful was Sitarama Shenoy whom Nityananda asked to open a restaurant across from the Vajreshwari temple.

Others found the Master without even looking. A story goes that Mrs. Muktabai and several Bombay devotees had gathered for a picnic near Vajreshwari. As they ate they spoke of Nityananda, lamenting the fact that three years had passed since they had seen him. At that moment a dark figure emerged from the jungle at the base of Mandakini Mountain and approached the ecstatic group.

In 1957, Mr. Krishnamurthy, a journalist and biographer, wrote the following: "Two decades ago Nityananda lived for years in a tree in the heart of the Vajreshwari jungle. Once a young man asked him, "Man cannot do the impossible but a yogi can. Won't you awaken the kundalini in me?" Moved by his earnestness, Nityananda touched his spinal cord and, in a split second, the seeker experienced the dynamic charge of the kundalini. The confines of mortal hope blended with the divine light. He felt as if a magnesium wire burned in his head and unfolded a mystery and a wordless music."

"When kundalini returns to its spiritual cave, the light is extinguished and the flute broken. Only when one puts the eyes of logic and reason to sleep, can one grasp reality's mysterious flash. For an intellectual understanding of kundalini, we can read books. But in our very own day we have Nityananda as a living emblem of the kundalini process. To him, it is not a mental trap. It is action."

"From the moment Nityananda opens the first window of our consciousness, we no longer feel bound by time. Indeed, his greatness lies in time's annihilation. The past becomes a memory. We cease to reach toward future passions. We live in the intuition of the moment. This transforms us from invalid to knower!"

Ganeshpuri--The Beginning 1936

Nityananda arrived in Ganeshpuri one morning in 1936. Some people think he came at the goddess Vajreshwari's bidding. We know he did tell Kanhangad devotees of his intention to visit the Bhimeshwar temple, but he said nothing of moving there. In those days Ganeshpuri was surrounded by a dense jungle inhabited by tigers and other wild animals. Access to the temple was via a footpath over a hill known as Mandakini. The area's only other inhabitants lived on the west side of the hill at a sanatorium. There, a doctor had diverted sulfur water from the natural hot springs into specially constructed therapeutic baths for his patients.

When Nityananda reached the Bhimeshwar temple that morning, he was wrapped in a checkered blanket. Thinking him a Muslim, the attending priest's young wife Gangubai refused to let him enter the Hindu shrine. The Master said nothing and retraced his steps to sit by an old well overgrown with vegetation and full of stones. [When the well was later cleared, these stones were touted for their healing power and eagerly collected by ayurvedic physicians.] Late that afternoon a Vajreshwari devotee arrived and found him still seated by the well. Hearing the tale, the devotee hastened to rectify the mistake. Apologies were immediately offered and soon a temporary structure was built for Nityananda on the temple's west side. It was small, with barely enough room for him to crawl inside and rest.

Before the door stood an ancient pipal tree that was home to many snakes. As he had done with the cobras in Kanhangad, Nityananda issued vibrational orders and they disappeared into the jungle--except for one. The oldest cobra would not leave, preferring death at the Master's hands. The story goes that one day he instructed devotees to stay away and some time later announced that the old snake's wish had been granted. He then ordered villagers to cut down the enormous tree that was now festooned with sacred thread and sprinkled with the red kumkum powder used in Indian rituals.

As word spread of Nityananda's arrival, villagers from surrounding areas began gathering around his hut in the evenings. A large pot of rice porridge, of which the Master would partake, always stood ready for them. Devotees were soon flocking to Ganeshpuri as well. To accommodate them, a building was constructed east of the hot spring water tanks.

At first, due to a lack of potable water, visitors only stayed the day. However, once the old well was refurbished, sulfur water was used for everything. One particularly hot afternoon the Master offered a plate of rice with spicy pickle sauce to a visiting devotee. It so happened that the woman found sulfur water distasteful and declined the food, knowing she would crave something to drink afterward. Nityananda again held out the plate to her, saying, "Don't be concerned. You will drink rain water." Venturing a look at the blue sky, she still ate nothing. Within minutes, however, a solitary cloud appeared overhead and rain poured down. The Master said, "Go and get your water," and she jumped up and collected rainwater for both of them.

Within a short period of time, three rooms were added to the temple's south side to form a compound. Today this is called the "old ashram." Nityananda's room with its small cement porch stood in the middle. There were two adjoining rooms that were fully enclosed, one on each side. But the walls of his room only rose seven feet and had a knee-high sliding panel for a door. The dirt yard in front was paved in 1943. Until then he saw devotees in either the building near the bathing tanks or the temple quadrangle.

The only route to the ashram was a winding footpath through the jungle. To reach this path, visitors had to use the neighboring sanatorium's private road. Soon the caretakers there, disgruntled at devotees getting off the bus at the sanatorium gate, began charging them a fee to use the path. This practice continued until, one day, words and blows were exchanged.

Hearing of the incident, Nityananda asked nearby villagers to recruit fifty laborers. The next morning, with the Master working alongside them, they began to clear trees and build a proper road from the ashram to the bus route, which incidentally still conveys regional buses to Ganeshpuri. At the time, however, the district's British magistrate and forest officer received complaints about the unauthorized project. They asked the local forest ranger, who happened to be a devotee, for a complete report.

Fearing the worst, and at Nityananda's insistence, the man complied. He described the new road as a public service and stressed the growing influx of devotees needing access to both the ashram and the Bhimeshwar temple. Finally, he concluded that the district benefited considerably from the Master's efforts and that he really should have undertaken the project himself.

The curious British officials drove to Ganeshpuri after reading the report. Parking well beyond where the Bhadrakali temple now stands, they approached the ashram as Nityananda sat watching them. Suddenly he turned his back to them and they returned to their car. The magistrate later admitted to subordinates that, while rarely moved by charitable thoughts, upon witnessing how this simple yogi worked to help the local poor, he decided to take no further action.

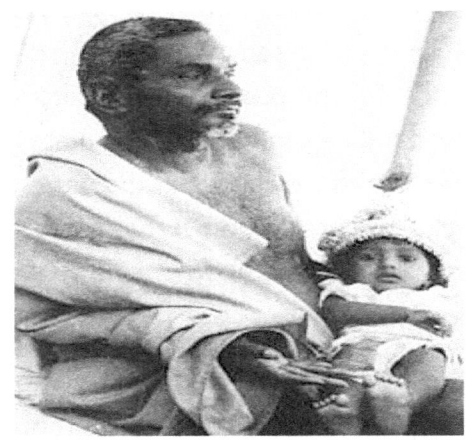

The Old Ashram: Part I

1936-1950

One afternoon a visitor took leave of Nityananda, planning to take the footpath through the woods to the Vajreshwari temple. As he walked off, the Master told him not to look back until he reached the temple. Along the way he encountered a cobra in his path but, following the directive, did not turn around. Instead, he waited for the snake to leave. Continuing, he soon heard someone whispering behind him. Once more, controlling his curiosity, he did not look back until he was within sight of the temple. Then, unable to stand the mystery, he turned and saw a gigantic figure with folded arms standing in the river repeating a mantra--which was what he had heard. Quite shaken, he managed to reach the temple where he remained in a dazed state and had to be hospitalized. It took two months for him to fully recover his senses.

There are many such examples of Nityananda's watchfulness. For instance, he always advised devotees not to venture out alone at night. One time, however, Mrs. Muktabai rose after midnight and went to the hot spring tanks to bathe. As she entered, she saw two uncommonly handsome youths run away and disappear inside the temple. She hurriedly returned to the ashram to tell Nityananda, who admonished her for disobeying his instructions. She apologized and then asked about the young men. He replied that they were sanatkumars, two of Lord Brahma's four sons born of his mind alone.

In 1965 some of the older devotees told Captain Hatengdi that the young Master often used the phrase "tortoise drishti" (or sight) when speaking of his constant mindfulness of their welfare and development. He told them to consider how a mother bird's physical warmth hatches her eggs. In contrast, a mother tortoise climbs onto the beach, lays her eggs, covers them, and returns to the sea, all the while mindful of her eggs. It is her constancy of thought that makes them hatch.

On another occasion, a devotee performing an act of service (seva) around the ashram was told to stop at midnight. He did so and then went off to bathe before retiring. En route, he saw an enormous muddy footprint near the statue of Shiva's bull. Though a man of courage, the devotee was shaken by the sight and rushed inside. There the Master waited and immediately asked, "Did you bow before the footprint?" And he quickly returned to do so.

Nityananda said that through time, sages had often frequented the grounds of the old ashram and he considered the hot springs water there to be holy (koti teertha). This phrase indicates the waters that saints have bathed in or meditated near. In Ganeshpuri the Master always asked even his oldest devotees to, upon arrival, first bathe in the kunds.

Throughout the uncertain light of early morning Nityananda would maintain a vigil until all the devotees returned from bathing. Once, coming from an early bath, Madhumama, a long-time devotee who sometimes cooked for the Master, encountered him at the ashram entrance. he asked the devotee, "Did you see it?" and pointed to a tiger sitting under a mango tree only twenty yards away. Clearly, the Master was standing guard.

Rajgopal Bhat, a regular visitor for two decades, spoke of a similar incident. In 1949 he brought his family to Bombay for the first time and, on finding no accommodations, was told by Nityananda to stay with a certain Mr. Gandhi in Ganeshpuri. Rising the next morning for a three o'clock visit to the hot springs, he felt himself followed and noticed a faint light behind him. Remembering the Master's perennial advice, he did not look back but continued walking. When he reached the present site of the Bhadrakali temple, the uncertain feeling disappeared. He took his bath and forgot the incident. In the evening Mr. Gandhi visited the ashram. Nityananda told him a tiger had followed Mr. Bhat that morning but his faith in the Master had protected him.

According to another story, Bhagawan Mistry, who handled the ashram's construction work, ran in one evening in obvious agony, shouting that a cobra had bitten him. Nityananda calmly told him to sit down. He asked someone to bring him the snake balm, instructed the bewildered Mistry to rub it on the Master's leg at the spot corresponding to his own wound, and told him to go to sleep. The devotee awoke the next morning fully recovered.

An even more dramatic intervention is related in this story from Dr. Deodhar about Sitarama Shenoy, a Mangalore devotee mentioned earlier in the book. After suffering a severe heart attack, he was taken by his family directly from the hospital to Ganeshpuri. His doctors vehemently protested this action.

Arriving in the village, Sitarama was helped from the car and placed on the ground before Nityananda, who proceeded to take his hand and drag him to the river. There Nityananda splashed water on the ailing man's face, telling him that he was fine and could walk back on his own. And so he did, completely recovered. Shortly thereafter, to his doctor's astonishment and at Nityananda's bidding, he opened the restaurant across from the Vajreshwari temple and worked there until his death in 1954. The restaurant is still maintained by his family.

One afternoon Nityananda announced that Narayan Maharaj of Khedgaon was coming. Seeing Achutamama's skepticism, he insisted that the celebrated teacher was in Vajreshwari en route to the ashram. Five minutes later, they heard a car stop to deposit the maharaj, who went directly to the hot springs. Following his ablutions, he approached Nityananda and asked him to cure his skin disorder. But the Master replied, "Inside you are pure. Why bother with the outside?" And the maharaj went away. That evening Nityananda spoke: "Everything was ready for him--the bed made and his head about to touch the pillow. But instead he got up and left." Referring to the spiritual stage previously reached by the maharaj, the Master told devotees that datta devata siddhi only lasted fourteen years and required a renewed effort at that point.

In contrast, the attainment of divine wisdom carried no such limitation. Jnana, he said, was infinite.

A man destined to be a longtime devotee made his first visit to Ganeshpuri in 1938. Most people came by bus but, after winning the Goa lottery, Golikeri Lakshman Rao was a rich man. he hired a taxi for the trip and arrived bearing a fruit basket. Nityananda accepted him as well as the fruit. After several visits, he asked Rao to come on a particular date and accompany him on a pilgrimage (teerthayatra). As Rao arrived that day, again in a taxi, the villagers fell at Nityananda's feet, pleading with him not to leave. He told them to fall at Rao's feet instead--and they did, much to the devotee's embarrassment. Nityananda motioned for Rao to acknowledge them, and they set off on their journey.

At the train station, over his companion's protests, Nityananda insisted on third-class tickets. And in Poona, their first stop, Nityananda took a hotel room with a bed for Rao-- and a space on the floor for himself and a cloth (chadder) for a blanket. The next day they went to Alandi. Here Nityananda encouraged the devotee to follow his usual manner of worship, and so Rao proceeded to the river Jnaneshwar. Meanwhile, the Master stood for several seconds with his hands at his sides in each corner of the shrine, and then left.

The next stop was to be Pandarpur. But Rao suffered a malaria attack in the night and asked Nityananda's permission to return to Bombay. He made no objection but asked Rao to leave his chaddar for him. Protesting, Rao said he would gladly buy the Master a new one but, again overruled, he sadly departed.

Nityananda traveled on to Pandarpur and other places before returning to Bombay. For several months in early 1939 he lived in the Kanheri caves at Borivli. Adjoining his cave was another where a guru lectured daily on Vedantic philosophy.

Focusing on the inconsequential and transitory aspect of the human body, he loudly exhorted his disciples to ignore its many attractions and afflictions. As fate had it, one day the guru was bitten by a snake. The resulting agony was expressed visibly and, as usual, quite vocally on his part. His distressed disciples asked Nityananada to help. While we know his mercy was boundless, the master nevertheless chuckled and asked if they had already forgotten their guru's words to ignore the body's physical aspects. Then he directed them to splash water from the nearby pond onto the wound. This done, their guru recovered--and immediately came to bow at Nityananda's feet.

Another of the Kanheri caves was occupied by a sanyasi who was a Mahakala worshipper. Following his daily worship he would bring the ritual light and incense (arathi) he had waved before his personal shrine and wave it before Nityananda. Taking no notice, the Master told devotees that it was just a sign of the sanyasi's deep devotion.

As always, devotees found Nityananda, and this time they flocked to Kanheri. One was the deeply attached Mrs. Muktabai. She related that one time, in her haste to arrive, she lost her way. Her anxiety grew until an asthmatic old man suddenly appeared and offered to show her the way. As they neared the ashram, he began to lag behind her and at the entrance was nowhere to be seen. Nityananda refused to discuss the incident and reprimanded her soundly for traveling at that hour in such a dangerous region.

Prior to his return to Ganeshpuri, Nityananda told devotees not to come to Kanheri only to see him. He urged them to visit the rock caves built by yogis and sanyasis centuries earlier and marvel at their arrangements for collecting and storing water.

Nityananda returned to Ganeshpuri in 1939, and Rao immediately came to see him. But again, he suffered an attack of malaria. In a fever-induced delirium, he admitted that as a youth he had once received sandwiches from the Muslim sage Baba Jan, which he had thoughtlessly discarded. Hearing the story, the Master shook the ailing man and asked him to repeat it. After listening to it again, he went to the pantry, opened several tins of food, and mixed the contents together on a piece of newspaper. He then carried the huge serving to Rao and ordered him to eat it. The sick devotee did so and immediately fell asleep. He awoke fully recovered, realizing that he had finally atoned for the insult of throwing away a saint's prasad.

The Old Ashram: Part II

1936-1950

In 1941 Swami Janananda traveled to Ganeshpuri to seek Nityananda's guidance on some financial and construction issues regarding the Kanhangad ashram. On his arrival, and prior to speaking to the Master, he was told to sit down. Within minutes a taxi drove up, a rare occurrence in the days, and Nityananda left, saying he would soon return. And he did--twenty-four hours later in the same taxi. Then, glancing at Swami Janananda, he said, "Go home. Everything is taken care of."

Without a word, Swami Janananda made the return trip, one that involved the usual number of trains and buses. Reaching the ashram, he heard that Nityananda had been there earlier with money and instructions. Let me add that even with today's improved transportation conditions and utilizing the new Netravati Bridge, it is impossible to complete a round trip between Bombay and Kanhangad by taxi in twenty-four hours...

Nityananda was never interested in attracting disciples or organizing an ashram. He was egoless in both words and actions. When pressed, he would say, "**This one is not flattered when important people come or sad when devotees leave**."

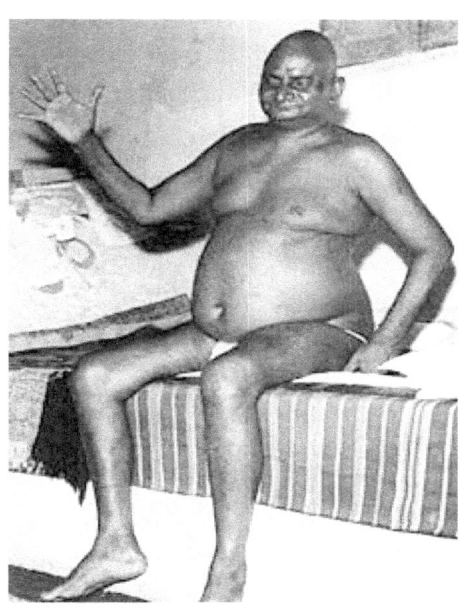

Students of other spiritual teachers sometimes came to Ganeshpuri, but the Master always steered them back to their own ashrams. He would tell them that their gurus were quite capable of solving their problems and that it was inappropriate as well as disrespectful to change loyalty on a temporary basis. One morning, as devotees of Shirdi Sai Baba filed before him, Nityananda was heard to shout, "Go back to Shirdi! Does the old man there sit differently than this one does here?"

A similar situation involved the affluent Bhiwandiwalla brothers, then devotees of Narayan Maharaj. When they first learned that Nityananda was in Ganeshpui, they set off to see him. But when they arrived, Nityananda shouted, "Go back to your guru!" and refused to speak to them. The brothers nevertheless continued to come. It was only when Narayan Maharaj died that the Master finally addressed them and accepted their devotion.

There was once a devotee who had lost a flourishing business prior to the Second World War. On his first visit to Ganeshpuri, he kept hearing Nityananda repeat the word "junk" and, try as he might, could not stop thinking about it. When the man returned home, the word still rang in his ears and he went for a walk. Lo and behold, he came upon an auction selling discarded odds and ends to the highest bidder. Without hesitation he bought the entire lot and soon sold it at a profit. Within months he was on his way toward recouping his earlier losses. Within the ashram he was called Raddiwalla, or "the head of junk."

Raddiwalla became a frequent visitor to Ganeshpuri, often bringing his entire family. Always anxious to have Nityananda touch him, he sometimes took the liberty of placing the Master's hand on the head of a relative he wished to have blessed. This annoyed some of the older devotees who had been around since the days in Mangalore. Back them, Nityananda had told them not to prostrate themselves before him, that their inner prayers would reach him. One afternoon Raddiwalla took his leave after placing Nityananda's hand on the head of every member of his family. Unable to contain themselves, the envious devotees asked the Master why he had never favored them in this manner after their many years of devotion. He rebuked them by saying, "**A blessing is not given by placing the hand on the head. It is an inner transmission--not an outer demonstration.**"

One day when the Master complained of fatigue, Mrs. Muktabai admitted her surprise, saying that he rarely left the ashram and spent most of his time resting on the floor of his room or on the bench outside. He quipped, "Yes, but the devotees remember, don't they?" On another occasion he said: "one established in infinite consciousness becomes silent and, while knowing everything, goes about as if knowing nothing. While doing many things in several places, outwardly one appears to do nothing."

One day a new devotee brought his wife to Ganeshpuri. After first greeting Nityananda, they sat down a little apart from the others. Some of the visitors were discussing the building of a small school in the area. Thinking this a good opportunity to contribute something, the husband rose and placed a thousand rupee note on the plate by Nityananda's bench. After resuming his seat, the man was astonished to find his single note transformed into a pile of smaller denomination bills.

Nityananda basked in the spontaneity of life and delighted in saying that things rarely went according to plan--even the best laid ones. After all, he would tell devotees, "*God's will always prevails.*"

In 1949, a devotee from Kerala was filled with dismay when a renowned astrologer announced that the devotee's young wife would soon die due to an affliction of Saturn in her chart. Distraught, the man rushed to Ganeshpuri. As he arrived and sat down, Nityananda turned to him and said, "Saturn is there but so is God." He then told the husband to stay on at the ashram and to perform certain rituals that were never explained. The devotee faithfully followed his instructions to the letter. When the day predicted for the calamity came, it passed without incident--and Nityananda told the happy man to go home.

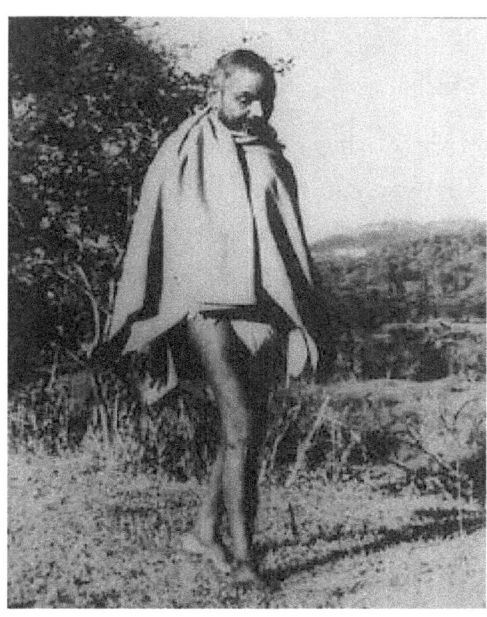

One morning as Nityananda reclined on his bench with legs outstretched, three stalwart sanyasis appeared in the entrance behind him. One carried a large, brightly-polished trident. [The trident (trishula) symbolizes the three powers of the Absolute: Will, Knowledge, and Action. It is often associated with Shiva.] Quietly they took a stance behind the Master and waited for him to acknowledge them, but he uttered no sound and made no gesture. Time passed. The visitors grew restless and the watching devotees uncomfortable. Suddenly, the trident bearer thrust it forcefully into midair where it remained of its own accord. Still Nityananda did not turn, but whenever he glanced from the right corner of his eye, the trident swayed slightly.

After some moments, Nityananda shook his outstretched foot-and the trident fell with a clatter. Bowing, the sanyasis asked to stay in the ashram for three days. During this time they said they were followers of a powerful guru in the Himalayas. The conceded, however, that Nityananda was himself a great leader of *the nath* order of monks (*Matsyendranath*), and demonstrating great respect and affection, they departed with his blessing.

It was around 1942 when Kamath and a friend spent Shivaratri, the annual festival of Shiva, in Ganeshpuri. Staying in rooms opposite the hot spring tanks, they rose at midnight to bathe and them entered the darkness of the Bhimeshwar temple. To their surprise, the beam of their flashlight revealed Nityananda standing with one foot on the linga and repeating, "Shiva is gone, Shiva is gone." And the two men knew that for Shiva to have gone he must first have come.

Mrs. Muktabai once asked Nityananda whether he could see God. His reply was *More clearly than I see you*." He also said that physical contact with the teacher was unnecessary. "*This one is here, there, and everywhere*," he assured. "*There is no pinhole where this one will not be found.*" And a certain incident in the life of G.A. Rao illustrates this.

Rao was the devotee mentioned earlier who had won the lottery. Always generous with his unexpected wealth, he unfortunately lost everything during the war. Nityananda asked a devotee living in the same town as Rao to let the impoverished man stay in his warehouse. One day Rao sadly considered that he did not even have a photo of his guru to wave incense in front of. That night he had a dream. In it, Nityananda had him search the wall above his pillow for a nail hole and instructed him to wave incense before it. The next morning when he awoke, Rao found such a hole and began waving incense before it daily for the duration of his stay.

Some time passed before he finally saw Nityananda in the flesh again. On that occasion the Master remarked that he was enjoying the fragrance of Rao's incense.

One day as visitors from Saurashtra were bowing before Nityananda, one of them began to shiver uncontrollably. Afterward a devotee took him aside to ask why he had reacted so. The man said that before leaving his village he had seen the Master in a nearby cave and was shocked to find him here as well. Then evening when the devotee remarked on the unlikelihood of such an occurrence, Nityananda replied, "**Anything is possible**."

Anything is possible. To Nityananda this was abundantly clear. When, in the mid-1950's, he asked Madhumama to go to Badrinath, the devotee stopped over in Rishikesh. There he was approached by a tall stranger who, in passing, warned him in Kanarese: "Don't eat anything offered by a sanyasi on your way to Badrinath. Only eat temple food." Madhumama was mystified by both the message and messenger. How would anyone know that he understood Kanarese and was en route to Badrinath? Turning to ask him, he found only empty space.

On his subsequent return to Ganeshpuri, he told fellow devotees that when he bowed at Kedarnath he felt as if his head touch the body of the Master. Some devotees laughed, but Nityananda remarked, "There is no need to doubt his experience. The body without the head (Munda) is in Kedarnath while the head without the body (Runda) is in Pashupathinath. If Shiva's body can lie in Kedarnath and his head in Pashupathinath, then a devotee would not be surprised to feel Nityananda's body anywhere."

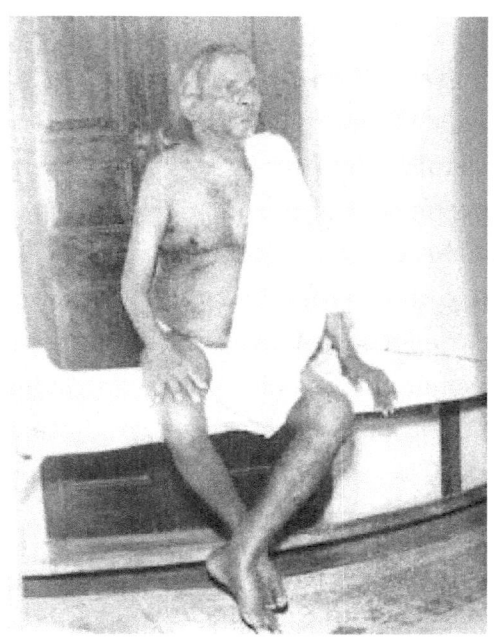

The Old Ashram: Part III

1936-1950

M. Hegde, a young relative of Sitarama Shenoy, was posted to Bombay during the Second World War as an apprentice in the Naval Dockyard. On his regular visits to Ganeshpuri, he was sometimes asked to prepare the Master's tea. During one visit to the jungle ashram, he found himself questioned by Nityananda. Did he wish to improve his prospects? Did he know about the government-sponsored Bevin Boy's Training Program in Great Britain? Hegde said he had read about it in the newspaper but thought himself ineligible because quotas were determined by province and he was not really from Bombay.

The Master told him to think big and apply anyway. The boy did and was accepted. However, at his medical examination, the local doctor contested his candidacy and declared him medically unfit. When Hegde hurried to Ganeshpuri, Nityananda again advised him to think bigger and appeal the decision. Hegde therefore wrote to the surgeon general and received an appointment. Puzzled at the sight of a healthy young man standing before him, the surgeon general asked the local doctor to explain his ruling. Because he was unable to do so satisfactorily, the decision was overturned.

During his year of training in Great Britain, Hegde began dating an English woman. One time, while the two were strolling in a park, Hegde suddenly saw an apparition of the Master before him. His stern face seemed to say, "Was this why you came to this place?" The apparition disappeared and Hegde began sweating profusely even though it was winter. The look on his face apparently was startling enough to make the woman end their relationship on the spot.

When he returned to India, Hegde went directly to Ganeshpuri to ask Nityananda what he should do next. The master told him to put on a suit and walk up and down one of Bombay's major commercial streets from ten in the morning to five in the afternoon. This was a tall order, but the young devotee resolved to follow his instruction to the letter. Exhausted, he later returned home and wondered how he would get a job by pacing up and down. Nevertheless, the next day he faithfully repeated his vigil. By noon he found himself staring aimlessly at a notice board outside the Macropolo shop. From the corner of his eye, he saw a foreigner enter the shop. Exiting some time later, the foreigner was surprised to see Hegde still staring at the notices. He asked the young man what he was doing and Hegde admitted that he was looking for work. The stranger inquired into his qualifications and whether he was prepared to go the Calcutta that night. Gulping, Hegde said yes and followed the man to the Lakshmi office building where he accepted a good opening position plus traveling expenses.

Predictably, Hedge caught the first train to Ganeshpuri. A hundred yards from the ashram, he could hear Nityananda shouting at him to return to the station immediately if he intended to catch the train for Calcutta. And joyously saluting the Master from that distance, Hegde set out for his new job.

Nityananda's understanding of life was light years beyond the people around him. Time after time, someone would express concern or sorrow about an event only to have the Master explain, sometimes in exasperation, that many things occur beneath life's apparent surface. Stories abound, of course.

Captain Hatengdi's mother was among those who first sought out Nityananda. In 1924, however, she turned instead to Swami Siddharud in Hubli, being quite taken with the many miracles attributed to him. Two decades later, as her son's connection with Nityananda evolved, he wrote to his mother and invited her to the ashram. And so it passed that in February 1944, accompanied by a brother and his family, she traveled to Ganeshpuri. Upon seeing her, and with characteristic brevity, Nityananda asked, "How long?" unprepared for this greeting, the woman mumbled, "Perhaps twenty years."

"No," came his reply. "Twenty-two. Anyway, where is Siddharud now?"

"He is no more."

"Where has he gone? Can you see him when you close your eyes?" he asked. When she said yes, he repeated, "Are you so certain he has gone anywhere?"

The Hatengdi family was assigned a room near the baths for the night. That evening Nityananda visited, sitting without saying a word. When one woman quietly asked about his silence, another said that he must be meditating because it was sunset. The Master immediately spoke, "All that was over in the mother's womb."

Another time a couple arrived in Ganeshpuri. After first bathing, they were arranging to prepare a meal for the Master when they saw him rush across the compound. He shouted at them to leave at once. The startled devotees hurriedly packed and left--just catching a bus to make the rail connection at Bassein. The instant they arrived home, a fierce gale began to rattle the shutters and windows. It was a precursor to a formidable storm that severed railway connections in the region. In fact, had the couple not caught that particular bus and train, they would have been stranded in Ganeshpuri for ten days.

Once again a hardship proved to be a blessing when a devotee and his wife arrived in Ganeshpuri for a few days. After settling in, they hired a horse-drawn carriage to take them to Vajreshwari. But as the wife climbed into the vehicle, she fell and broke her ankle. Witnessing the occurrence, Nityananda told the husband to take her to a certain bone-setter in Bombay as opposed to the hospital. When an anxious friend of the couple asked Nityananda how such a thing could happen in Ganeshpuri, he replied, "**She has young children. A fatal accident would have brought distress to them.**" It was clear to everyone that a fatal accident had been averted.

Around 1950, Dr. Deodhar recalls seeing two cars arrive. From one car servants emerged carrying bedding and headed for the ashram's back door. It seemed that the Bhiwandiwalla family was preparing to stay for some time. Family members emerged from the other car and walked toward the main entrance. One man gingerly carried an inert child in his outstretched arms. Not ten minutes later, the servants returned to the cars with the bedding. Next came the family, the same man holding the child. The entourage drove off and Dr. Deodhar hurried inside. There he learned that the child suffered from pneumonia and had been unconscious for three days. The family brought the child before Nityananda and begged him to open the child's eyes. Passing his hand over the small face, the child's eyes opened, but moving his hand back, the child's eyes closed. Nityananda then told the family to perform the last rites because the child was dead.

Mistry had been in charge of the ashram's construction work for many years and felt comfortable around his guru. Without thinking, he remarked how unfortunate it was that the child had died in Nityananda's presence. Angrily the Master said, "What do you know about it? This is the fourth time that the child has come from its mother's womb seeking liberation. It has wanted freedom but karmic law has dragged it down again and again into the same family. Now fulfilled, this soul will not have to return." Overcome by curiosity, Dr. Deodhar later questioned a family member, who confirmed that four infants had died shortly after birth--the last one only after receiving darshan from Nityananda.

In another instance, a Bombay couple had their first child late in life. When he contracted smallpox. the parents rushed him to Ganeshpuri. There they placed their beloved son at Nityananda's feet in full view of a group of devotees and ashram children. Aware of the risk to those present, the Master ordered the couple to take their sick child home immediately. The Nityananda stood up and entered his own room. For ten days he stayed inside seeing no one, until one morning he emerged and walked directly to the hot springs to bathe. Following him, anxious devotees noticed a number of skin eruptions on his body. Later they learned that in Bombay the sick child had miraculously recovered.

The following story occurred some time before Dr. Deodhar became a devotee. On his jungle estate near Panval stood a small shrine to Shiva. Installed by his family at this shrine was a certain Swami Ramananda who performed the daily rituals. Once a week the monk went to the Deodhar compound to collect supplies, and one time he arrived as the gamily was deciding whether to excavate an old rubble-filled basement that lay directly beneath the present house. Listening to the discussion, Swami Ramananda excitedly said the basement held a golden treasure guarded by a large cobra, and he offered to retrieve it for them. Rather doubtful, Dr. Deodhar said they were not seeking treasure-only a basement. But the family agreed to let the swami supervise the project.

Two days of digging passed without producing any sign of a basement. Meanwhile the family grew increasingly anxious, fearing that the house might collapse. Swami Ramananda pleaded for one more day, and spent the night in the trench breathing so loudly that no one slept. The next morning he climbed out and said they could replace the excavated dirt because nothing would ever materialize. Angrily, he added that a certain langotiwalla (literally "one in charge of the loincloths") was preventing their success, and he would go to Ganeshpuri and demand satisfaction.

The swami said he had known this langotiwalla in Rishikesh. He recalled that in those days Nityananda was already a powerful yogi known to lie on the bank of the Ganges for long periods of time without taking food or water. He explained that, in the case of the basement, Nityananda had obviously "blinded" Swami Ramananda's powers (siddhis). In short, it was not that the basement with its treasure did not exist; it was simply that Nityananda was not allowing the swami to find it.

Now it seemed that Dr. Deodhar was already in the habit of visiting holy men residing in Maharashtra. He had even heard about Nityananda from his patients and wanted to accompany Swami Ramananda to Ganeshpuri. However, when they missed their travel connections in Thana, he returned home. Swami Ramananda continued on, promising to tell the doctor later about his intended confrontation.

Swami Ramananda returned a few days later, a changed man. He admitted to having been severely chastised by Nityananda. "This is the third time you have used your siddhis in recent years," he told him. "You have far to go in your spiritual work and should know that you will never succeed by using your powers for vain and selfish reasons. Why did you do it?" Swami Ramananda meekly replied that he was only trying to express his gratitude to the Deodhar family. But Nityananda admonished him again, saying that it was the wrong way to do it. He then ordered him to move to a certain spot on the Narmada River and continue his personal practice. The humbled swami left immediately after telling his story and the family never saw him again. Dr. Deodhar felt compelled to meet Nityananda and became a lifelong devotee.

There is still an air of mystery around Nityananda's age, background, and movements. For instance, the only information known about his visits to the northern regions is that he traveled north between the ages of 12 and 16 or so, after leaving his foster father in Benares. In 1944 he told devotees of his presence when the ancient Ananteshwar temple was built. He described himself then as having an unkempt beard and matted hair. The confines of time and space did not appear to affect him. [The Ananteshwar Temple was built in the mid 16th century, making it over 400 years old.]

The Old Ashram

1950-1956

Devotees gathered late one evening in 1950 on the west side of the ashram. Here Nityananda sat on a small ledge bordering a six-foot drop into the darkening fields behind him. Silence prevailed. Suddenly in the distance a pair of bright eyes appeared and, weaving its way slowly through the fields, a tiger came up to the ledge and stopped. The animal then rose lightly on its haunches and rested its forepaws on Nityananda's shoulders. Calmly the Master reached up with his right hand and stroked the tiger's head. Satisfied, the tiger jumped back down and disappeared into the night. Later Nityananda observed that as the vehicles of the Goddess Vajreshwari tigers should be expected around her temple. He also said that wild beasts behave like lambs in the presence of enlightened beings.

Many stories tell of his uncanny ability to understand animals. In Udipi he once told its captors to release a certain caged bird because it constantly cursed them. Another time he reassured a frightened devotee that a nearby cobra was too busy chanting to harm anybody. Others remember a devotee who always came for darshan accompanied by his pet parrot. And in May 1944 Captain Hatengdi heard Nityananda say that a bird told him it would rain in three days, and rain it did.

Among the many distinguished visitors seen in Ganeshpuri was a certain swami from Shirali. This enlightened yogi was the ninth guru of a small community that had demonstrated an enviable performance record in all spheres of endeavor for nearly a century. A shining example of kindness and humility but too mild mannered to exercise his authority, the gentle guru found himself dominated by a committee of lay advisors. For many years he had expressed a desire to visit Ganeshpuri but the trip was always thwarted by the committee.

Finally asserting himself in 1951, the swami departed on his pilgrimage. He was accompanied by a Shirali entourage that included three Nityananda devotees- Mrs. Muktabai, her brother, and his wife. The trip's organizers, still unenthusiastic about the trip, drove the swami to nearby Akroli where they started to hurry him from the car to the nearby hot springs. But their guru asked where Nityananda was. Hesitating, they admitted to being several miles from Ganespuri. The swami demanded to continue on, saying he would only bathe at the ashram. And so the group continued on.

Now it seemed that on the previous day Nityananda announced that a visitor would arrive at eleven the next morning. He then asked a devotee to heat some cow's milk and set it aside. When the swami and his entourage arrived, precisely at eleven, they proceeded directly to the hot springs. However, Mrs. Muktabai ran to the Master's room and excitedly exclaimed, "Deva, our Swamiji has come!" Nityananda replied, "Everything is known. Milk has been put aside. Place a chair on the temple's outer veranda, put a shawl on it, and offer the milk to the swami."

And so it passed that the swami had his bath, he worshipped at the Bhimeshwar temple, and he gratefully accepted the milk. He then rose and proceeded to the ashram's western hall. As the swami and his lay followers passed the room where Nityananda sat, the lay followers, still determined to prevent a face-to-face meeting, silently bowed before the Master's door and conveniently blocked him from view. Oddly, the swami no longer asked about Nityananda. He simply sat in the hall repeating over and over, "We are feeling blissful here and do not feel like leaving." (To avoid saying "I," mathadipathis customarily refer to themselves in the first person plural.) Although pleased that he seemed to have forgotten about Nityananda, the lay advisors still worried. They tried to hurry him by saying that he would miss evening services in Shirali if he did not leave immediately. The swami replied, "Why the concern about being late for one service? We are in a state of bliss and do not feel like leaving." However, eventually they persuaded him to leave, and the motorcade departed.

Staying behind, Mrs. Muktabai again rushed to Nityananda's room, this time to say with sorrow that the swami had left without seeing him. The Master replied, "You are wrong-- the meeting did occur. But his coming to Ganeshpuri was unnecessary. It could have happened anywhere and so many people tried to prevent it." She then knew that the encounter had been on a subtle level, leaving the swami in a state of bliss and immobility. She also realized that the Master himself had made the swami temporarily forget about him. Several other Ganeshpuri devotees belonged to this community and Nityananda had always told them that the swami was a good sanyasi and a true yogi.

When the party from Shirali was ten miles from Ganeshpuri, the swami awoke as if from a reverie and exclaimed: "Oh, but we did not meet Nityananda!" His advisors responded that they had driven too far to turn back. To this the swami said, "I believe he came to Shirali once but we were quite young at the time. We have long desired to meet him." But as was their custom, his advisors chose to ignore the swami's gentle hint.

Meanwhile Mrs. Muktabai's brother was upset with the subterfuge. He returned to Ganeshpuri the next day and told Nityananda what had occurred on the return drive, adding that he personally would bring the swami to meet him. But the Master replied, "It is unnecessary because the meeting took place. Moreover, the good man suffers from diabetes and is unfit for another tiring journey. Remember that he is a Mathadipathi and must listen to his people. [Math (pronounced mutt with an aspiration at the end), means monastery. A mathadipathi is a leader of a math or monastery; an abbot.]

One day Mr. Mudbhatkal's Muslim landlord told him that he had always wanted to meet Nityananda but ill health prevented him from traveling. The devotee promised on his forthcoming visit to Ganeshpuri to bring his landlord some prasad. However, when he found a large group of visitors from Bombay seated before the Master, he timidly decided to wait until another day to mention his landlord. At the end of his visit the devotee went to bow before the Master, still conscious of his broken promise. As he turned to go, Nityananda called him back and purposefully handed him a coconut. His landlord's desire was fulfilled.

Similarly, a devotee from Santa Cruz tells of a childhood journey to Ganeshpuri in the company of a group that included a follower of U. Maharaj. Learning of the disciple's intended visit, his guru gave him a coconut to offer Nityananda. When the group neared the ashram, it found Nityananda leaning against the wooden gate waiting. The moment he saw them he said, "The coconut has been received"--as if to say a thought was as good as a deed. And we know that in the Mangalore days he told devotees that inner salutations expressed with purity of feeling and motive (shuddha bhavana) made physical obeisance unnecessary.

During this time Shankar Tirth, a sanyasi who had wandered for years without finding inner peace, first appeared. Hearing one day about Nityananda, he journeyed to Ganeshpuri where, upon receiving darshan, he finally found happiness. Asking the Master where he should stay, he was told to occupy the nearby Nath temple that Nityananda had restored two decades earlier. Shankar Tirth did so but the next morning, visibly shaken, said he had experienced such frightening nightmares of attacking cobras telling him to leave--that he asked to live elsewhere. Instead Nityananda told him to go back to the temple and announce on whose orders he was there. The sanyasi did this but returned the following day with the same story. Again Nityananda told him to go back and tell the threatening forces who had sent him. This time his announcement produced peace and quiet.

A year or two later the Shankaracharya who had initiated Shankar Tirth into his particular order of monks was camped at Banaganga. When he sent word for the sanyasi to report for final initiation, Shankar Tirth asked Nityananda if he should go. He was told that it was unnecessary, and so he informed the Shankaracharya that he would not come.

The Old Ashram: Part II

1950-1956

Another Shankaracharya visited Ganeshpuri in the mid-fifties. Details of his visit reached Captain Hatengdi in an unusual way. In fact, it was in 1977 at a harikatha, which is a scriptural story told in song and narrative, that he heard the story:

The Shankaracharya of Puri was spending his chaturma in Bombay. Traditionally, a chaturma was the four months of monsoon during which a wandering sadhu would stay in one place, but these days it referred to a period of special study. At the end of his time there he visited the Dattatreya shrine in Vakola, where he expressed a desire to visit the Vajreshwari temple. Having just written a book on Shakti, he wanted to visit the shrine of the goddess before it was published. The then young harikatha performer was hired to drive two men, the elderly Shankaracharya and a shastri learned in the scriptures, to Vajreshwari. The old swami was not very strong and had to be helped up the steps leading to the shrine. Afterward, the Shankaracharya suddenly uttered a desire to see Nityananda and the three companions found themselves unexpectedly en route to Ganeshpuri.

When they arrived, the Master was resting on his narrow bench with a few people seated before him. The three new visitors quietly joined the others. Silence reigned. After some time the scholar stood up and announced who they were. He said that the Shankaracharya had written a book on Shakti and that they had come for Nityananda's blessing. No one else spoke, and the silence continued. At some point the Master raised his head and nodded to an attending devotee, who left and quickly reappeared with a mysteriously prepared tray of fresh flowers, fruit, and coconuts. The attendant respectfully placed the tray before the Shankaracharya and withdrew. Although it was clear that Nityananda had been expecting the holy man, he still did not speak. Several minutes passed before the scholar again stood up, this time to say that what was transpiring in silence was new to him. He nevertheless recognized that the flowers and fruit represented Nityananda's blessing and announced that his party would take its leave. Bowing deeply, the three visitors left the silent ashram.

In 1954, G.L. Rao was staying with Shankar Tirth in the Nath temple opposite the Vajreshwari temple. One afternoon Godarvarimata, a holy woman from Sakori, drove up to the temple and asked whether she could be taken to Ganeshpuri. Shankar Tirth asked Rao to accompany her. They found Nityananda resting in his room with his feet extended onto the cement platform. Rao announced the arrival of the visitor who sat down near his feet, and Nityananda grunted in acknowledgement. Wishing to be hospitable, Rao asked whether he could bring Godavarimata something to drink, and Nityananda said yes. While Rao was away, the Master came out of his room and sat on the platform. Godarvarimata stayed for two days, later saying that Nityananda had given her the darshan of her guru. She had originally come to ask Nityananda to grace a Vedic ceremony in Bombay with his physical presence. He refused, saying he would observe the ritual from Ganeshpuri--but she continued to press her invitation. When finally he replied that "one has to come only if one is not there already," she stopped asking. Later it was reported that on the final day of the yajna the holy woman was granted the darshan of Nityananda.

In 1954, Sitarama Shenoy suffered a heart attack in Vajreshwari and died. Grief stricken and inconsolable, his wife was determined to take the body to Ganeshpuri. Accordingly, she hired a car, had the body placed in it, and proceeded toward the ashram. A quarter mile away, the car stalled and would not start up again. At this point the driver announced that he would neither repair the car in the dark nor help carry the body the remaining distance. Undeterred, the widow left the body with the driver and set off for the ashram on foot. When she was still some two hundred yards from the gate, she heard Nityananada shouting, "Go back and perform the last rites!" She pleaded with him but was ordered away.

The devotee Rao was present that evening and asked Nityananda why he had not revived her husband as he had done some years earlier. The Master responded that their children had been young then and needed a father, and in compassion the Divine Force worked that way. However, present conditions were different. His interference, he said, would cause people to stop going to Chandanwadi, Bombay's crematorium, and come to Ganeshpuri instead.

Nityananda often tested a devotee's mettle, as in the instance of a Brahman devotee who came weekly to read the scriptures aloud in the Master's presence. After several visits he asked to be cured of his tubercular condition and constant cough. Nityananda agreed and told him to eat a small frog fried in ghee every day. A strict vegetarian, the Brahman was horrified--but having asked for Nityananda's help, he dutifully complied with the instructions. Soon his lungs improved and he developed a taste for frogs in the bargain.

The Master never took credit for the endless instances of healing that occurred around him. In fact, he often directed devotees to rely on their own traditional medical physicians. When pressed, he attributed everything to the Divine Force. He would say: "**This one had no desire to do good deeds. Everything that happens does so through the will of God.**"

Nityananda was tolerant of his devotee's humanness; his actions indicated that one's heart was free to turn to God only after the basic human needs were fulfilled. He made no demands, issued no commandments, and frequently concerned himself with their worldly comfort. In return, all he asked was that followers be prapared to receive that which he offered in such abundance. This is a story of an attorney from the distant state of Kerala who regularly visited Ganeshpuri on weekends. As the years passed, however, the devotee felt keenly the loneliness of his unmarried state and finally announced he wanted a wife. Listening, Nityananda pointed to the surrounding throng and said, "Take one from here." The prospective bridegroom instantly froze, concerned that his mention of a private problem had triggered a casual response. Bewildered, he sat as the people around him slowly dispersed until only one man remained, likewise from Kerala. Eyeing the attorney, he told Nityananda that he and his wife were having difficulty arranging a suitable match for their daughter. Nityananda pointed to his devotee.

Everything seemed settled until their families sent the potential couple's horoscopes to a group of astrologers who unanimously pronounced the match unsuitable. When informed of this, Nityananda without a glance at the offending charts pointed out that a certain aspect nullified the negative signs correctly discerned by the astrologers. When this information was relayed to Kerala, the astrologers agreed, amazed at their failure to notice this vital detail, and the couple married.

A longstanding devotee from the Mangalore days was a woman whose ill- tempered husband never allowed her to handle any family financial matters. In fact, she had never dared to ask him for money. Then one day following their recent move to Bombay, the wife asked her husband for some rupees. He demanded to know why. She replied that she wanted to visit nearby Ganeshpuri and he quipped, "And what will you achieve by going there?" Seconds later he literally threw a five-rupee note at her. Normally she would never have touched money so humiliatingly offered, but determined to see Nityananda she picked up the note and departed at once.

Reaching the old ashram at a little past noon, she found the devotees restless and the atmosphere tense. The Master had not taken his afternoon meal and as a result no one had eaten. They told her that when he was approached earlier about his food, Nityananda had become very upset and sent the questioner away. The devotees implored the woman to speak to him, and she approached the small room where he sat across from the Krishna temple. Seeing her, the Master visibly relaxed and asked, "Well he hasn't changed yet." His faithful devotee replied, "I don't know whether people ever change their inborn habits--but I have brought some food for you. Will you eat now?" And he did.

Late one evening in 1955, Nityananda asked his attendants to count the money in the Krishna temple donation box. When told the amount, he asked them to remove all but a quarter of it. The next morning worshippers found the box broken and the money stolen. When informed, the Master nodded. He said that on the previous night he had noticed a starving man silently praying for enough money in the temple box to feed him. And so Nityananda obliged him with an adequate amount.

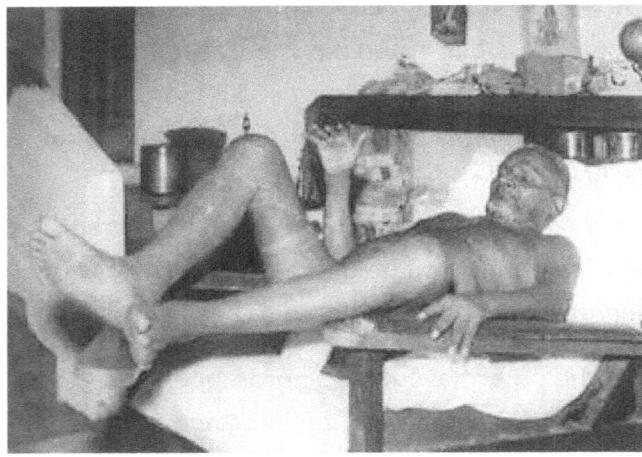

The New Ashram at Kailas

1956-1961

In 1956 a new ashram at Ganeshpuri was inaugurated and named "Kailas" after the Himalayan mountain home of Shiva. Here Nityananda lived for five more years--until two weeks before his mahasamadhi. Changes accompanied the new living situation. The Master's devotee attendants now monitored access to his private quarters and put darshan on a schedule. Visitors wishing to see Nityananda at other times were forced to make special arrangements.

Early one evening Nityananda sat in the middle of the inner platform with a pile of pillows at his left. Before him a window revealed steps leading to the terrace. Suddenly the young head of an important monastery in Udipi appeared at the entrance. He was accompanied by a number of followers, one of whom announced to Nityananda's seated devotees that their swami required a mat to sit on. The devotees watched the Master for a clue as to how to proceed--but he continued to gaze out the window without acknowledging the visitor in any way. Finally, the swami respectfully pushed the pillows against the wall and seated himself on the platform's edge. He then addressed Nityananda in Kanarese.

"Why do they call you God?" he asked.

Looking to his left, the Master replied, "Everyone is a God including yourself and those sitting here."

"But they call you an incarnation," insisted the young man.

Nityananda answered, "Does an incarnate ever make such a pronouncement? Does a jnani ever project himself as enlightened?"

"Yes, Krishna does in the Bhagavad Gita."

"No, Vyasa does so in telling the story--Krishna does not."

"But," the swami argued, "Krishna showed the universal form of God to Arjuna. it is recorded in the Gita!"

"How can the Absolute's form be seen or shown?" the Master said. "Vyasa wrote it to inculcate faith among the devout."

Trying to open an intellectual debate, the youth then raised certain points mentioned in the Gita. However, always impatient of such dry discussions, Nityananda waved him aside, saying: "What is in the Gita? From beginning to end, it is simply advice to renounce, renounce, renounce! To renounce worldliness and its inherent desires."

Considerably moved, the swami rose and thanked Nityananda for his darshan. But when he left, two of his followers stayed behind. The Master shrugged and said, "When there is yoga, there will be darshan."

A week later, the Master mentioned his young visitor. He hinted that in a previous incarnation the swami had been the elderly priest from Udipi who, recognizing the then youthful Nityananda's divine presence, had ordered the villagers not to harass him. This past connection had brought him to Ganeshpuri and Nityananda foresaw a bright future for him.

On another occasion, a small band of renunciates came and stood before him as he rested on the inner platform of his room. Nityananda nodded to them from his sleeping posture and they left without a word. When some of the devotees present expressed their surprise at not recognizing the renunciates, the Master said devotees did not just reside in Ganespuri. He said some lived in jungles, some in cities, and others in foreign lands.

Mrs. Kaikini of Dadar was a faithful follower of a great scholar who held audiences spellbound during his brilliant lectures on Jnaneshwar's famous translation of the Bhagavad Gita. Each year she was among those who accompanied him to Pandarpur on an annual pilgrimage known as Wari. Because Mrs. Muktabai occasionally attended these lectures, she became friends with Mrs. Kaikini and eventually invited her to Ganeshpuri. However, Mrs. Kaikini demurred, saying that it did not sound like an atmosphere she would enjoy. She admitted hearing that Nityananda was taciturn, gave no meaningful talks, and often rebuked visitors.

Some time later, just before the annual Wari, Mrs. Kaikini missed one of her scholar's regular lectures. Instead she went to a talk by a rival who, new on the scene, was beginning to attract a following. As fate would have it, her scholar/teacher had both noticed Mrs. Kaikini's absence and heard of her attendance at the other lecture. He angrily proclaimed that she was never again welcome in his presence or at the Wari.

When Mrs. Kaikini heard this, she was deeply shocked. To be punished so severely for what she considered a minor transgression was more than she could bear. Friends feared for her mental balance and Mrs. Muktabai again asked her to come to Ganeshpuri. This time Mrs. Kaikini agreed.

Their party arrived to find Nityananda sitting on his bench. When Mrs. Muktabai told him what had happened, he responded with characteristic brevity. "*In divine wisdom (jnana) how can there be difference (bheda)?*" The two young women took this to mean that if Mrs. Kaikini was truly listening to the saint Jnaneshwar, would it matter which lecture she was at? Then the Master pointed to the ground and shouted, "Besides, this is Pandarpur. There is no need to go in Wari!" He repeated this and as he did, Mrs. Kaikini's relief was immediate and she returned home calmed and at peace.

The following year as the month for the Wari approached, her anxiety returned, and she decided to go to Pandarpur on her own. But when she started to pack she fell ill. By the time she was well enough to travel, it was too late. The following year followed a similar pattern. Again, as she began to pack she became ill. Only then did she recognize the significance of Nityananda's words--and from that moment she no longer felt compelled to attend the Wari. Some years later she suddenly weakened and took to her bed. Stopping her son from rushing for a doctor, she said "Please don't. I see Nityananda standing there and he has come to take me." Within minutes she passed away.

Narayan Shetty, popularly called Sandow Shetty, was a familiar figure in Ganeshpuri in the last ten years of Nityananda's life. He was a big, gregarious man looked up to int he ashram-- although he sometimes went too far acting the buffoon. Now it happened that he was quite fond of fruit, especially those brought as offerings. Often he would seek the Master's permission with silent gestures and then slyly slip the best ones aside for himself. When a few devotees objected to such audacity, Nityananda retorted, "Never mind. His desires are simple--let him have the fruit."

Some years after the Master's passing, Sandow was hospitalized following surgery. Captain Hatengdi, going to visit his friend, found him semi-conscious and speaking as if to Nityananda.

"Remember, Master, that you promised me a place," he muttered. "Don't forget." And to the shock of the doctors who expected a full recovery, he died.

Once a famous singer visited Ganeshpuri at the invitation of a devotee. While fans and critics alike considered the man outstanding in his field, they agreed that he was also a little arrogant. Upon entering the ashram to perform, the man found a group of tribal people seated around the Master reclining on his bench as usual. Mud floor, an uncultured audience, and Nityananda's apparent indifference instantly upset the artist who decided his talents were wasted on this gathering. Without a word, he turned and went to his room. Later that evening a woman from a distinguished school of music arrived and performed for over an hour. Overhearing her, the disgruntled artist decided that he would perform the next day. To his dismay, however, that morning he could not utter a single note. He fearfully approached Nityananda who said, **"Sing? Why not? God gave you the voice--sing his praises. Why should you care who hears and who does not?"**

Please note that Indian music is an ancient science intended to enhance the individual's communion with the Infinite. Fame and wealth are incidental to its spiritual aspect. For this reason most songs relate in some way to reuniting the individual with the Supreme.

A year or two after K.S. Lulla began visiting Ganeshpuri, Nityananda took him aside. He told the attorney to go to Kanhangad and then to Dharmasthala to receive darshan at the famous Manjunatha Temple. He also told him to travel by air. This was the devotee's first trip to that part of the country and he planned it with care. He first proceeded to Kanhangad and from there to Mangalore. He then intended to take an early taxi to Dharmasthal and return to Mangalore in time for his 11:30 a.m. flight to Bombay. Accordingly, he rose, procured a taxi, and arrived at Dharmasthal at six in the morning. But when he tried to enter the Jain shrine for darshan, he was stopped. The attendant priest informed him that he could receive darshan only after first participating in the ritual puja--which would occur at noon. Lulla explained his predicament but the priest was adamant, explaining that tradition required this protocol of even the highest in the land. However Lulla persisted and was finally taken before the hereditary head of the temple, who simply repeated the temple rules. Nityananda's devotee in turn repeated his plea, saying, "Bhagawan sent me for Lord Manjunatha's darshan but my return flight is at 11:30. If you cannot help me I will go back and explain to Bhagawan why I did not receive darshan." Intrigued, the gentleman asked to whom he referred. When Lulla said "Nityananda of Ganeshpuri," the priest was told to let him enter the temple at once.

Lulla quickly returned to Ganeshpuri to tell his tale. To his surprise, however, the devotees already knew of the successful pilgrimage. He then learned that at the exact moment of his entry into the Jain temple in Dharmasthal the Master had smiled in Ganeshpuri, announcing, "Lulla is having darshan of Manjunatha."

This incident is unusual because Nityananda seldom urged participation in traditional ritual or public worship. Instead he often said that for it to lead to liberation devotion should not be demonstrative but practiced secretly. "Gupta bhakti--mukti!"

Once a devotee spoke of her spiritual experiences to friends in Bombay and implied that she was developing rapidly. On her next visit to Ganeshpuri the Master asked, "What do you do when you season food? Don't you cover it for a time and let it simmer?" This, he explained, allows the flavor to permeate the dish rather than escape into the air. *Similarly, spiritual experiences should be kept private until one has evolved enough to speak of them without arousing the ego.*

A cooking analogy is not surprising considering Nityananda's knowledge of the subject. He sometimes instructed a cook on how to grind the masala and what spices to use. It was customary for his devotees in Ganeshpuri to each prepare a dish as a daily offering to him. And Nityananda would always know if an ingredient was missing or make suggestions about blending spices or some aspect of its preparation. He once told a devotee that as a person became more spiritually evolved, he or she would instinctively be able to cook well and combine ingredients in the right proportions without having to measure them.

Nityananda's personal knowledge of the culinary art was legendary. G.L. Rao recalls that the Master once repaired a superb festival dinner for him. Serving Rao most of the food, he saved a little for himself on a sheet of newspaper. This he mixed with some curry, at a few bites while still standing, and then threw away the paper. Captain Hatengdi had a similar experience in 1945 when Nityananda prepared some rice and a regional potato dish peculiar to his devotee's native region. Carrying it to the guest room, he handed it to him. Moving a discreet distance away, the self-conscious devotee began to eat as the Master watched. Though delicious, it was an enormous portion and only after some time did Nityananda suggest that he could stop eating. Another year passed until one day, as they sat together, the Master remarked, "It is good to know how to cook." Captain Hatengdi took it as a casual utterance until thirty years later he found himself forced to learn the elements of cooking.

The New Ashram at Kailas

1950-1961

Nityananda could be very modern in his views. Once a devotee with a growing family brought his fifth and youngest child to Ganeshpuri. Oddly enough, no one else was around. The Master gave the baby his blessing and played with him for a while--and then turned to address the father. "Why must you reproduce like the cat family? Go and have an operation.

Another time, on an evening in 1947, he broke ashram silence to speak about Prohibition. "How is it possible to stop a poor man from drinking?" he demanded. "What can one offer a weary man who trudges home every night with little to feed his family and even greater debts? How should he forget his worries and fall asleep? Currently, every household in this region brews its own liquor from plantains. Make drunkenness a crime--but not drinking. Until people are properly fed and have healthy recreation, drinking will exist."

In another instance a mutton shopkeeper decided his hereditary avocation was unclean. After much thought, he shut down his butcher shop and reopened it as a general store. The new enterprise, however, was a failure and the man sought the Master's advice. Nityananda's advice was simple--the man should follow his true avocation and not be swayed by external considerations. In speaking to his devotee, he used the word dandha in referring to the duty a person must perform in this lifetime.

Lastly, there was a boy who wanted to become a pilot. When his devotee parents disapproved, he appealed to Nityananda--who took the son's side. The Master told the parents not to worry about his safety. Accidents, he said, were more likely to occur on the ground. But another crisis arose when, during the boy's eye examination, doctors detected a condition that inevitably would lead to blindness. In despair, the boy returned to Ganeshpuri where, again, Nityananda said not to worry. He then gave him a small bottle of oil to massage regularly onto his scalp. And three months later, when he retook the eye exam he was declared completely fit.

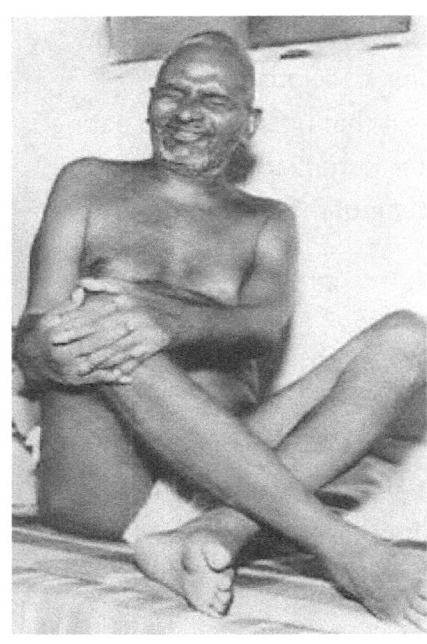

M.D.Suvarna, who took most of the later photographs of Nityananda, remembers one of the more remarkable visitors to Kailas. Swami Chinmayananda first came for darshan sometime around 1956. He returned often and frequently spoke of Nityananda to his own disciples, always calling him the living *stithaprajna of the Bhagavad Gita*--one who never wavers from consciousness. One day in 1960 he decided to take his students to Ganeshpuri. Organizing a group of musicians for the occasion, the Master received them with the honor due a visiting religious dignitary. He first invited Swami Chinmayananda to address the combined assembly from a terrace of the newly opened Bangalorewalla building and then told the swami to use the wisdom and power of Saraswati to spread the message of the Upanishads. Humbly, Swami Chinmayananda replied that he and the others present were spiritual infants compared to the great yogi. He also said that anyone attempting to describe Nityananda to the world would be trying to write "*a saga of one hundred Christs living together, each exhibiting his wondrous powers to ameliorate the sufferings of the poor.*"

Physically, Nityananda was showing signs of age. By 1957 his teeth had deteriorated so much that two devotees threatened to fast if he did not have them removed. He finally agreed but, refusing the then typical anesthetic injection of cocaine, experienced considerable pain and bleeding. When the two devotees later offered him some food, he refused. "How can one eat when the teeth have just been removed?" he said. "You may not realize it, but yogis do experience pain. The difference is they pay it no heed."

The relationship between the spiritual and the physical was sublimely simple--at least for Nityananda. When some devotees complained that travel conditions and old age hindered them from more frequent visits, he countered that his physical presence was unnecessary for their spiritual growth. "*Devotees will find this one wherever they meet and talk. Fish are born, live, and die in the holy Ganges without attaining liberation, but devotees have only to think of the guru.*" He had been saying this for years.

And when asked about the benefits of performing selfless service, the Master would reply, "Who wants it? God? Of course not--people only do it to get something in return. you should dutifully do your own work to the best of your ability without seeking a reward. That is the highest seva you can render. *The only thing required for spiritual growth is a detachment from worldly pleasures. If you don't listen to this, you will fail in the end*. "[The Master said this over and over again throughout the years. He said that the thoughtless state, the state of detachment is the highest state. How can there be desire in the state of detachment? It is not the world the yogi gives up, it is desire for worldly sense pleasure. The true yogi is full and content whether he is a pauper or a rich man. If pleasurable things come your way, experience them, but never go looking. Always be content in yourself wherever you are and whatever your circumstances.]

One day a devotee saw that Nityananda's feet were extremely swollen and asked about it. "**People come here for some benefit**," he told her, "**and then leave their desires and difficulties at this one's feet. While the Ocean of Divine Mercy washes away most of these tensions, a little is absorbed by this body--a body assumed only for their sake**."

Whenever Nityananda intervened on a devotee's behalf, he always gave destiny the upper hand. During the monsoon of 1959, a long line of devotees and petitioners waited outside for their turn to enter the ashram. The wife of an old Gujarati devotee pleaded with Suvarna to be allowed inside. As the doorkeeper was about to open the doors, Nityananda shouted at him to stop - and he did. But as the woman kept calling through the window and Nityananda continued shouting at him, Suvarna grew agitated. Throwing open the doors, he nervously admitted a group that included the Gujarati couple. She waited until the others had departed and then begged Nityananda to heal her husband, who was obviously gravely ill. He was silent for some time before saying, "Take him first to the hot springs and then to the dispensary for an injection." Greatly relieved, the woman thanked the Master and, half carrying her husband, left. However, en route to the kunds she spotted the dispensary and, deciding it more convenient to stop there first, took her husband inside for his injection. They then proceeded to the hot springs where, upon entering the water, the old man died.

It was in the early 1920's, following his studies in England, that Dr. M.B. Cooper received from a Himalayan saint the secret preparation for a drug with broad curative properties. The doctor spent the next decades studying the compound, which yielded astounding results. In 1959, after hearing his friend and colleague Dr. Deodhar speak of Nityananda, Dr. Cooper asked to accompany him to Ganeshpuri. he wanted to talk to the yogi about the future of the drug.

Arriving, they found Nityananda seated in his room. Dr. Cooper gazed in silence as tears streamed down his face. After a time Dr. Deodhar led him away to a restaurant where, over a cup of tea, he reminded his friend about mentioning the drug. Dr. Cooper shook his head. "*You come here so often,*" he said, "*that you only see his outer form. But I saw a dazzling crystal in his head! In a split second I was overwhelmed at his purity and acutely aware of my own separation from the Divine. I could only stand before him and cry.*"

Dr. Cooper was correct. Nityananda's unconcern with his physical body was reflected in his devotees constant awareness of it. And they were perplexed. By 1945, although he ate very little, the yogi was clearly--and mysteriously--putting on weight. In those days overnight guests cooked for themselves, always offering something to Nityananda--who declined more often than not. In fact, meals were not organized in the ashram until the early 1950's when the old west room was converted to a simple kitchen. Nonetheless, by 1960 his body had grown to huge proportions. his eating habits had not changed. If anything, now being toothless, he ate less.

Alarmed, four devotees finally voiced their concern. The first was Sandow Shetty, who as a youth had been fond of gymnastics and feats of strength. The Master told him that his heaviness was due to lack of exercise. The second inquirer was Rao, who will be recalled as suffering from chronic malaria. Nityananda told him that his swollen stomach was a result of a malaria-induced enlarged spleen. The third devotee, a practitioner of pranayama breathing exercises, was told his size was a result of breath retention. Finally Mrs. Muktabai came to him full of concern for his health and comfort. To her he said that the love of his devotees had settled around his gigantic belly. Regardless of cause, by the time Nityananda took mahasamadhi in August 1961 he was once again thin.

Feeding the poor was a standard occurrence at Kailas because the food offerings brought by visitors to Ganeshpuri were distributed to local poor children. In later years, as the number of devotees grew, so did the piles of flowers and fruit baskets. Most were distributed as usual, but Nityananda allowed some to rot and then ordered them buried. One day Sandow Shetty ventured to ask about this apparent waste. He was told, "It does not go to waste. Those for whom it is meant are consuming it."

In 1958 Nityananda asked that the poor children of Ganeshpuri be fed on a permanent basis. And it was done. Within three years a hundred children a day were receiving morning meals; within twenty years the numbers surpassed 700. Today, besides the children, meals are served several times monthly to the region's adivasi, nearly 2,500 tribal people shunned by other communities. The ashram coffers are always full, not surprisingly, with unsolicited donations for food.

Nityananda's Passing

August 8, 1961

On the afternoon of July 25, 1961, a weakened Nityananda asked Gopalmama, his attendant, to arrange for a chair to carry him to the nearby Bangalorewalla building. He said he would remain there a fortnight (14 days), and exactly two weeks later the yogi took mahasamadhi. His bed still stands in the building's main hall and is revered as a shrine.

Confusion was evident in the months preceding his passing. One rumor had Nityananda moving to the city of Bangalore, a plan primarily fostered by Lashmansa Khoday, who oversaw construction of the Bangalorewalla building. He went so far as to charter an airplane. Hearing of this, devotees rushed to Ganeshpuri to argue that it would make Nityananda less accessible to them. Nityananda said he had no intention of leaving and that "an assembly of sages" had already suggested that "it be here only." [*Nityananda was referring to Masters from the subtle realms, such as Siddhaloka.*] But unable--or unwilling--to understand the implications of this statement, Khoday and others continued with their plans. The day before the scheduled flight, however, the Master developed diarrhea and the trip was cancelled.

In hindsight, his move to the Bangalorewalla building appeared premeditated. It was the only building in Ganeshpuri large enough to encompass the multitude who would soon come to see him one last time. Remodeling the old ashram was likewise timely. In early June Nityananda learned that it was still unfinished; the voluntary backers had postponed the roof until after the monsoon season. But the yogi insisted that there was no time to lose. He ordered them to lay the slab immediately and to use ashram funds if necessary. These instructions were followed, and it was in the rebuilt section of the old Viakunt ashram that his earthly remains were later interred.

Of the many signs revealed to devotees in those last months, most were misinterpreted or ignored. For instance, Mrs. Muktabai recalled that shortly after his move to the Bangalorewalla building, Nityananda told her there would be a major pilgrimage to Ganespuri in two weeks time. She wondered, but never thought to ask, why so many people would come during the monsoon. However, one person understood--a woman devotee from Dadar called Mataji by her followers and Mantrasiddhibai by Nityananda.

In May 1961, the day before she arrived for a visit, he experienced a discharge from his ear. He did not complain and the secretion was odorless, but devotees nonetheless called in a respected specialist. Although he had never met his patient, the doctor prostrated himself and refused to prescribe any medication until Nityananda promised to recover. The Master nodded his assurance and the doctor gave Gopalmama some capsules with instructions for administering them. He then departed. The yogi accepted a capsule, saying he did so because the good doctor had shown great sensitivity. But later he refused a second one. "One is enough," he explained. "His bhavana has worked." Mantrasiddhibai, learning of the discharge, began crying and begged Nityananda not to leave. She interpreted it as a sign that he was cleansing his system of toxins--and for only one purpose. The Master admonished her, *"Why cry? Stop it. Greater work is possible in the subtle plane than in the gross."* To the others, including Mrs. Muktabai, he said he had injured his ear long ago in a fall in the Kanheri caves.

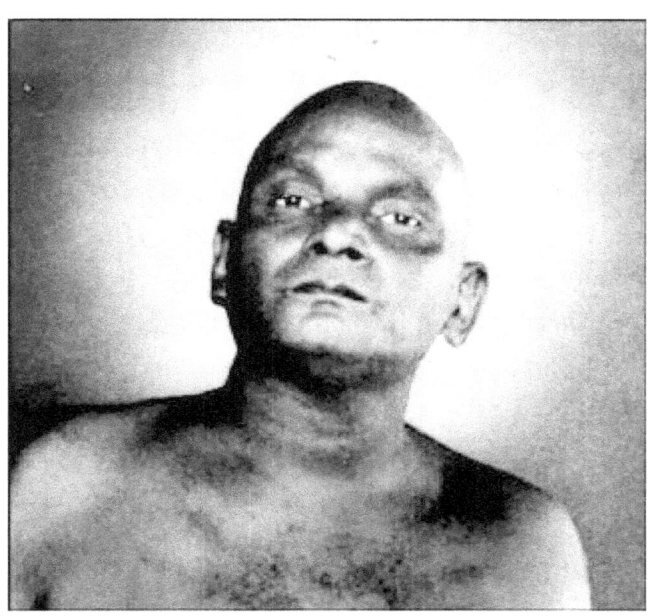

The way Dr. Pandlaskar heard of the mahasamadhi was decidedly odd. Early that morning the doctor's nine-year-old son had confronted his parents with the words: "What are you doing here? Go to Ganeshpuri. He leaves today because the assembly of sages says that he alone can help in the forthcoming ashtagraha yoga. Astrological indications are for great evil to the world in general and to India in particular." The parents were so astonished at the boy's bizarre words that they reprimanded him for talking nonsense. But that evening they heard of Nityananda's passing and departed at once. The boy was so affected by his experience that he did not fully recover for years. His message was thought to refer to the conjunction of all planets in a single sign, the next occurrence being in February 1962 when all eight entered Capricorn, the sign of India. It was a hot May afternoon in 1961 when M.U. Hatengdi first heard what he called a telepathic bell announcing that Nityananda would soon take mahasamadhi. This is his story: Fearing the yogi had already discarded his human form, I tried not to think about it. The next morning I reluctantly opened the Delhi paper even though it would hardly mention a nonpolitical event in Bombay. All the same I was relieved to find nothing in the obituaries.

The prospect haunted me for the next three months. I grew insecure about my own spiritual practice even though Nityananda had told me there was nothing to read or study. Even worse was the thought of being unable to contact him in a physical form. I had not yet heard of his assurance that greater work was possible on the subtle plane, and since 1948 my visits to see him were infrequent and largely in the public eye. No longer did I quietly sit with him in private. True, he once said that when a child learns to walk, the mother, still watchful, must allow it freedom to run around. Perhaps he should have added, even if the child tries to hang on to the mother! I knew his grace was with me wherever I was stationed in the Navy-but I also knew that I could contact him if necessary.

Unable to leave the naval station, I made a plan. Knowing that Mrs. Muktabai still went to Ganeshpuri every two weeks, I wrote asking her to report on Nityananda's health after each visit and enclosed some self-addressed envelopes. Her letters began arriving regularly, the first few indicating that he was well. Her third or fourth letter, however, referred to some debility as well as talk of his undertaking a trip to Kanhangad. This confused by did not worry me. He had told me in 1944 that he would remain in the Ganeshpuri ashram, and even if he changed his mind, I was used to traveling great distances to see him. Besides, I was planning a visit in early August and it was the mid- July. But my anxiety continued and it was an unhappy period for me. The last letter from Mrs. Muktabai was dated August 4 and reached me on August 7. It was a dark and rainy evening and I grew despondent reading it. She wrote me to come at once because the Master was very weak.

Back in December I had made a small altar in my home. On a corner shelf lit by the first rays of the morning sun I kept a framed photograph of Nityananda along with flowers from our garden and a silver lamp. The lamp held just enough oil to burn for an hour and it was my custom to light it every evening at sunset. The day after the distressing letter I came home for lunch to find the little lamp already burning. In turn, the picture was decorated with flower garlands and flanked by two vases, each containing sweets traditionally prepared on the festival of Ganesh's birth. When I asked my wife why she had arranged such a display, she said she had simply felt like it. I had never shared with her my fears about Nityananda's passing and so her demonstration was all the more remarkable. She lit the oil lamp at nine that morning and it had never gone out. She collected every flower in the garden including the water lilies, something she had never done before, and then prepared the modaks--all this without knowing why. The mystery was solved the next morning when I learned of the mahasamadhi. While I was so absorbed in the world, the Master sent this sign of his blessing from nine hundred miles away.

Nityananda occupied a room directly above the entrance of the Bangalorewalla building. For the first three or four days, though weak, he walked a little. July 27 was his last Guru Purnima, a day on which Hindus traditionally honor the teacher, and he addressed the assembled devotees for nearly 45 minutes in a surprisingly strong voice. He said that the boxcars of a train going up a hill might slip backward without sand thrown on the tracks for traction. To maintain a lasting connection with the engine, each boxcar must forge a bond of unshakable faith and conviction. Everything else he said would happen automatically. He then mentioned plans for building a hospital in Ganeshpuri.

A day or so later, with only Madhumama present, he stood on the balcony watching the sun set in a sky that was unusually clear for July. Nityananda said, "Anyone wanting to see the sun should do it now for tomorrow he may not be seen." The following morning dawned cloudy and stayed that way as a noticeably weaker Nityananda was moved to the main hall. There he stayed until he died.

On August 7 around four in the afternoon he asked for B.H. Mehta, popularly called Babubhai Lokhandwalla. Mehta, who was in a restaurant having tea at the time, learned of the summons and hurried to the main hall. There the yogi handed him a large parcel wrapped in a piece of cloth and asked him to look after Kanhangad. The bundle contained cash, gold, and other valuables that Mehta eventually used, along with funds he collected, to build the two Kanhangad temples above the rock-cut caves and at Guruvana.

Guruvana is the area of jungle where Nityananda was found as an infant. A temple dedicated to Nityananda stands there today, along with many other temples in India dedicated to the Master.

For months devotees had noticed in Nityananda a growing sadness that often approached tears. We can only surmise that the great yogi felt as Krishna did in the Bhagavad Gita when he said he granted supplicants what they prayed for. But more often than not, the only thing they wanted was worldly success or material gain. *Too many fools, he said, passed his dwelling without asking for the liberation he offered*. Likewise people brought Nityananda their earthly cares. These he relieved hoping to inspire in them a hunger for the spiritual gifts he was empowered to bestow. But in the end, like Krishna, he was disappointed. Some people actually came to Ganeshpuri for a lucky number to gamble on. They might count, for instance, how many of his fingers were visible at a given moment or the number of steps he took. Usually this was when Nityananda threw stones or shouted.

This is only my view from the heart, but it is understood what Nityananda meant by "*More work can be done in the subtle.*" *Nityananda, while incarnate, was with people, all the people who asked for the liberation he offered received it*. As in the case of remarking to Rao that he was enjoying the incense, even though it was being waved in front of a hole over one hundred miles away, he showed that he was wherever there was devotion. Though in the gross, he suffused the lives of all who desired what he offered through his permanent establishment in the subtle. *Having merged with the formless Absolute, yet he projects subtle form from the realm of Siddhaloka now*, and *suffuses and permeates all who seek him within and without. In this way, only the earnest seeker with a pure heart can find him, and the numbers he can reach are limitless*. By pure it is not meant a person with perfect behavior, but rather, *perfect love for the master, a perfect desire to merge with God Shiva, and his gift of divine liberation and understanding*. All who desire may fall under the protection of the Siddha lineage and the Bhagawan Nityananda, *the essence of love*.

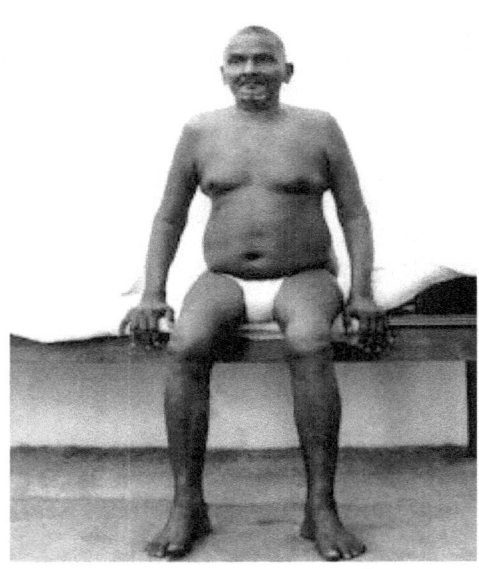

On the evening of August 7 the engineer Hegde felt drawn to Ganeshpuri. Traveling alone, he gained entry to the samadhi hall with some difficulty and found Monappa at Nityananda's bedside. The doctor had just announced that there was no need to worry and was walking out with Sandow Shetty--when he dropped his medical bag with a thud. Opening his eyes, the Master asked what the noise was and then inquired who was at his feet. Hearing that it was Hegde, he told Manappa to leave. Hegde started to massage the Master's feet and was alone with him until four that morning. A little after midnight Nityananda startled him by speaking:

"People only come here for money, and the more they get the more they want. Their greed is boundless. Sometimes they arrive hungry and with only the clothes on their backs but soon they start demanding luxuries like cars and houses. *One would think that with their basic human needs satisfied, they would seek something higher. Something spiritual. But they persist. There is little point in allowing this body to continue. Tomorrow I will take samadhi.*"

This last sentence he repeated three times. Hegde was stunned because, while Nityananda was very weak, doctors had found nothing clinically wrong with him. Most devotees fully expected him to recover. Soon he began calling for Swami Janananda, demanding to know why he had not come. When Hegde begged him to postpone his mahasamadhi, Nityananda replied that he would if asked by someone with selfless devotion and love. After all, was not Pundalika a great devotee who made the Lord of Pandharpur wait for him? And was there no such person here? One would be enough to put off the samadhi. With such a person present, he said, not even God could leave without permission. He would be unable to break that bond of pure love. And pointing his index finger at Hegde, Nityananda asked, "*Can you offer this one selfless devotion?*" But Hegde tearfully replied, "*I don't know.*"

Nityananda's Passing: Part II

August 8, 1961

In the remaining hour or so, Nityananda asked for certain other devotees by name but they arrived too late. He told Hedge not to worry, and at a quarter to four again muttered something about Swami Janananda, who also came too late and only after receiving a telegram. Hegde asked if he could help but Nityananda said he needed a sanyasi. At around four o'clock he sent the engineer to bathe.

Returning, Hedge offered to pour some coffee into the Master's mouth but the devotee in the next room woke up and told him to stop, saying that his plan was to bathe and then prepare Nityananda's coffee himself. And the yogi waved the engineer aside. But when the other devotee went for his bath, Hedge ran down to the hotel and asked the grateful manager to prepare some special coffee. Quickly Hedge carried it back, served it to Nityananda, and then departed, leaving him in the care of the others wishing to attend him. Among them, sometime ofter seven, were several women devotees from the early days, including Mrs. Wagle, a professional nurse.

In the early days Nityananda had served sugar cane juice to visitors. When Mrs. Muktabai had once asked why, he said, "Why? Because it is this one's juice." However, that morning Nityananda requested coffee and food for those present, something he had been doing for several months. Coming from Bangalore, Lakshmansa Khoday arrived around this time.

Among those assembling since six that morning was Chandu, a longstanding devotee who had come some days before. When Nityananda suddenly asked him for some kasthuri, a type of musk oil, Chandu began to weep. Years ago in Kanhangad he had told the devotee that before leaving this world he would ask him for kasthuri. In an attempt to calm him, Nityananda asked his old companion if he knew of a train that could carry then to Kanhangad. Chandu answered, yes, there was a scheduled train. But when the yogi asked, "How can this one go without strength in these legs?" Chandu was silent.

C.C. Parekh had arranged for a lift to Bombay. He planned to leave by seven that morning, tell his staff that he would remain in Ganeshpuri a few more days, and return to the ashram that afternoon. However, as he entered the car, he suddenly stopped. Asking his friend to wait, he hurried to the hall--where he was shocked to find the Master struggling to breathe. He administered oxygen at once and Nityananda's breathing improved, but Parekh decided not to leave. Remaining at the head of the bed, he was soon joined by Dr. Nicholson, a devotee and respected eye specialist from Bombay. Dr. Nicholson's wife joined them shortly, having telephoned a doctor at the neighboring sanatorium. Soon he arrived, examined Nityananda, and prescribed some medicine. But it was too late. Nityananda had them remove the oxygen mask and, breathing normally, asked Parekh for some water. Then at a quarter of nine he asked Lakshmansa khoday for some lemon juice. Khoday offered him fresh coconut milk instead, which he accepted. He took nothing more.

At nine-thirty Gopalmama noticed that Nityananda's body was radiating a lot of heat. Speaking for the last time, he repeated what he had said often that summer: "*A sadhu became a swami. The swami become a deva to some, a baba and a bhagawan to others. This deva will now enter constant samadhi.*"

[sadhu--literally, good; holy man. swami--literally, master of one's Self; title given to monks of the orders organized by Shankara. bhagawan--godhead; one who possesses the six treasures; one who is full of light. Deva--Literally, a shining one; a God. This is the last reference that Nityananda made of himself.]

Ten minutes later he took several very deep breaths, the final one expanding his chest fully. He straightened his legs, the one arthritic, as far as he could, clasped his hands above his navel, and lay perfectly still. After a time Parekh called Swami Muktananda and others from the adjoining room to take charge of Nityananda's body.

Between that afternoon and the following evening, there was much discussion about where to inter the holy remains. The devotee responsible for the Kailas ashram's construction proposed building a subterranean room there. Other devotees suggested a site on the hill behind the present museum building. Another group wanted it to be where the yogi's body now rested in the Bangalorewalla building, a proposal that Khoday offered to oversee. However, the site ultimately chosen for the samadhi shrine was the recently reconstructed old ashram building. Nityananda had always said that sages gathered there, and it was remembered with what urgency he had ordered the slab roof installed during that summer's monsoon.

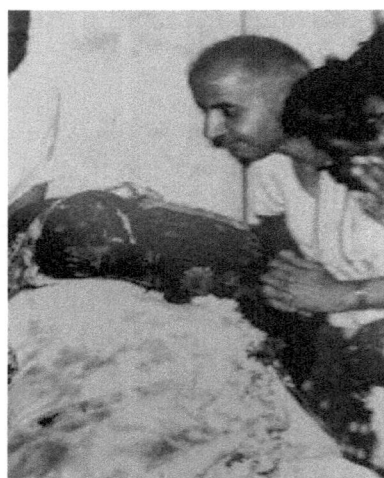

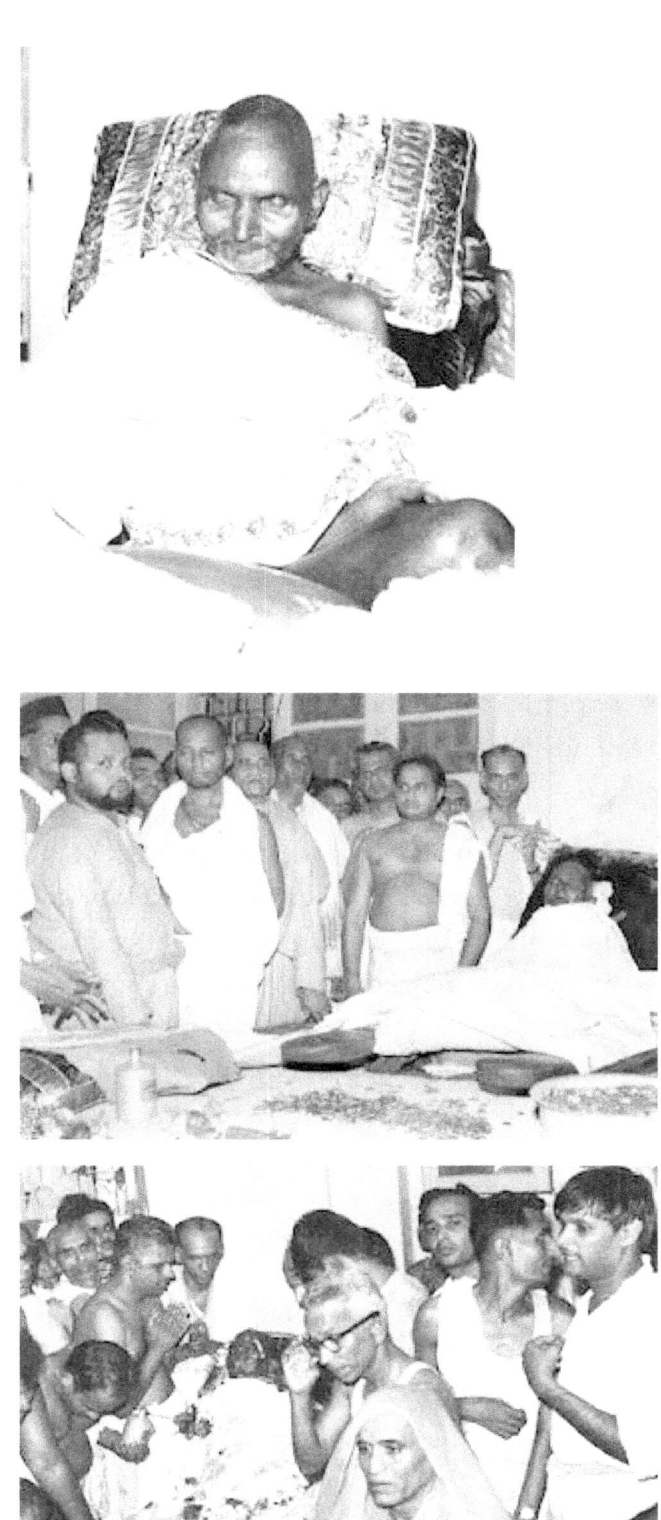

On the morning of August 9 Captain Hatengdi arrived at his office to find a telephone message. Calling home, he learned that Mrs. Muktabai had sent a telegram saying that Nityananda had taken mahasamadhi the day before and interment would be in three days. He somehow managed to reach Bombay at eleven that night only to learn that the ceremony would occur the next morning. At that hour there were no trains or taxis and he spent a dismal night waiting for the morning train, which he caught. He pulled into Bassein, now the Vasai Road, around five-thirty to find 150 other people stranded en route to Ganeshpuri. The state transport office was still closed and the area was deserted-- except for a growing crowd of anxious devotees. Captain Hatengdi joined the line, resigned to what seemed inevitable. He was 25 miles away and would never arrive in time to see Nityananda one last time.

As he stood musing, five people stepped out of line to flag down a solitary taxi. But the driver refused to make the trip and they trudged back to the throng. By now the hopelessness of the situation drove Hatengdi to pace up and down--from the station to the fork in the road. To the right lay Ganeshpuri; to the left, Bassein and the fort. Pacing this 200-yard stretch several times, he again came to the fork in the road. This time, however, he saw an old but empty seven seat vehicle approaching from Bassein. He hailed the driver, who agreed to take Hatengdi and six other devotees who quickly piled in. The driver kept remarking on their good fortune. It seemed he rarely came this way and had been surprised to find himself at the fork in the road. At seven-fifteen he dropped them off at the Bhadrakali temple.

Captain Hatengdi, overjoyed to be there, had no idea where to find Nityananda's body. He managed to push through the crowd and five minutes later saw the body being carried from the Bangalorewalla building and placed on a jeep. At that moment the sun broke through the drizzle to light up the Master's face and Hatengdi rushed forward to catch hold of the vehicle. The hour-long procession would circle the buildings before proceeding to the old ashram's eastern entrance. As the entourage slowly began to move, the sun seemed to bow out and the drizzle resumed. The body had been arranged in the lotus position and sat in an easy chair conveyed by means of two logs tied to the chair arms. Hatengdi did not release his hold on the jeep until the chair was lowered and carried into the low building.

The old ashram was filled to capacity and there was no possibility of entering. So Hatengdi went first to bathe and then to pray. By now he knew the samadhi shrine was situated right where he used to sleep following the ashram's move to Kailas. He finally and truly understood Nityananda's earlier words to him that "*this spot alone was good.*"

Nityananda's life exemplified nondualism. He made no distinction between people, never caring about their religion, their sex, or whether they were poor or wealthy, backward or educated. He was the common man's friend, the spiritual aspirant's guide, and the devotee's constant companion. He taught that devotion to God went hand in hand with the performance of one's earthly responsibilities. In fact, he demanded that people work in the world, saying that work properly done was the same as worship. He felt people should be of the world without being worldly. He particularly favored charitable works as opportunities to serve God. Always fond of feeding the poor, he built a small school in Ganeshpuri and a dispensary in Vajreshwari. Even while crediting the will of God and karmic law for the suffering of individuals and nations, he never let this justify callousness toward others.

He did not want followers. But when they came, he only asked for purity of motive and faith (*shuddha bhavana and shraddha*) and the freedom to do his work from within. His greatness lay in the key he held to the inner consciousness of the faithful. His power radiated without effort or notice on his part. Words were unimportant to him. Free of earthly ambition, he distributed whatever gifts people brought him. It says in the Bhagawatam that the divine power of such a guru remains hidden, manifesting itself for those who truly desire Truth. With Nityananda, this was so--and his manifestations were many. *While emanating steadily from the spiritual plane, his divine presence reflected the viewer's inner state of consciousness*. While some saw in him the terror of Kali, others found the compassion of Vajreshwari. Dualism was always unmasked as an intellectual pursuit that toyed with separate aspects of the same reality.

In his final months Nityananda complained that people only came to him for material gain. *"What sort of grace is possible in such cases?"* he would ask before adding, *"They don't need a guru--they need a soothsayer."* He called it an abuse of his physical presence, likening it to spiritual window shopping. *Where was their spiritual aspiration? Why ask the ocean for a few fish when, with a little effort, one could have the priceless pearls on the ocean floor?*

He spoke of the *antarjnanis, self realized* beings who lived in the world and experienced pain like everyone else. The difference between them and the rest of humanity was their ability to detach their minds from their suffering. *Once established in infinite consciousness, they became silent.* And, while all-knowing, they lived as if knowing nothing; while manifesting simultaneously in unlikely places, they appeared idle. They viewed life as if it were a movie-- from a state of detachment. *For Nityananda, being detached from life's circumstances, pleasant or otherwise, was the highest state. He was an antarjnani.*

Let the mind, he said, be like a lotus leaf floating on the water, unaffected by its stem below and its flower above. *While engaged in worldly pursuits, keep the mind untainted by desire and distraction. Keep the mind detached and faith in God firmly established in the lotus of the heart, never letting it be swayed by happiness or despair. Devotees will find themselves subjected to various tests, he said--tests of the mind, of the emotions, of the body. With every thought that pops into the mind, God is waiting for a person's reaction. Therefore, stay alert and detached.* See everything as an opportunity to gain experience, improve oneself, and rise to a higher level. *Desire alone causes suffering in the world.* Humankind brings nothing into this world and takes nothing away from it. This ashram, for instance, is full of things for devotees to use when visiting, but if this one (Nityananda) leaves he will take nothing with him. Whatever is need will come. This one is not flattered when important persons come or distressed when devotees fall away. Whether visitors come or not, whether they bring offerings or not--it is the same. This one has no desire to go anywhere or see anything. Let one's thoughts and actions reflect one's words. This ashram's practice is not in doing good deeds. *This ashram's practice is learning to be detached. Anything else that happens does so automatically by the will of God--although this one will speak when somebody is genuinely interested.*

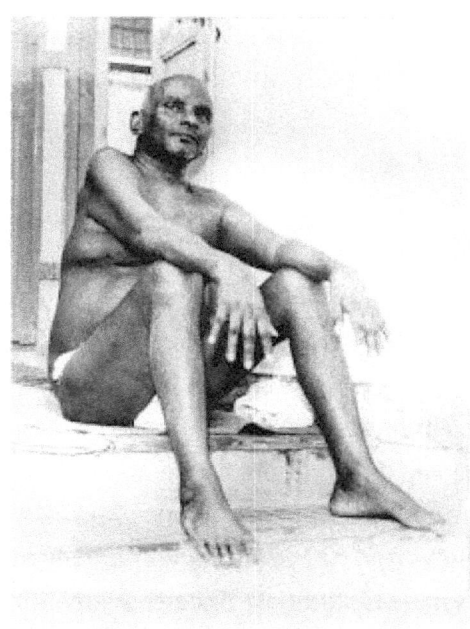

Afterword

The Shrines of Ganeshpuri

Since ancient times Ganeshpuri was considered a holy place and Nityananda often recounted episodes from the ancient Puranas attesting to this. Of the area's numerous shrines, several were built and maintained by Nityananda and his followers.

The old Bhimeshwar temple, situated near the old ashram, was one of these. Dr. Deodhar recalled than on a visit around 1950 he noticed that the silver cobra--the Naag--was missing from the temple's linga. But he kept forgetting to tell Nityananda. This continued for some time until one day he asked another devotee to mention it for him. Hearing the belated news, Nityananda said, "Have you come here just to tell me this? Deodhar always forgets! Tell him this one said to have the Naag remade--but this time in copper." He then gave detailed instructions for its size and features, directing the devotee to use a thread to show the dimensions. Finally, he said he wanted it installed on the following Monday-four short days away. Receiving these instructions, the doctor hurried at once to the marketplace where he was directed to a certain artisan. This man, the district's only coppersmith, announced the project would take him ten days to complete. Anxiously, Dr. Deodhar explained the urgency and the coppersmith agreed to finish it by Sunday.

When he arrived to pick up the Naag, the doctor saw that the cobra's eyes did not glisten as instructed. The coppersmith explained he had left off the shiny beads, fearing they would fall out and leave empty sockets. At that moment a statue of Shiva was carried in from the workshop, its eyes brightly painted and shiny. The men looked at it and decided to do the same for the snake. Nityananda was satisfied with the results and kept it in his room until the installation, which occurred the next morning.

An unusual feature of the Bhimeshwar temple was the continuous trickle of water from the ceiling at the rear of the dome. It had begun seeping from a number of places behind the main linga sometime in the early 1940's after Nityananda moved to Ganeshpuri. As time passed the amount of water increased, even during the hot summers. Captain Hatengdi heard this from his uncle who added that Nityananda had cautioned him not to step on the small lingas that sprang up wherever the water fell. And indeed, two discernible lingas were forming in two water-filled holes directly behind the main linga. Projections of various shapes also appeared in a rough semicircle around them. Whenever Nityananda mentioned the water, he would laugh heartily at the thought of scientists coming to investigate the phenomenon. It is said that once the yogi left the old ashram for Kailas in 1956, the water slowed to a trickle and stopped completely the day Nityananda's statue was installed in the Samadhi Mandir temple.

On one of his monthly weekend visits in 1945, Captain Hatengdi noticed a small shrine 200 yards from the road to the ashram. Nityananda said he built it for the village deity, or gramadevata, because the spot had the power of samadhi. And it was here that Swami Muktananda later made his ashram.

The current Krishna temple stands where once there was an old stone relic of Nandi, the bull of Shiva. Its presence had always been a mystery. Captain Hatengdi recalls watching Nityananda sit on it occasionally, both feet dangling down its left side. When they began building the temple, workers tried to move the stone--but it would not budge. Hearing of this, Nityananda ordered them to break a coconut near the bull. Once they did, two of them easily lifted the great stone. At the Master's instructions, they the bull's head, placing it on the cow statue that stands behind Krishna.

With the Krishna temple finished, Nityananda immediately turned his attention to the Bhadrakali temple. He would set a specific day for its inauguration and the work had to be completed. In this instance, Mistry had a single day to make the goddess's statue and, per

Nityananda's instructions, he used the same cement mixture employed earlier for Krishna. But when it was finished, the priest anxiously said her face was not attractive enough. This, Nityananda reassured him, would be taken care of--and ordered the statue covered with a white cloth. At the following morning's consecration ceremony the cloth was removed to reveal a changed face that satisfied even the priest's aesthetic expectations. Later, when asked why the hurry to build this particular temple, Nityananda replied that Bhadrakali had followed him from Gokarn, desiring a place in Ganeshpuri. And she was not prepared to wait!

Besides those actually built by him, numerous shrines were dedicated to Nityananda after his mahasamadhi. The first temple built on Kanhangad rock opened in April 1963, the one in Guruvana in May 1966. The rock temple was commissioned by B.H. Mehta from funds he collected.

Known as Samadhi Mandir, the samadhi shrine was the creation of Prabhashankar Sompura, who designed the renowned Somnath Temple as well as the two Kanhangad temples. The samadhi shrine with Nityananda's earthly remains is located on the site of the original Ganeshpuri ashram. Rising a hundred feet into the sky, the shrine and hall capped by a 24-foot high dome have an imposing beauty. The Tansa River flowing a short distance away adds to the tranquility of this holy site.

Additional temples dedicated to Nityananda range from simple altars adorned with his photograph to more elaborate temples such as the one built by M.L. Gupta in Koilandi near Calicut. With its large hall, this shrine wits where the young Ram once roamed with his adopted father Ishwar Iyer.

With the Krishna temple finished, Nityananda immediately turned his attention to the Bhadrakali temple. He would set a specific day for its inauguration and the work had to be completed. In this instance, Mistry had a single day to make the goddess's statue and, per Nityananda's instructions, he used the same cement mixture employed earlier for Krishna. But when it was finished, the priest anxiously said her face was not attractive enough. This, Nityananda reassured him, would be taken care of--and ordered the statue covered with a white cloth. At the following morning's consecration ceremony the cloth was removed to reveal a changed face that satisfied even the priest's aesthetic expectations. Later, when asked why the hurry to build this particular temple, Nityananda replied that Bhadrakali had followed him from Gokarn, desiring a place in Ganeshpuri. And she was not prepared to wait!

Besides those actually built by him, numerous shrines were dedicated to Nityananda after his mahasamadhi. The first temple built on Kanhangad rock opened in April 1963, the one in

Guruvana in May 1966. The rock temple was commissioned by B.H. Mehta from funds he collected.

Known as Samadhi Mandir, the samadhi shrine was the creation of Prabhashankar Sompura, who designed the renowned Somnath Temple as well as the two Kanhangad temples. The samadhi shrine with Nityananda's earthly remains is located on the site of the original Ganeshpuri ashram. Rising a hundred feet into the sky, the shrine and hall capped by a 24-foot high dome have an imposing beauty. The Tansa River flowing a short distance away adds to the tranquility of this holy site.

Additional temples dedicated to Nityananda range from simple altars adorned with his photograph to more elaborate temples such as the one built by M.L. Gupta in Koilandi near Calicut. With its large hall, this shrine wits where the young Ram once roamed with his adopted father Ishwar Iyer.

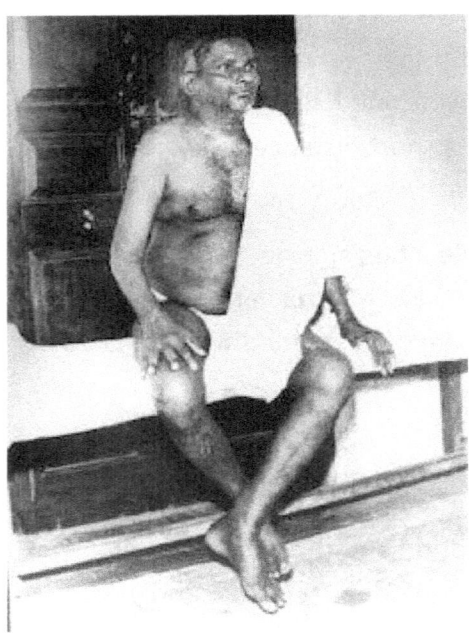

Nityananda's Photographer

Nityananda hated being photographed and only a handful of images from the early days exist. Most of the photographs we have of him were taken decades later by M.D. Suvarna.

Devotees often wanted a picture of Nityananda with their families. Typically, the young Nityananda discouraged people from revering his photographs and actually admonished them for doing so. Mr. Krishnabai felt that since he had obliged the photographer in her own compound she might be permitted to keep his picture in her house. Accordingly, she asked the photographer to send one to her mother's house. When she arrived to pick up the framed photograph, it was nighttime. Mangalore still lacked electricity in those days and with only kerosene lamps burning Mrs. Muktabai did not notice Nityananda sitting in a dark corner. As she was asking her mother about the picture, the yogi exclaimed, "So you want a photograph, do you? You will find it in the dung heap!" Running outside, she looked to no avail. It was then that her mother said Nityananda had smashed the framed picture with a rock. The shards, of course, now lay buried in the dung heap. [Nityananda frowned on such things, as he did not want his image to become an object of retail commerce.]

Photographs of Nityananda only became readily available when M.D. Suvarna, originally a press photographer, came to Ganeshpuri in the early 1950. He and a colleague, learning of Nityananda's growing popularity, knew people would soon be demanding photographs. But when they arrived at the ashram, Nityananda thundered at them and they retreated in haste. Suvarna, however, decided to try again. This time his persistence was rewarded. Permission was granted, after considerable pleading, under the following conditions: there should be no disturbance, no fuss, no posing.

Suvarna first traveled to Ganeshpuri as photographer but he soon became a devotee. Whenever work brought him to Bombay, he made a point of visiting Ganeshpuri on Thursdays and shooting a roll of film. *The resulting images consistently portray Nityananda's mystical power, compassion, and inner bliss*. Some are so good that they may be mistaken for posed portraits. Others show considerable variance in Nityananda's physical appearance from picture to picture, a fact pointed out by the sculptor, Mr. Wagh, who utilized them for the altar statue in the samadhi shrine.

As an experiment, in the late 1950's Mr. Suvarna exposed several hundred feet of motion picture film, taking snippets at odd moments and later splicing them together. It was the first time he had handled such a camera and his results were remarkably good. Oddly, however, on occasion the developed film was completely blank. For instance, once he wanted to photograph Nityananda returning from his morning walk, After having a hole bored in the wall of a nearby hotel, Suvarna waited with his pre-adjusted camera and took several shots of the Master passing. But the developed film was blank. he repeated the experiment--with the same result. Suvarna recalls Nityananda sometimes asking him, "What is the value of so many pictures? Are you still not satisfied?" And then he would smile.

One last time, on a particularly important occasion, Suvarna's cameras unaccountably malfunctioned. it was August 10, 1961, two days after the mahasamadhi. The body had been placed in an easy chair, mounted on a jeep, and driven slowly around the Ganeshpuri compound, a procession that, despite a steady drizzle, Suvarna managed to capture on film. Then the body was taken inside the old ashram for burial. From different vantage points in the room, Suvama and his cousin each took a roll of film during the ceremony. But later they discovered that not one exposure came out.

Shri Nityananda Arogyashram Hospital at Ganeshpuri

The beginning of Shri Nityanadna Arogyashram is in a way connected with the late Dr. M.B. Cooper and the herbal wonder drug revealed to him by a Himalayan saint long ago. Through vibrational guidance and his own genius he successfully prepared an inject able solution from the original formula, which he initially prescribed for tuberculosis. However, Dr. Cooper knew the Himalayans took it both to combat disease and to maintain health, and further research proved the compound's broader curative properties. As a result, over the years he helped patients suffering from asthma and other lung ailments, skin diseases, arthritis, cysts, as well as tuberculosis--even advanced cases. He named the remedy mahawaz--"the great sound"--because of the cosmic sound that seemed to direct his research.

Dr. Deodhar had been Dr. Cooper's assistant since the late 1930's. A decade later he became a devotee of Nityananda and, after seeking the Master's advice, left general practice to concentrate on mahawaz. He was told the remedy would be successful if administered through an ashram hospital but that such a project would require great patience and perseverance on his part.

Eventually, Dr. Deodhar and B.C.S. Swamy, a fellow devotee, brought Dr. Cooper to Ganeshpuri. Upon first seeing Nityananda, the doctor was overwhelmed and had to leave. But he returned later with an ampule of mahawaz to show the yogi. Again, Nityananda said it would succeed. A few months before the mahasamadhi Dr. Deodhar and Mr. Swamy presented a proposal for a hospital to be built at Ganeshpuri. Nityananda immediately approved the idea and asked for a map of the ashram's property. He indicated where he wanted the future hospital built, giving them the piece of land along with a cash donation. he said to proceed in three stages, indicating with his hands and saying, "First small, then big, and then very big!"

In 1963 the Nityananda Arogyashram Trust was formed, and in December 1966 the hospital's foundation stone was laid by Swami Chinmayananda in the presence of a distinguished audience. Today one of the district's finest hospital buildings, its spacious and airy rooms are within walking distance of the samadhi shrine.

Dr. Cooper donated the mahawaz formula to the Trust. Although he and Dr. Deodhar received fabulous offers for this formula, they were determined to maintain its availability to common people. Similarly, his daughter, Dr. M.H. Pavri, and his son, Mr. Cooper, gave up their rights to any entitled royalties. Upon the death of her father in August 1980, Dr. Pavri assumed responsibility for the hospital as well as for the manufacture and development of the herbal extract.

So Say The Stars

There is considerable interest today in Vedic astrology, and ancient science predating its Western counterpart by millennia. To this end readers may be interested in a horoscope prepared for Captain Hatengdi in March 1970. (Incidentally, the Western word "horoscope" is of ancient Greek derivation and refers to "looking at time.") In such instances, sages with intuitive wisdom chart all possible permutations and combinations to develop the pattern of a subject's life.

In India these are called Nadigrantha readings. Full of great detail, they include the names and charts of individuals influencing the subject in good or bad ways, often referring to previous incarnations. However, such readings are primarily useful in understanding a subject's past and inherent tendencies. Present and future predictions often prove unreliable because of the ongoing play of human will and divine intervention. In Captain Hatengdi's case, at the age of 28 he was shown to meet a great being who would affect his life quite favorably. There was a lengthy description of this being, which we include here in an edited form.

He came to the world for the sake of his devotees, a great yogi. Nothing is known of his birth or his age. He has fed thousands of sanyasis and sadhus. While ever in samadhi, he talks. While ever with the Atman, he is never in the body. He talks directly to God. Long- limbed with a vibrant personality, he sometimes goes naked and some- times wears a loincloth. Although few recognize him, *he is God in human form*.

He is called by a name beginning with the letter N. He sits near hot springs and a Shiva temple and does not engage in outward activities, giving the impression of doing nothing. Money he takes from his loincloth as needed. He removes difficulties and occasionally prescribes medicines. Ignorant people never see his true nature.

While these words cannot possibly relate his greatness, a devotee will come in due course and describe him properly. Others who write about him will succeed only if they are inspired by him--and then only if he wishes it.

Eventually books will be written about him and many will make money in his name.

At the time of this reading, he is no longer in human form. His many devotees include highly evolved sanyasis and members of royalty. Numerous ashrams and shrines are built in his honor--but he never recognized or initiated disciples. No one was fit to receive the knowledge of God from him. Although he has taken mahasamadhi, his blessings remain with his devotees. *When you think of him, he is with you. Anyone who approaches him with purity of motive is granted their wish.*

How can we describe such a being? He might deliver harsh words or actions, saying "Matti, matti--it is of no consequence," but blessings always fall on the recipient. He sees with equal-sightedness, treating everyone the same regardless of social position. But people pursue him with material desires--not with spiritual aspirations. Still, his guiding light is always available to both the devout and the spiritual seeker. Sadly, most devotees never really knew him. No one was powerful enough to succeed him or receive what he could grant. But he still blesses the devotees--and he remains without disciples.

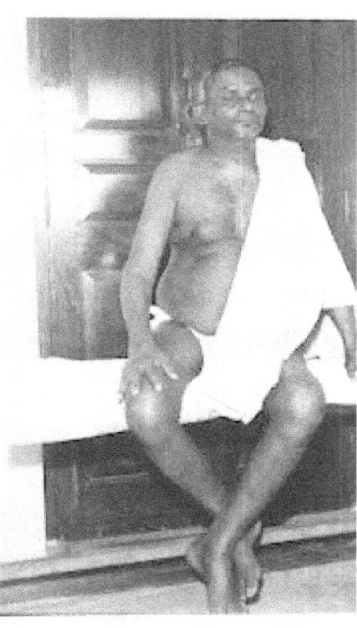

Remembering The Master

Captain M.U. Hatengdi, retired Naval Secretary at Naval Headquarters in New Delhi, was a long-time disciple of Nityananda. This chapter is his story.

I remember first seeing Nityananda when I was five years old. It was 1920 and he was in the cattle shed of the late Colonel V. R. Miraijkar in Mangalore. Many years later the famous surgeon recounted that on returning home after eight years abroad he had argued with his mother about the young Master to whom she was devoted. He did not understand how a woman so fastidious about cleanliness could tolerate him. This was because in those days the reclusive, rail-thin youth was as likely to be found on a doormat or a dunghill as anywhere. The colonel's mother ordered her son to mind his own business. He regretfully told me that decades passed before he recognized Nityananda's greatness for himself.

In the early 1930's Nityananda still wandered South India and a long time passed before I saw him again. In fact, it was only when I felt an urgent desire for a spiritual teacher that a cousin who visited Ganeshpuri whenever he traveled to Bombay agreed to take me to the ashram. And so it passed that on June 10, 1943, I had my first darshan with the Master. The experience evoked in me feelings of reunion with a long-lost friend and an unusual inner peace. I remember not being nervous despite his silence that morning. Later as he stood on the tiny porch outside his room, I boldly asked him three questions. He gave suitable answers although the third concerned mundane matters and his response seemed to imply that I should have known better than to ask it.

After that I saw the Master every Sunday for a while. On one visit a young man ran up to me outside the ashram and asked if he could come. Saying that I thought everyone was welcome, I brought him along. Nityananda was away but we soon saw him approaching from the direction of the river. He seemed to be shouting at the stranger by my side. Entering the ashram, the Master shouted again, asking the startled man who had brought him, and then told him to leave. Turning to me, he said, "Never put yourself out to anyone here. People come with different predilections (vasanas) and it's not for you to interfere." My subsequent strict compliance with this directive brought me problems not becoming distracted from my spiritual practice.

On these early visits the Master was often away when I arrived, and it might be an hour before he appeared. I always waited anxiously until I saw him because there were few people about and the ashram felt empty. Unaware of his habitual and sudden disappearances, I thought that perhaps he traveled to Kanhangad periodically and so I asked him. He replied, "This one won't go anywhere in the future-only here." As if to avoid further queries he added, "Moreover, traveling these days is difficult." This was during the Second World War when civilians were advised to travel only when necessary. After that Nityananda was always present when I came, either sitting on the cement porch or in his room.

The years from 1944 to 1948 were golden for me. Happily stationed near Bombay, I spent a weekend every month in Ganeshpuri, often alone with the Master. He always greeted me affectionately in Konkani, asking "Have you come?"

Certain other patterns developed during these visits. For instance, he would point to the room I was to occupy, there being only two--one on either side of his own. The peculiarity was that I always stayed in the rooms by turn without deviation. My activities also followed a routine. First I would bathe in the hot springs and then sit to the left of the entrance. Invariably, he always sat on the first step with the narrow doorsill completely blocking my view of him. He never sat facing me. In fact, he would sit for half an hour or more and then walk around only to return to the same spot. This usually went on throughout the waking hours of my visits, which mostly passed in silence. In the beginning, the moment Nityananda sat down near me I would become drowsy and utilize all of my self-control to stay awake. Gradually this experience subsided. I never asked its significance, thinking that sitting near him was simply a form of meditation.

Punctually at ten o'clock every night, he asked me to retire and close the doors. Then, after extinguishing the small kerosene lamp, I lay in total darkness listening to a jungle serenade of frogs and crickets and watching glowworms light the trees with rhythmic regularity. The Master would slowly push open my door at the same time every morning and stand there. And I can't explain how, but my eyes opened every time he stood there in the darkness. As soon as he saw that, he would say, "It's four o'clock," close the door, and walk away. I would rise at once, bathe, and take my place near the entrance. He then joined me for coffee, usually served black and sweetened with ghee (clarified butter) because milk was scarce. The affection he showed me was particularly evident when we sat by ourselves after these morning coffee sessions. Such weekends of peace and happiness made me long for his company, and I eagerly awaited the monthly rituals.

Many people have told me that the Master's presence in their lives gave them a tangible sense of security. I know I always felt that he watched over me and an incident from 1946 illustrates this:

It was dark and the grounds were slippery and treacherous. On my way to the baths, I fell and cut my leg on the sharp stones. In pain and bleeding badly, I washed the wound with rainwater until I thought the bleeding had stopped and then had my bath. Later I was evaluating the injury in my room when Nityananda appeared suddenly, poured a little sandalwood oil on the exact spot, and left as he had come--without a word.

I have stated that our time together mostly passed in silence. however, he did occasionally speak and his words to me at the close of my third visit were particularly significant. "In life," he said, "when a person overcomes one obstacle, another presents itself. This process continues until one's experience is complete and the mind is able to face any situation with the right perspective." To me this was a disheartening idea because I was still young and nursed a number of worldly ambitions. To view life as an obstacle course was not a happy prospect. Still, having sought him out for my spiritual development and not worldly gain, I knew there would be no ultimate disappointment. Already I felt blessed with a strong inner security and a longing for more of his grace.

The Master's conversation could appear casual and years might pass before I appreciated his meaning. For instance, he broke one evening's silence by uttering the solitary sentence that the words of Jesus could also be found in the Bhagavad Gita. This was something about which I was quite ignorant at the time. At other times I discovered that words spoken by him earlier were destined to be fulfilled. Later I heard that when asked how to recognize someone who had attained divine wisdom Nityananda replied that the words of such a person (jnani) were always fulfilled.

In 1944 I suffered a tormenting period of inadequacy regarding my spiritual practice. I did not ask him what I should do in fear that he would prescribe some severe breathing exercises or mantra intonation. One night as we sat together I hesitantly asked whether there was a particular book he would advise me to read. His response was instant: "*It's not necessary. But if you must, read the Bhagavad Gita.*"

Nityananda's general disinterest in worldly events never surprised me--but I knew he was aware of them. it was two days after Lord Mountbatten became Viceroy that I arrived at the ashram for my monthly weekend. Sitting near me, the Master said, "While Mountbatten is a good naval officer, he lacks experience in politics." And certainly today an objective historian could substantiate this view. [Nityananda's awareness of global events was amazing, particularly in the early days at Ganeshpuri, due to the fact that the jungle ashram was isolated, with no television or newspapers of any kind.]

One Saturday night, with India's independence only four weeks away, Nityananda made some weighty pronouncements about the future. First he asked, "What does swaraj mean?" Defining it as "freedom" or "self-rule," he said that India needed additional time to complete its training, hinting that considerable begging and suffering remained for our country. He seemed to say that India's continued dependence on outside assistance would limit our freedom. He added that greedy parties were forcing the situation in the same way that people try to force fruit to ripen before its time. He even predicted our country's division into several states because of petty rivalries and jealousies. And everything he said has come to pass.

I was unable to understand at the time, being overwhelmed like others by the euphoria of India's potential future and greatness. I remember foreigners saying that with so much horsepower we only had to press the accelerator. Alas, today's reality falls short of yesterday's hopes.

Months later, in September 1947, I again heard the Master speak about a great national leader. He said that little time remained for this individual and he wondered whether he was satisfied yet with his fame and accomplishments. Why, Nityananda asked, did he not simply retire from politics, close his eyes, and think of God--for God would come to him, implying that he was a spiritually advanced soul. He added that a person alone, regardless of greatness, cannot do everything. Instead we should each treat life as a relay race, covering the bit of track meant for us as fast as possible before passing on the baton. Four months later, Mahatma Gandhi was assassinated.

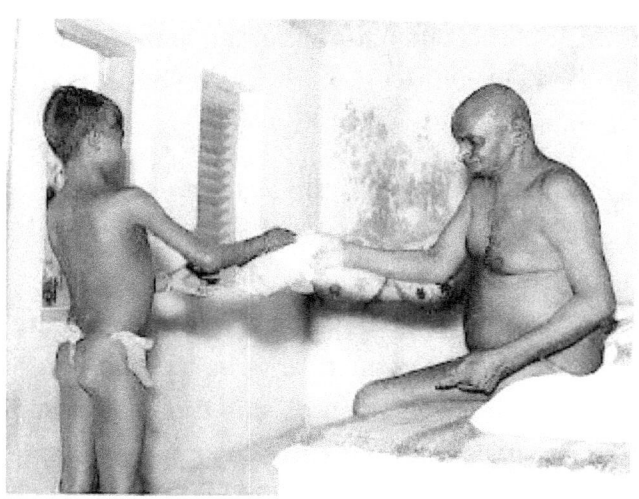

Remembering The Master: Part II

On a dark night in June 1945, I was at my usual place by the door to the room nearest the baths. Oddly, Nityananda was sitting behind me some twelve feet away. We were both facing south and peering into the darkness when suddenly he shouted in Konkani, "Who's there?" I had to strain my eyes to see a person slowly moving toward us. "It is I," the man replied. Another shout erupted behind me, "Who?" demanded the Master. This time the man said, "Satyanarayana prasad." The Master shouted back: "Prasad for whom?" Repeating this a second time, he added, "Is anything known about this place (meaning himself)?" I had considered Nityananda to be an incarnate personality since I first received his darshan. This incident only strengthened my belief and I wondered why he seemed angry. Turning to look at him, I saw him in a posture radiating such power that I quickly averted my eyes. With great kindness he said to me, "*Prasad means something received with God presenting Himself fully satisfied in the chosen form and bestowing the gift. You may have it now.*" By offering it to me I knew the prasad had been consecrated. Pointing to the stranger, he then added, "That man did not come for prasad but for sankalpa." *A sankalpa is a vow taken to perform some action if a prayer is answered, a practice that the Master generally discouraged*. As the man began telling his story, my guru admonished him and ordered him to return to the ashram from which he had come.

Several months passed until one evening the Master said: "*Mothers are more important-- they know what fathers only think to be so. It is the mother who points out the father, brothers, and sisters to the child; this the child believes without question. The mother is to the child what the guru is to the disciple. The guru reveals God to the disciple and enables the disciple to experience His presence.*"

Sometimes he denied responsibility for his actions--even benevolent ones. One morning in 1946 as we sat in our usual places, a man approached. Nityananda rose, took a stick from the roof, struck him four or five times, replaced the stick, and sat down again. The man left without uttering a sound. Seeing my confusion, the Master said: "This one has not beaten him. He came to get beaten." And it is indeed true that many people believed such beatings to be blessings that would ward off trouble.

This reminds me of a story about the great Vyasa, author of the Vedas, the eighteen Puranas, and the Mahabharata with its beloved Bhagavad Gita. It is in his honor that we celebrate Guru Purnima every July in India. As he sat one evening on the banks of the river Jumna, some milkmaids carrying pots of curds approached desiring to cross over. Because it was dusk and the river was high, they asked the sage to use his good offices to make the river open a path for them. Vyasa asked them for something to eat, partook of the offered curds, and then addressed the river: "If I have eaten nothing, make a way for these milkmaids." The river complied at once. Because Vyasa always identified with the Absolute (atman) and not with his physical body, his true form had not eaten. Nityananda was often described in the same way.

My visits to Ganeshpuri were infrequent between 1948 to 1954, estranging me from a new generation of devotees. Then, restationed in Bombay from 1955 to 1957, I often felt lost during my monthly visits. In addition, my few overnights were spent in the big hall since the one's flanking Nityananda's room were no longer used by visitors. One was now a kitchen while the other was kept closed and used for storage.

One rainy September night, rather than stay in the big hall I made up my mind to sit outside the kitchen near the Master, who sat there on a bench. At seven o'clock he called to a devotee whom I did not know, asking him to open the closed room for me. I spent the night there surrounded by gifts and other offerings to Nityananda. I departed early the next day, later learning that Nityananda departed the same morning for a new ashram in Kailas.

After 1957, I only visited Ganeshpuri once or twice a year. Because of what I had understood him to mean years earlier, I always kept to myself, courteous but not overly friendly with other devotees. When Nityananda moved his living quarters to the new ashram in Kailas, specific hours were set for darshan. The old ashram's central hall was now usually empty because most devotees gathered in the west hall. On my sporadic visits, I usually occupied a corner of the old hall near the bench where the Master used to sit. My habit was to arrive in the early afternoon and leave by seven the next morning. However, to catch even a glimpse of Nityananda meant knocking hourly at the Kailas doors until they were opened at five o'clock or later. Sometimes special arrangements were made for devotees who had traveled great distances but, a virtual stranger to the new ashram's attendants, I was overlooked. Frustrated, I wondered why the Master failed to make special arrangements for me.

Finally I saw him one evening. He said to me, "Where do you stay these days?" Since he had always seemed to know what I was doing even when stationed to remote areas. I was irked at the question. Petulantly, I replied, "Where else? There." With an admonishing tone, he used his index finger to point to the place I had occupied in the old ashram and said, "Only there is good." I confess that his response was unclear to me at the time. I was too busy thinking that if this were so, why was he in Kailas? But I kept quiet. Only when he left his physical body and his remains were interred near that very spot did I understand.

My last visit before he took mahasamadhi was in October 1960. Late in the evening, and after numerous hourly knocks on my part, an attendant opened the door and asked me to sit beside his chair. The Master was resting in his room. About ten minutes passed while two devotees in the passage were trying to work a new tape recorder. The particular words they had managed to catch were of Nityananda repeating, "*Without the guru's grace, nothing happens.*" Thinking of myself, I wondered whether my five-hour wait was due to a lack of grace in my life. What, I fretted, had I done to merit such treatment. As this thought entered my mind, he emerged from his room to lay down again--this time facing me on the adjacent platform. The only light was above my head and he looked directly at me as I nervously shifted my gaze. Nothing was said. Fifteen minutes later, he slowly rose and returned to the platform in his room. I was disturbed by the enormity of his body and wondered how he managed to breathe. My wonder was even greater because I knew how little he ate.

When I informed the attendant of my intended early departure in the morning, he told me to meet him at the baths at four o'clock. I entered the main hall to receive darshan at six. Finding Nityananda asleep on the platform and turned toward the wall, I bent over to see his face. he opened his left eye and nodded to indicate that I could go. Again, no words were spoken. Even when my visits became infrequent, he had always said something to me. This was the first and only time that silence reigned. Perhaps he thought I had reached a higher level of understanding--but if so, I was certainly unaware of it. In truth, I left the Master recognizing that a long struggle lay ahead of me. *Nevertheless, today as I remember the golden weekends spent in his divine presence, I am filled with inner peace and happiness. I am eternally grateful.*

This ends the book entitled "*Nityananda: In Divine Presence.*"

It is hoped that this small glimpse into the Master's life gives you as much hope, joy, and satisfaction as it has me.

Source of this book: https://amritananda-natha-saraswati.blogspot.com/p/bhagavan-nityananda.html With thanks to my Sri Vidya teacher *Sri Guru Amritananda Natha Saraswati*.

With thanks to M.U. Hatengdi, Swami Chetanananda's book *Nityananda: The Divine Presence*

The guru is the means. — *Shiva Sutra 2.6* Lord Shiva tells Parvati, "That master who is the cause of your attaining the creative energy of Lord Shiva and who then establishes you in that state is as good as me." (*Malinivijaya Tantra 2.10*)

This book is a supplementary reading material to:

- Ricardo B Serrano's Youtube Channel https://www.youtube.com/@RicardoSerrano-q6y
- Om Nityananda Guru Om https://bhagawannityananda.org/
- *Akashic Records Reading with Tao Chang* by Ricardo B Serrano https://amazon.com/dp/ 0988050285
- *Oneness with Shiva* by Ricardo B Serrano https://amazon.com/dp/0988050226

Epilogue on *Shaktipat meditation* (Diksha) by Bhagawan Nityananda's devotee Ricardo B Serrano: *It is through a guru, master that the Shakti is awakened - by word, touch, look, or thought.* Kabir

He is the real Guru Who can reveal the form of the formless before your eyes;

Who teaches the simple path, without rites or ceremonies;

Who does not make you close your doors, and hold your breath, and renounce the world;

Who makes you perceive the Supreme Spirit wherever the mind attaches itself;

Who teaches you to be still in the midst of all your activities.

Fearless, always immersed in bliss, he keeps the spirit of yoga in the midst of enjoyments. KABIR

The mission of the Shaktipat Intensive by Acharya and Qigong Master Ricardo B Serrano is to facilitate *Diksha* - Shaktipat Meditation, and Qigong - to realize Self and Qi-healing. Realization is the merging of the mind in the Self (Divine Consciousness). In the Self-realized state, the mind becomes stable and free of thoughts; it becomes still. We experience supreme bliss when we go beyond thoughts. As the mind becomes one with the Self, it acquires the power of the Self that can be used for healing, creativity, rejuvenation, stress management, and for opening the heart to unconditional love, quieting the restless mind to attain personal transformation and freedom.

The technique for developing and realizing the Self, Buddha nature or Krishna nature must preferably be learned from a living spiritual teacher who can impart the proper technique, spiritual help and blessings. The spiritual technique alone is not enough. The help and blessings (Shaktipat initiation) of Acharya Ricardo B Serrano are necessary and of utmost importance. Acharya Ricardo's powerful inner blissful transformative experiences with Sadguru Nityananda's Grace while performing the tantric and spiritual practices during his three months vacation, from November, 2009 till February 2010, in the Philippines, which drove him to write about it, have convinced him that he has become just like an Acharya with the ability to do Shaktipat. These experiences include dreams where he met face to face his late mother and Siddhas in Siddhaloka, and Self-Realization experiences such as overwhelming God's love and universal oneness, inner peace and quiet mind he hasn't felt before. The most powerful and unforgettable experience while practicing Shaktipat was being in the flow of a powerful loving Shakti (Qi) opening his heart greatly to God's (Shiva's) unconditional love and expansion of his consciousness uniting with the universal or Cosmic consciousness. He has to ground himself, connecting with Mother Earth, with Qigong to enable his physical body to handle this powerful expansion of consciousness and overwhelming Qi flow. This liberating and enlightening experience through the Grace of Bhagawan Sadguru Nityananda would be similar to a pond of water (you) reuniting and becoming one with the vastness of the ocean (God) through a river path (Sadguru).

Without God's grace through a Guru, represented by his energy or spirit ("Shakti"), there can be no fulfillment or realization (enlightenment, liberation).

The Guru is like a boat that takes us across the ocean of worldliness toward oneness with God.

Sadgurunath Maharaj Ki Jay (Hail the true Guru).

What you meditate on you become. I meditate by chanting the great redeeming mantra OM NAMAH SHIVAYA, SO HAM (I AM THAT) and also on the form of my Shaiva Guru Bhagawan Nityananda to imbibe the Guru's shakti. - Master Ricardo B Serrano

Om Namah Shivaya, a five syllable mantra purifies the five elements: Na (earth); Mah (water); Shi (fire); Va (air); Ya (ether).

I have been healed of my plantar fasciitis in my right foot with Nityananda's help. - Ricardo

The following articles on Qigong and Chinese medicine should assist to remove *Shen Qi Jing* blockages and balance yin/yang energy in the body:

- Distance healing and Soul Healing 90 Psoas and 5 Tibetan Rites 92 Qigong 94
- Kundalini syndrome and Treatment 97 TCM and Sexual Dysfunction 98
- What is Kundalini Shakti? 100 Sri Yantra, Mantras and Chakras 102
- Names of 32 Liu He Ba Fa movements 104 Opening and Closing the Gates of Heaven 105
- Chen Tuan 115 Hara & Energetic Pathways 117 Movement as medicine 118 Caring for the Spirit 119 Three Treasures 120 Three Dantians 123 Soul Healing 125
- Wei Qi Field 130 Grounding 132 Buteyko Breathing 136 Love Peace Harmony 137 Mantras 138 Conclusion 139 Heart Sutra in Sanskrit 140 Neuroscience in mantras 143

Distance Healing with Soul Healing

Distance healing is based on the principle of directability and the principle of interconnectedness.

Distance healing is basically healing spiritually someone at a distance or remotely in another location (city, country) by a spiritually developed healer. The date and time for distance healing is synchronized between a client and a healer, so that a client or patient is receptive to a distance healer's Qi-healing. Consultation by Zoom or picture of a patient is helpful to establish a stronger etheric link with a patient.

Why does it work?

The following principles are based on the principles of Qi-healing:

Principle of Transmit ability. Life force or vital energy can be transmitted from one person to another person.

Principle of Receptivity. A patient has to be receptive or at least neutral to receive the projected pranic energy. Being relaxed also helps increase the degree of receptivity. Without receptivity, the projected pranic energy will not be absorbed, or only a minimal amount of it will be absorbed. Patients may not be receptive because: they are biased towards this type of healing, they do not like the healer personally, they do not want to get well, or they are in general not receptive about anything.

Principle of Interconnectedness. The body of the patient and the body of the healer are interconnected with each other since they are part of the earth's energy body. On a more subtle level, it means that we are part of the solar system. We are interconnected with the whole cosmos. The principle of interconnectedness is also called the *Principle of Oneness*.

Principle of Direct ability. Life force can be directed. It follows where attention is focused; it follows thought. Distant pranic healing is based on the principle of directability and the principle of interconnectedness.

Healing Benefits of Distance healing

The same physical, psychological and emotional healing benefits are obtained in distance healing as in a regular one-on-one Qi-healing session. Most clients have noted that their spirits have lifted with an overall experience of tingling all over the body, inner peace, psychological and emotional healing. Some clients have noted that they felt lightness, revitalized, energized and joyful.

When you open your heart to unconditional love, you invite more peace into your mind, more clarity into your decisions, and a deeper connection within your soul, heart, mind and body.

Conclusion:

Regular one-on-one Qi-healing session is generally a preferable mode of healing, however, because of distance and time restraints between a healer and a patient, distance healing is another viable option to those who prefer remote distance healing.

Ricardo's principal healing Spiritual guide is *Buddha Kuan Yin* who assists his distance healing work and mission. Other ascended healing masters also are at hand assisting during the distance healing session. Divine spiritual (God's) energy or *Tian qi* through the higher soul is directed by a spiritual healer to heal a patient's disease at a distance.

Saints called upon for distance healing are: *Padre Pio*, Patron Saint for pain, healing and suffering; *Bhagawan Nityananda*; *Mother Mary*; *Namo Amituofo* and 87 Buddhas of Da Bei Zhou mantra.

Distance healing by Tao Healing hands practitioner Ricardo B Serrano may also assist in the recipient's *Merkaba activation* which initiates the holistic healing and enlightenment process.

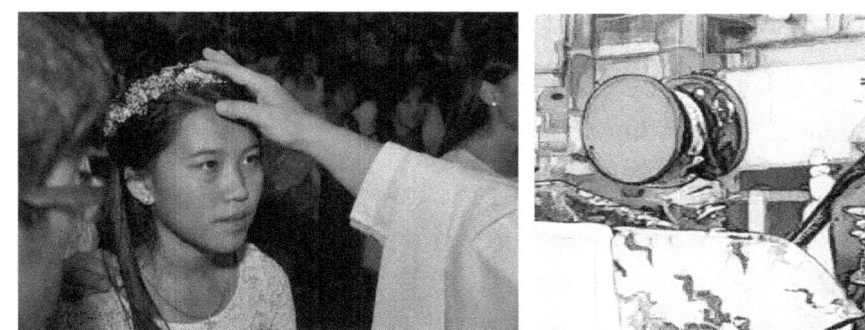 

Shaktipat initiation (Diksha), page 88 **Chod Damaru with Bell** to awaken kundalini, page 164

The predominant sign of such a yogi is joy-filled amazement. – Shiva Sutra 1.12

What kind of amazement is this? This yogi, upon entering into that limitless state of bliss (*ananda*), is never satiated with the experience. On the contrary, he feels bathed with the amazement of joy. This is the predominant state of yoga of a yogi who has become one with the supreme Lord, the supreme *tattva*, Shiva *tattva*. And by this, you can surmise that he has ascended to the state of Shiva.

When he perceives his own nature through subjective perception, then he perceives that he is one with this reality. For him, being wonderstruck and filled with wonderful joy, there is no possibility of traveling the path of repeated births and deaths. (*Spanda Karika 1.11*)

Excerpts from *Shiva Sutras the Supreme Awakening revealed by Swami Lakshmanjoo, 2007*

Psoas (Muscle of the Soul) and the 5 Tibetan Rites

The 5 Tibetan Rites are a sequence of 5, simple yoga-like movements performed 3–21 times daily to boost energy, strength, and longevity. The routine includes spinning (clockwise), leg raises, camel pose, table top, and switching between upward/downward dog. It is best performed in 15–20 minutes and can be modified for beginners.

The psoas muscle, often referred to as the "*muscle of the soul*" by Taoists and somatic practitioners, is a deep core muscle connecting the legs to the spine, playing a crucial role in physical, emotional, and energetic well-being. It is often described as the seat of the soul, storing emotional tension, stress, and survival instincts. The "5 Tibetan Rites" are a set of exercises often used in combination with yoga to strengthen, lengthen, and release this crucial muscle.

The Psoas: "Muscle of the Soul"

- Location and Function: The psoas major is the only muscle connecting the spine to the legs, extending from the 12th thoracic vertebra (T12) and the lumbar vertebrae (L1-L5) to the femur.
- Emotional Connection: It acts as a primary sensor for the reptilian brain, tensing in response to fear or stress (fight-flight-freeze). A tight psoas is linked to accumulated fear, trauma, and anxiety.
- Benefits of Release: Releasing the psoas—making it "juicy" or supple—is believed to Ground the body, improve breathing (due to its connection to the diaphragm), alleviate lower back pain, and improve hip mobility.

5 Tibetan Rites for the Psoas

The 5 Tibetan Rites are designed to activate and balance the body's energy centers. Several of these movements specifically engage the psoas:

- Spinning (Rite 1): Improves balance and circulation.
- Leg Raises (Rite 2): Actively strengthens the psoas through hip flexion.
- Kneeling Backbend (Rite 3): Stretches the front of the hips, releasing the psoas.
- Tabletop/Bridge (Rite 4): Strengthens the hips and opens the core.
- Upward/Downward Dog (Rite 5): Opens the hip flexors and shoulders while stretching the spine, directly targeting the psoas muscle.

Regularly working with the psoas muscle through the 5 Tibetan Rites can help transition from a state of chronic stress (tight) to a state of ease and "*soulful*" connection (released).

5 Tibetan Rites

1. 1st Rite: Spinning (Twirling): Stand up straight, extend arms parallel to the ground (palms down), and spin clockwise 3–21 times to improve balance.
2. 2nd Rite: Leg Raises (Supine to Upward): Lie on your back, hands by sides, inhale to raise straight legs (and optionally head) to 90 degrees, then exhale as you lower them.
3. 3rd Rite: Camel Pose (Backbend): Kneel with toes tucked, hands behind thighs, inhale as you lean back (arch spine), and exhale to return upright.
4. 4th Rite: Tabletop Pose: Sit with legs extended, hands beside hips, inhale to lift into a table-top position (knees bent, torso parallel to floor), and exhale to return to sitting.
5. 5th Rite: Upward to Downward Dog: Start in upward-facing dog (chest up), move to downward-facing dog (hips high, V-shape) while inhaling, then exhale back to upward-facing dog.

Key Guidelines

- Repetitions: Start with 3 reps of each in the first week, adding 2 reps each week until reaching 21.
- Breathing: Deep, conscious breathing is essential to the flow.
- Modifications: Knees can be bent in leg raises, and range of motion should be adjusted to avoid pain.

I have been practicing the 5 Tibetan Rites and I can attest that the practice works in alleviating emotional stress, trauma, back, hip and foot pain because the practice strengthen, lengthen, and release the crucial psoas muscle which is nicknamed the "muscle of the soul".

Qigong, the grandparent of Chinese Medicine

Qi is the basis of Traditional Chinese Medicine (TCM) which includes acupuncture, herbology, massage and Qigong as taught by my classical Chinese medicine teacher Dr. Kok Yuen Leung and practiced clinically at the Hangzhou Hospital of Traditional Chinese Medicine, China where I had my TCM internship in 1993. Historically, Qigong is both the Mother/Father of the later branches of oriental medicine and as a pillar of Classical Chinese Medicine. Drawings depicting Qigong movements have been found in Chinese tombs at least 3500 years old, with other references going back 5000 years or more. This makes it the grandparent of many eastern energy-based healing modalities such as acupuncture and acupressure, tui-na (meridian) massage, chi nei tsang (deep organ massage). It probably guided the development of the internal martial arts such as Tai Chi Chuan and Ba Gua Chuan, and the many derivative Japanese/Korean healing arts such as shiatsu, Do-in, as well as the numerous martial spinoffs of Aikido, Judo, etc. Some historians speculate that Qigong even travelled into India where it became part of the repertoire of yoga and sacred temple dance training.

Thus, Qigong is what Chinese medicine since prehistoric times is based on!

The Yellow Emperor and the Han Dynasty

The earliest written record of Qigong as a healing technique is found in *The Yellow Emperor's Classic of Medicine,* or Huang Di Neijing Suwen written during the Han Dynasty (240 B.C.). It shows that classical Chinese medicine is a quasi-religious system relying heavily on ancient doctrines and a small number of ancient texts that offer a philosophy of balance and harmony between human beings and the environment. It describes the fundamental natural principles that lead to good health, implying that all phenomena of the world stimulate, tonify, subdue, or depress one's natural life force, and that humans are the offspring of the universe and therefore are subject to its laws:

"In the past, people practiced the Tao, the Way of Life. They understood the principle of balance, of yin and yang, as represented by the transformations of the energies of the universe. Thus, they formulated practices such as Dao-in (Qigong), an exercise combining stretching, massaging, and breathing to promote energy flow, and meditation to help maintain and harmonize themselves with the universe.

"They ate a balanced diet at regular times, arose and retired at regular hours, avoided overstressing their bodies and minds, and refrained from overindulgence of all kinds. They maintained well-being of body and mind; thus, it is not surprising that they lived over one hundred years."

"Health and well-being can be achieved only by remaining centered in spirit, guarding against the squandering of energy, promoting the constant flow of qi and blood, maintaining harmonious balance of yin and yang, adapting to the changing seasonal and yearly macrocosmic influences, and nourishing one's self preventively. This is the way to a long and happy life."

As a seeker of truth, holistic healing and enlightenment (oneness with Spirit) since I was in my 20's, I have been fortunate and grateful to have studied under classical Chinese medicine and Qigong teachers and have read the classical references of TCM with Tao Master Lao Tzu's Tao Te Ching, Huang Di Neijing, Shen Nong Ben Cao, and the other classical teachings of my Qigong teachers which assisted me greatly to the eventual realization that with no understanding, application and mastery of Qi through the practice of classical Qigong and without the wisdom of the fundamental correct doctrines of the classics, deeper and faster healing of clients or the fulfillment of the goal in becoming a self-realized Qi-healer will be just a pipe dream.

"The teaching focuses essentially on the purification of Jing-Chi-Shen into its final product: the elixir of pure-person." - Door to All Wonders, Tao Te Ching

The practice of Qigong is essentially oriental medicine without needles. The Qigong craze is spreading like wildfire in the west because it is easy to learn, easy to do, and produces fast results, whether you need healing or are just a bliss junkie. It may be the greatest blessing ever for Oriental Medicine. If tens of millions of Americans graduate from jogging and muscle-building to the more subtle practice of Qigong, they will become educated about qi flow. That means millions of more people who will feel comfortable seeing an acupuncturist /herbalist to diagnose and help balance their Qi. This is the real grassroots foundation of the revolution in energy medicine occurring in the west today...

On a more basic level, all qigong is so simple yet powerful that many energy healers use Qigong to repair themselves from "*healer burnout.*"

The Taoists are famous in China for their medical qigong. They claim to use neigong to tap into the universal pool of pre-natal *jing*. Medically, this means you can replace the "*acquired jing*" from your parents that is gradually spent, the depletion of which causes one to age. A high level practitioner of neigong is considered an "*immortal*", since death now becomes a voluntary event, not an unconscious process that forces us out of our body. There are many cases of people claiming to regrow hair, teeth, repair diseased organs, or recover from near death conditions.

This focus on tapping into the universal pool of pre-natal jing defines one of the differences between "*classical qigong*" (largely suppressed by the Communists as being too spiritual) and "*modern TCM qigong*". Classical qigong might also focus more heavily on the Eight Extra Meridians and the role of the five vital organ shen (*zhang fu spirits, or intelligences*) that regulate the flow of qi in the five elements cycle. In Taoist neigong, these practices include the famous "*Microcosmic Orbit*" and the more secret *"Fusion of the Five Elements"*. The five types of qi are fused into a "*pearl*" of concentrated or purified consciousness that has the power to dissolve deep physical or emotional trauma...

When Qigong is combined with acupuncture, Qi is sent through the needles to regulate meridian flow, allowing for much faster and deeper healing than using needles without Qi emission... The main limitation of Qigong is the skill of the healer or the willingness of the patient to practice. Acupuncturists are in the best position to introduce this healing modality into the west, and they can gradually increase their Qi skills to complement their needle/herbal practice and TCM diagnostic knowledge. Learning to do so is both fun and rewarding for the acupuncturist."

Excerpts from Six healing Qigong sounds with Mantras http://amazon.com/dp/0988050269

In the Advanced form of *Liu He Ba Fa*, I have: See *Names of 32 Liu He Ba Fa movements*, p. 102

- Expanded my understanding of the 6 Unities and 8 Principles — and how they calm the mind and instill movement with fluidity, spirit, and connection
- Cultivated Yin and Yang in movement — Yin as soft, yielding, inward energy (contraction, stillness, adaptability) and Yang as strong, expanding, outward energy (extension, structure, expression)
- Deepened my experience of how Qi flows through breath, intention, and movement — which must be cultivated, and not forced
- Experienced how the Bow Stance, Horse Stance, Cross Resting Stance, Empty Stance, and Drop Stance create stability and grounding — and how these stances affect balance, root, and the way Qi flows through the body
- Increased Gu Jin (bone strength) — and how true strength comes from the bones, tendons, and alignment — not brute force
- Understood the role of Yi (Intention) in strength — how Yi provides clarity and control, ensuring Qi moves efficiently, and how movement is scattered without Yi
- Learned why action should be guided by a calm, elevated Shen (spirit) — not forced or erratic, and how movements flow smoothly and efficiently when Shen is balanced

It is possible to experience internal power and flow with the advanced Liu He Ba Fa. - Master Ricardo B Serrano, With thanks to my Liu He Ba Fa teacher Master Helen Liang

Liu He Ba Fa, Wai Qi Liao Fa and 3 Dantians (See Akashic Records Reading with Tao Chang)

This article provides the Qigong solution to the kundalini syndrome experienced by yoga practitioners! *Heal the soul first, then healing of the mind and body will follow*!

Kundalini syndrome and its treatment

Theorists within the schools of Humanistic psychology, Transpersonal psychology and Near-Death Studies describe a complex pattern of motor functions, sensory, affective and cognitive-hermeneutic symptoms called the Kundalini Syndrome.

This psychosomatic arousal and excitation is believed to occur in connection with prolonged and intensive spiritual or contemplative practice (such as meditation or yoga) or as a result of intense life experience or a near encounter with death (such as a near-death experience).

According to these fields of study the Kundalini syndrome is of a different nature than a single Kundalini episode, such as a Kundalini arousal. The Kundalini syndrome is a process that might unfold over several months, or even years. If the accompanying symptoms unfold in an intense manner - that de-stabilizes the person - the process is usually interpreted as what Stanislav Grof has termed "*spiritual emergency*".

Interdisciplinary dialogues within the mentioned schools of psychology have now established some common criteria in order to describe this condition, of which the most prominent feature is a feeling of energy travelling along the spine, or progressing upwards in the body.

Motor symptoms are said to include tremors, other spontaneous or involuntary body movements and changes in respiratory function.

Sensory symptoms are said to include subjective changes in body temperature - feelings of heat or cold - a feeling of electricity in the body, persistent sexual arousal syndrome, headache and pressure inside of the head, tingling, vibrations and gastro-intestinal problems.

Cognitive and affective symptoms are said to include psychological upheaval, stress, depression, depersonalization or derealization, intense mood-swings, but also moments of bliss, deep peace and other altered states of consciousness.

Within the mentioned academic traditions this symptomatology is often referred to as the Physio-Kundalini syndrome or Kundalini-experience Awakening.

Transpersonal literature emphasizes that this list of symptoms is not meant to be used as a tool for self-diagnosis.

Any unusual or marked physical or mental symptom needs to be investigated by a qualified Qigong teacher who specializes in treating kundalini syndrome. I practice Qigong to redistribute and balance my Qi after Sri Vidya meditation to prevent and treat kundalini syndrome. It works!

Beware of false meditation teachers: Most meditators get into kundalini syndrome symptoms and die young because they have *empty Jing* (*essence*) by not practicing Qigong to build the *Three Treasures*. Heaven is Yang energy and the body's *Jing is Yin energy*. If the *Jing* is empty, the body will get sick because of too much Yang energy. - Master Ricardo B Serrano

- Excerpts from page 69-70, Oneness with Shiva https://amazon.com/dp/0988050226

Soul Healing is not similar to Qigong healing. Qigong is energy healing. We go beyond energy. It's Divine Healing Hands or Divine Soul Healing. We can do one-to-one healing, group healing, and distance healing. There are all kinds of sickness in the physical, emotional, mental, and spiritual bodies. To heal and transform humanity, we must remove *Jing qi shen blockages*. *Jing qi shen* blockages are the biggest pollution. - page 7, Return to Oneness with the Tao https://www.amazon.com/dp/0987781960 Read *Soul Healing*, page 123

TCM and Sexual Dysfunction

Strengthening Jing and the Life-Gate are often the first approach when working with sexual dysfunction and general health problems, according to Traditional Chinese medicine (TCM).

Weakness of Life-Gate Fire-The Gate of Life or Ming men is (located on the middle of the lower back) is an essential part of traditional Chinese physiology. Called the "*Gate of Life*," it holds the Yin and Yang of the body from which all substances and functions develop. Along with the Yin-Yang theory, one of the most fundamental principles in Chinese medicine is that of the "*Three Treasures*." The Three Treasures consist of *jing* (essence/potential energy), *qi* (energy/function), and *shen* (spirit or spirits). In terms of understanding the *Ming Men* the concepts of *jing* and *qi* are primary. *Original Qi* is stored in an energetic center called Ming Men. The relationship between the Kidney organ-system and Ming Men is defined by the relationship between the elements of Water and Fire, or Kidney and Heart as explained above. Strengthening Jing and the Life-Gate are often the first approach when working with ED/Impotency and general health problems.

Erectile dysfunction (ED)/Impotence; Seminal discharge, white/cold

Dizziness/vertigo; Tinnitus

Pale complexion; Cold extremities; Listlessness of spirit

Weak aching lower back and legs; Frequent urination

Pale Tongue with white coating; Deep thready pulse

In cases of Kidney deficiency that require warming, moxibustion can also be performed at these acupuncture points. The moxibustion treatment involves the burning of a herb, Ai Ye-mugwort, to warm and circulate the energy in the local area, strengthening the Life Gate fire.

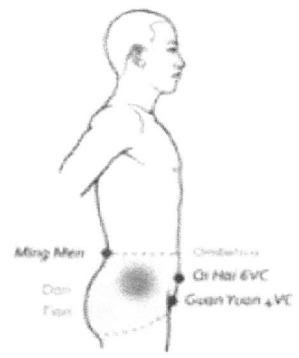

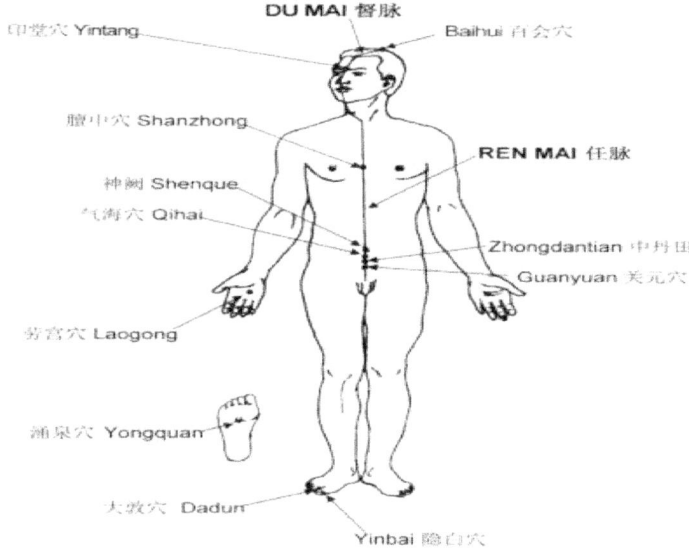

Fig 1 Ren Mai

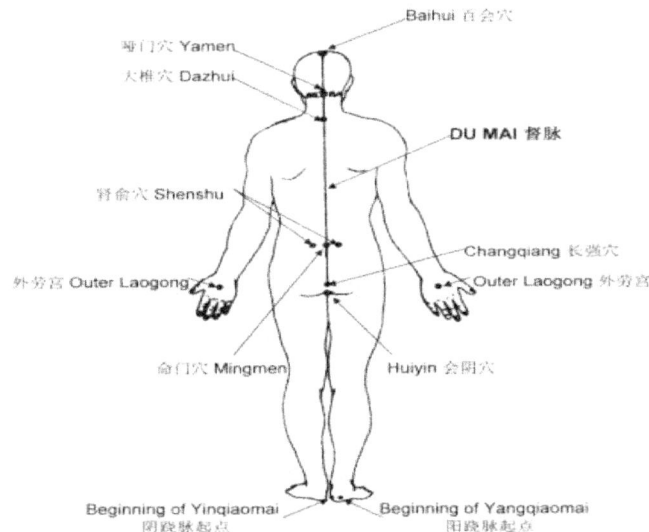

Fig 2 Du Mai

What is Kundalini Shakti?

According to my Sri Vidya Guru, Sri Amritananda Natha, Sri Devi: Hindus call her *Gayatri*, Christians call her *the Virgin Mary*, Buddhists call her the *Compassion*, Sufis call her the *Movement*; other ancient religions simply call her *Mother Earth*. She is our source, our sustenance and our end. *She is Kundalini*, the power moving us toward the unity of all life.

She combines in Herself the tenderness of all mothers and the passion of all lovers, wisdom and insanity, childishness and experience, cruelty and faithfulness.

She is an Angel and a Devil, fire and icy water, She smells of a musk of a barrel house and of an incense of a temple. On the final day of their construction, what is the difference between a bar and a temple? Absolutely none - and they will often have the same customers too!

Devi says, "I am Christ, I am Christian; I am Mohamed, I am the Muslim; I am Brahmana and I am Chandala; I am God and I am the Devil; I am the sinner and I am the virtuous; I am the wise man as well as the dunce; I am the disciple as well as the Guru; It is I that listen and I that speak; I am certitude and I am doubt; I am Heaven and I am Hell; I am darkness and I am light; I am Yoga and I am Bhoga; I am Freedom and I am Bondage; I am everything. Look, look, look close, I am there in every atom, in every molecule. How can you bear grudge or hatred against anybody? I am all; there is nothing which is not myself. I alone was in the past; I alone am in the present; I alone shall be in the future. Whomsoever you envy, you envy me, in this vast universe, it is I alone, who exist"

She is raw power (the living veritable tigress when She catches hold of you) representing on the one hand Thanatos - the death instinct, and on the other - irrepressible Eros. She represents the burning head of desire plus the detachment of the burial ground.

These are Her two poles; She is the bipolar entity, the unity of opposites. And the world manifests in the separation of Kali and Kala; it disappears in their union.

She is maya; dissolution of maya leads to mahasamadhi from which there is no return. This is the reason why it is insisted that you treat Devi as your mother; then the thought of enjoying Her does not arise that easily in the head, preserving your life. But think! what better way to die than in the hands of mother, to become Shiva, a death like corpse? If you are Her child, She feeds you with milk from Her ever full breasts; and the milk of life is sweet indeed. But in the total recognition there is no second - one does indeed become Shiva and Shakti in union; then there is no manifest world, except the continuous unending bliss. And one who has once tasted the sweetness of it, does not want to come back, except as a sacrifice of freedom brought about willfully! So long you have been sleeping under delusion; now that you have already known the nature of your own self by the grace of Guru, then why yet to hesitate? By leaving aside all your idleness and giving up all sorts of your weakness, raise up yourself, and with the shouting of 'DEVI', 'DEVI', awaken Her Dears from their sleep!

tavaivāsmi! tavaivāsmi! na jīvāmi tvayā vinā! iti vijñāya devi tvaṁ naya māṁ caraṇāntikam! 'I am Yours, I am Yours! I cannot live without You! O Devi! Knowing this, please take me to Your lotus feet!'

The Maha Meru Sri Yantra is the three dimensional projection of the great Chakra Yantra (Sri Yantra) that symbolizes Sri Devi Lalitha Tripura Sundari. The Maha Meru Sri Yantra is said to contain the energies of all other Yantras and all traditions. It is considered to be very auspicious when kept in temples, puja and healing rooms, and business places.

The Maha Meru Sri Yantra, queen of all yantra, is among the world's most ancient Hindu, Shaivite and Buddhist tantric symbols. For many millennia the Sri Yantra has been used to bring good fortune, wealth, health, protection and as an energetic aid to meditation and healing for Sri Vidya practitioners. The Meru is a communication and transmission portal between dimensions and between you and your highest self.

Mantra plays a vital role in the experience or realization of embodiment and identification with Sri Devi. Sri Vidya practitioners at Devipuram experience Sri Vidya in tangible and palpable ways, from physical sensations to optical visions, and the Sri Yantra is a core element in this experience. In Amritananda's narrative, his heart is the site of the pratishtha (Sri Devi's life force). Not only is Devipuram a manifestation of the body of the Goddess, the Goddess is established in Amritananda's heart and through him, within the community he was soon to lead.

Through the grace of Sri Devi, I have experienced the bliss of samadhi and healing via Sri Vidya upasana and Qigong. –Acharya Ricardo B Serrano

Kundalini is Sanskrit for "*snake*" or "*serpent power*," so-called because it is believed to lie like a serpent in the root chakra at the base of the spine. In Tantra Yoga *kundalini* is an aspect of *Shakti*, the divine female energy and consort of Shiva. The Sahasrara or crown chakra is often called the abode of Shiva. It is also the goal of Kundalini when, as Shakti, she rises to reunite with Shiva. In Tantric Yoga the Brahman Self is attained through the reunion of Shiva and Shakti in the Sahasrara – p. 47, Meditation and Qigong Mastery https://amazon.com/dp/0987781901

Guru Paduka, wheel of the supreme Guru Mantra: *Aeem Hreem Shreem – Aeem Kleem Souh – Hamsah Sivah Soham- Hasakhaphrem- Hasakshamalavarayum Hasoum – Sahakshamalavarayim Sahouh – Svaroopa Niroopana Hetave Sva Gurave – Sri Anna Poornamba Sahita Sri Amritananda Natha Sri Guru Sri Padukam Poojayami Tarpayami Namaha. Ka e I la hreem Amrta – Ha sa ka ha la hreem Ananda – Sa ka la hreem Janani*. Sri Devi is our source, our sustenance and our end. She is Kundalini, the power moving us toward the unity of all life.

Symbols of Sri Yantra, Damaru, Mantras, Chakras with Kung Fu

You enter the Source of the Cosmos, Sri Yantra, in the Womb of the Divine Mother. You become a part of Her, to live in waves of beauty. - Soundarya Lahari.

Sri Yantra and Sri Devi (Adi Shakti)

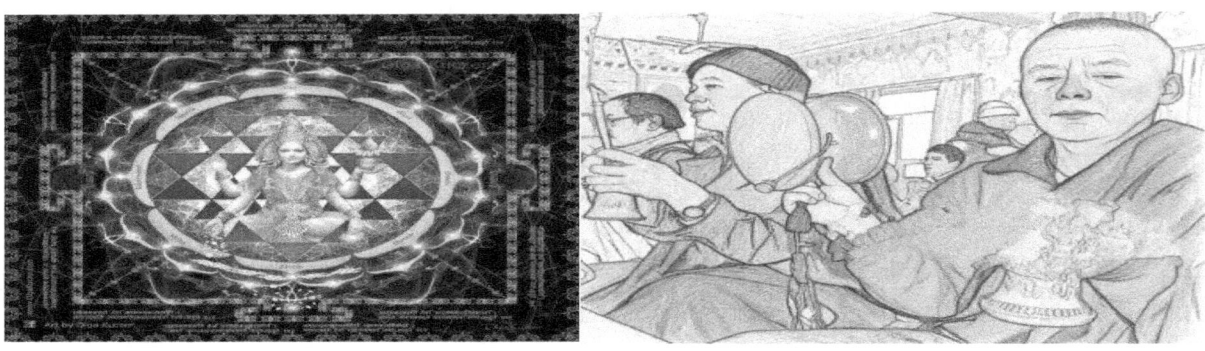

Sri Devi within the Sri Yantra　　　　**Chanting to Vajrayogini with Chod Damaru, Bell**

The purpose behind every human manifestation is to go through a process of transformation to become the embodiment of Love, Compassion and Wisdom. – Guruji Sri Amritananda Natha Saraswati

"One must seek the shortest way and the fastest means to get back home - to turn the spark within into a blaze, to be merged in and to identify with that greater fire which ignited the spark." - Bhagawan Nityananda

"The great redeeming mantra
OM NAMAH SHIVAYA
from my Shaiva Guru
Bhagawan Nityananda,
is practiced silently and vocally
often to realize SO HAM (I AM
THAT)."
- Master Ricardo B Serrano

"The heart is the hub of all sacred places. Go there and roam." - Bhagawan Nityananda

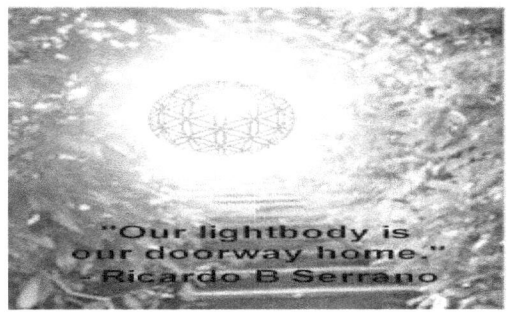

Hologram of Love Merkaba   Seven Chakras in the Central Channel

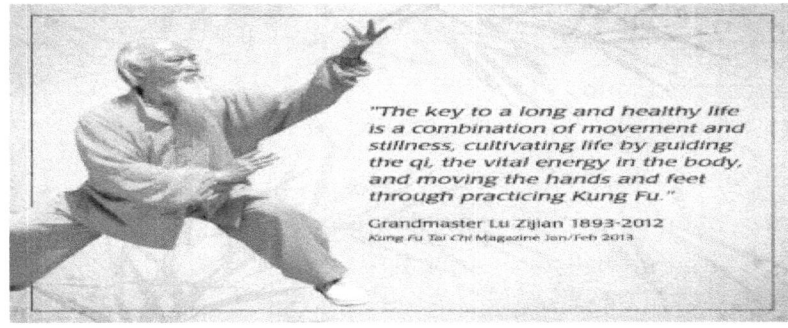

The mind benefits from stillness, and the body benefits from movement

Wuji Quan movements unite the Shen Qi Jing of
Heaven, Earth and Human to attain oneness with the
Tao by opening the Shen Qi Jing channels in the body.
- Ricardo B Serrano, Dipl.Ac.

Chant Ren Di Tian Tao Shen Qi Jing He Yi; S+E+M=1 (information, energy, matter join as one)

Names of Liu He Ba Fa 32 Movements: See *Advanced Liu He Ba Fa*, page 94

1. Stop the Wagon to Ask for Directions
2. Rein the Horse at the Cliff
3. Close the Door and Push the Moon
4. Rein the Horse at the Precipice
5. Close the Door and Push the Moon
6. Part the Clouds to See the Sun
7. Pluck the Stars and Exchange the Dipper
8. Wild Geese Flying in Formation
9. Lone Goose Leaves the Flock
10. The River Flows Unceasingly
11. The River Flows Unceasingly (2)
12. Wild Horse Chasing the Wind
13. Taming the Tiger, Listening to the Wind
14. Sound in the East, Strike in the West
15. Azure Dragon Extends its Claws
16. Elixir Refining Nine Transformations
17. Angry Horse Turns Its Head
18. Push the Boat With the Current
19. Startled Horse Turns Its Head
20. Flower Drops From a Vase Onto an Ink-Stone
21. High Mountain Flowing Water
22. Boy Presents a Book to the Master
23. Woodcutter Carries Firewood
24. Swallow Pierces the Clouds
25. Swallow Skims the Water
26. Heavenly Official Plucks the Stars
27. Support the Sky and Cover the Earth
28. Casually Drop Into the Well
29. 2 Phoenixes Facing the Sun
30. Intercepting Hands, Double Push
31. Warm Breeze Sweeps the Leaves
32. Double Pouncing Palms to the Face with Ending Posture

https://youtube.com/@RicardoSerrano-q6y

Helen Liang – Opening and Closing the Gates of Heaven by Martha Burr

Helen's amazing story of her triumph over cancer was the cover story of the July/August 2003 edition of Kungfu/Qigong Magazine. We are happy to share the article here, and hope you may find your insights and hope in its story.

Miracles are in short supply these days, though we seek them daily. Sometimes we find them, or possibly they find us. Seven years ago a beautiful young girl lay dying in a Vancouver hospital bed, victim of a rare and aggressive form of lymphoma. After a devastating course of chemotherapy failed to eradicate the disease, doctors told her that she had only two weeks to live. Her only hope was an extremely painful bone marrow transplant with a success rate of five per cent. Faced with death, many people would desperately cling to any offer of hope, but with courage rare in one so young, Helen Liang resolved to spend her final days out of the hospital, at home, trying to find a kind of peace with her family. Her father, the famous martial arts master Liang Shou-yu, refused to let her give up hope and embarked with her on a course of qigong, tai chi, meditation and alternative Chinese and Western medicine. Two weeks passed. She was still alive. Another two weeks, and then another. Week after week became five years. Whether to attribute the miracle to *Kuan Yin, the goddess of mercy*, to qigong, to bitter Chinese herbs, to a family's unwavering love, or Helen's own will to heal her cancer, the answer is still a mystery. But seeing Helen today, performing her favorite martial art form, *Liu He Ba Fa* (Water Style), is poetry of the soul in motion, a miracle in action, and a dancing light beaming steadily out of the darkness that nearly extinguished her life nearly seven years ago.

To the Edge of Darkness Upon graduation Helen got a job at a Vancouver bank. She was up for a promotion when all of a sudden she got sick. "It started with pulling wisdom teeth out and I got a bad infection. Even now they don't know what is the cause of lymphoma. I just remember I had a very high fever for nearly a month. I went to the hospital and they were trying to find out what it was; they thought it was some kind of infection. I stayed in the hospital for so long, getting different kinds of antibiotics. But nothing happened. Lumps started coming out, and it was very painful. It was awful. Once they were taking a biopsy, and I was there by myself early in the morning. Doctors came, and they took this huge needle, didn't give me any anesthetic, but drilled into me, and I fainted. My parents came while I was unconscious, for I don't know how long.'

The doctors did all kinds of tests. "One day my doctor came," Helen recalls, "he was also our family doctor and had always taken care of me. He referred us to this oncologist; I think he was already suspecting something. I remember one morning I was with my dad, just the two of us, and this doctor came in. 'I have something to tell you,' he said. 'I'm afraid Helen's got cancer.'"

"To me at that time, cancer was the end of the world. I was so young, and I'd been so healthy, and just graduated and had a whole life ahead of me, so I just felt I couldn't accept it. How could it be cancer? My dad was very quiet, he didn't say anything. The doctor continued, we have to treat her right away with chemotherapy. I didn't know what chemo was, I didn't have a clue. And then he left."

The doctors told Helen they could not give her any other treatment for her cancer. This was the last hope they could offer. She had been in the hospital for three weeks with a raging fever, which no medicine was able to cure. "That afternoon," she says, "we had to make a decision on whether to go for a bone marrow transplant or not. I remember that day. All my family was there for this decision, because it was an urgent issue. And nobody could make that decision. I had to make the decision. So eventually I was thinking about the pros and cons. I think my Dad was leaning towards not doing it and seeking alternative medicine, but he couldn't really make the decision for me. I was just sitting there and I was thinking, I've looked at those people and is that a life that I really want? And the chances were less than five percent. Do I want my last few days to be in that room, or do I want to be with people I love and do the things I wanted to do? It was a hard decision."

Helen went home, tended by her entire family and her family doctor. He practiced Western medicine but he had also learned qigong with Liang Shou-yu as well. This doctor supported Helen leaving the hospital and Helen's parents when they said they wanted to search for an alternative medicine treatment. Her father, says Helen, would do anything.

After seeing her life drain away in the hospital, Helen was at least glad to be home. She recalls, "After I made the decision I went down to the beach and all of a sudden it's as if I have thrown away all the burden. I feel it's OK. I'm just going to do what I have to do for the last few weeks, and every day I'm not going to give up. My dad's still telling me to do meditation, do qigong. And it so happened that day that there's a doctor, a close friend of my dad's, in Seattle. He called and said, 'I know this Chinese doctor from Beijing, maybe he can help.' My dad said, yes, let's try."

After contacting this Dr. Wang, Helen described her illness and symptoms to him over the phone. He wrote a prescription and faxed it immediately. "We went to get these Chinese herbs," says Helen. "My parents were forcing me, saying you have to take this, at least just to kill the fever for now. You have to just try. Of course the bowls of this bitter Chinese medicine... I was so weak, and I'd take just a little bit and I would throw up. But I forced myself. I'm not giving up, I thought, and I'll do whatever I need to do. So I took the medicine for a few days, and my fever did start to get better. I had diarrhea but that's how the medicine works, how the medicine gets rid of the impurities in your body, so that's supposed to help you. So at least my fever was more in control...

"I was more relaxed, and I was doing qigong and tai chi with my dad every day. We'd go out doing all kinds of qigong because it's good for you to stay outside and get a lot of oxygen. That's supposed to kill the cancer cells. So we're outside two-thirds of the day, my dad and friends and everybody taking turns, taking me out, walking on the beach. We had to stay away from the crowds because my immune system was really low, very weak. So I just took Chinese medicine, doing qigong and tai chi."

Helen did this routine for one week. Then another. Soon it was three weeks. "I say oh, three weeks, I'm still around. And I know everybody is feeling that way, they just don't want to say it. They don't want to get excited. They're very careful. And my dad is very strict, saying you have to go out every day, get as much oxygen as possible. And do qigong and a lot of meditation. And take the medicine. Then we combined it with another medicine, from another alternative medicine doctor, a Western doctor. Some kind of medicine that's supposed to boost your immune system. I was giving injections to myself. That was a very painful process, because I had to stay in bed for an hour or two just doing the injection to my stomach area. All the medicine, from China, from different places, it cost my parents a lot of money. Every month thousands and thousands of dollars."

Slowly, Helen's body began to heal. For the next six months Helen's cancer would come back a little bit, but then go away. The combination was working. Little by little her strength came back to her, and by the end of one year she was finally regaining her body and spirit.

Healing Light — Buddhist and Taoist Qigong As Helen's recovery progressed she practiced Buddhist and Taoist qigong with her father, and also a serious amount of meditation by herself. "Every day," she recalls, "I'd go in the backyard where we had flowers and bamboo. In the morning, facing the sun, with no noise, I'd sit and meditate. I'd combine methods, and shorten them, tailor them to me. I focused sometimes on the goddess *Kuan Yin*; I'd feel peaceful whenever I'd think of her. So I'd do something that has something to do with her, visualize an image of healing light.

"Another thing that really helped me, I found it myself. I would sit there and imagine I am one with the universe, almost that I'm not there. When you think about that, how immense the universe is… the good, the bad, disease and everything, how everything moves on, recycling, coming in a circle… you're no longer afraid of anything. I'd think, I'm not even sick right now, I'm the universe… feel how powerful the universe is… I'm not there and yet I'm powerful."

"Sometimes feeling pain, the side effects from chemo, I'd feel horrible, that's when I meditated the most. I'd wake up and feel refreshed… feel peaceful and powerful… I was the universe."

As her body healed Helen had the strength to practice more taiji and other internal styles, particularly her favorite Liu He Ba Fa (Water Style). In the quiet bamboo shade of her garden, or the salty air of the Vancouver beach, Helen's focus never wavered. She took in life moment by moment, day by day, becoming one with nature.

"Everyone tried not to talk about it at the beginning," she remembers. "Then three weeks passed, four weeks passed, then I just don't think about it anymore. One of the things I learned the most is let nature run its own course. Don't worry about the outcome. Worry about the process, and let nature go from there. Always try your best, but don't worry. If you fail and lose, it doesn't matter. That's part of nature."

"At the beginning when the doctor told me there was nothing they could do, and I only had a couple of weeks, I was in denial. I asked why? I never knew the answer. I couldn't pull myself out. And with this disbelief, I was scared and depressed."

"Then, I found some kind of answer. It depends on how you look at this thing and what you learn from it. Now, I can say I don't feel bad what I went through. I wouldn't say I'd want to re-live it, but the experience, and what I learned, it was a very special experience. I don't feel bad because I learned so much. There were enlightenments that I really, really treasure. I can feel it, I know it."

Many people have trouble with meditation because they don't know how they are supposed to feel, and have a difficult time disengaging from the mundane thoughts of everyday life. Few people achieve the kind of deep focus that was afforded Helen by being on the edge of the abyss, but the very fact that her meditation was a life or death matter may have produced an exceptional human experience.

"During meditation," she says, "if you could reach a stage where you're in a state of bliss, you don't feel yourself. It's hard for anybody to reach that kind of state. It is the ultimate state. A few times I reached that. That kind of happiness cannot be described. It's blissful. But only two or three times I had that kind of experience. I have not felt it recently. Meditation now, I do it in a different way. But then, my mind wasn't thinking about anything else just healing yourself everyday. Every second, every minute, healing yourself."

Helen recalls reading the martial art novels her father gave her as a teenager, and says she felt like one of those mystical Taoist hermits. Forced to stay away from people and crowds due to her low immune system, she found her real peace with herself and nature, in the backyard garden, in the park, on the beach. "It was a quiet and peaceful feeling," she says, "which I carry with myself from that time onward."

For All the World to See After a profound year of meditation, qigong, and internal martial arts Helen's hair had grown back. Still frail, the experience only seemed to make her beauty all the more ethereal. It was then 1997, and promoter Jeff Bolt was having a groundbreaking event in Orlando, a pay-per-view sanshou fight coupled with a live demonstration performance featuring the top wushu talent of North America. It would be the first broadcast of its kind, and was much anticipated by the entire American martial arts community.

Liang Shou-yu was one of the top stars, and Helen was invited to perform as well. She had not performed in a long time. Her body was still weak, and she was tentative about performing the Water Style form in its entirety. Again, it was her father who pushed her forward, nurturing her, encouraging her. She found the will and the strength and the courage to get on the stage, and by the end of the night she was the star of the show (though she will deny this with her characteristic modesty, I was there helping to coordinate the show, and can vouch for the star quality coupled with a spiritual serenity which made her beloved by both the audience and her peers).

Helen's healing remained on strict schedule. "My mom brought 3 jars of Chinese herbal medicine to Orlando. My hair had grown back a little by then. Orlando was a good experience for me. It was the first time after I got sick that I actually did the whole *Liu He Ba Fa*. I tried my best to do that. It was very tiring but it was good."

The Orlando event was an important milestone in her recovery, giving a much needed psychological and emotional boost to Helen, for not only was the physical wasting of lymphoma devastating to her body, but the mental trauma was also something difficult to conquer. Returning to the hospital that had both failed and given up on her was a hard road to retrace. "For a long period of time," she says, "I was afraid of going back to the hospital. I had very bad feelings as soon as I'd go in. My dad knows that. He'd say, go in, take it lightly, it doesn't matter if it's the hospital, park, or here. Make sure you have that peace inside you, no matter where you are."

Her experience with the oncologist, from the beginning, had gone from bad to worse. He was not only final in his pronouncement that Helen's illness was terminal, but he also openly scorned alternative medicine. "He told me nothing could be done. He couldn't accept the fact we did alternative medicine, and called my doctor bad names. After chemo and fever for so many weeks my body was all bones, I couldn't move, I was lying in bed. He saw where

I was giving myself injections, and was furious that I'd gone to that other doctor. Later on that oncologist also did terrible things to my family doctor, and tried to bring him to court."

"But my family doctor stayed by my side, and the Chinese doctor too. I refused to go back to the oncologist. Since I left the hospital have had no contact with him. Half a year later he called me once. My impression was that he called to see if I was still around! I heard later he was in disbelief. I never called him back. And refused to go back to the hospital to have him check me."

They say if you can last the first five years after cancer your survival rate is good. Even as the clock ticked away, Helen didn't count time quantitatively, but qualitatively, living each moment, each day to its fullest. She has never gone back to be checked for the lymphoma. "I don't think I ever got a confirmation," she says. "If I feel good, I feel good. I don't want to hear them say anything. Let it be. If I feel sick, I'll go to a doctor. I just want to feel normal. Of course this is a very special situation, and rarely anyone has one like it. My type of lymphoma was an extremely aggressive one. A rare type."

A careful regimen of continued meditation, qigong and martial arts practice continues to keep Helen healthy, though her immune system remains delicate and vulnerable. She still gets sick more than most people, and has to be careful about her health. But most of all, she realizes you can't take anything for granted. "My illness was an amazing growing up experience, even though I suffered so much growing up at that age. I had these youthful dreams and then it hits you all of a sudden the world stops for so many years."

"After all, you come to realize how much people care. I owe my parents so much. They love us so much. I couldn't believe how much energy they put in, and love. Also, I was fortunate to have friends and my parents' friends who were very good to me and there to care for me. So to me, I always treasure friendship, and material stuff is not important. I don't talk about what they have done, but I always remember. I keep it inside me."

Wushu, Water Style and the Way Today, seven years later, Helen still practices wushu every day, and teaches at her father's school in Vancouver. "Wushu remains an inseparable part of my life," she says. "I've been doing it since I was a little child. When I needed it so much it helped me. Before I loved it as an art, a very complete art. If you love something you find it always completes your life. When you're younger external styles seem more exciting, and they're beautiful, they have strength, require stamina, they train your will. I still love that, but now I do more internal martial arts. When I'm in an internal mode, I can find myself more. Whenever I do this form (*Liu He Ba Fa Six Unities/Eight Principles*, also known as *Water Boxing* or *Water Style*,) I'm totally with it. It's that meditation kind of feeling. Plus the theories and histories of Water Style, and my evolving understanding of it, has brought me to an even higher level."

Since her public performance of *Liu He Ba Fa* half a dozen years ago Helen has become one of its best-known masters. When Kungfu magazine first published her article on it in 1997, following her Orlando performance, dozens of letters poured in and the demand eventually produced Helen's instructional Water Boxing video. According to Helen's article, *Liu He Ba Fa* is believed to date back to the 10th century, created by a Taoist hermit Chen Tuan in *Huashan* to benefit one's health, strengthen the body, get rid of sickness and attain longevity. It is no wonder that she became a master of it.

"My love is Water Style, I feel it's my true expression," she says. "Naturally, I always like to associate Water Style with that element's characteristics, and I'm very fond of water. People say Helen, you look gentle, but you have strength and power. Later on I came to realize, yes, I am like that and even if I'm not, I'd like to be. As it says in the Tao Te Ching, *Under heaven nothing is more soft and yielding than water. Yet for attacking the solid and strong, nothing is better; it has no equal. (verse 78)*

"I love that passage. Water yields and receives. It has no edge, no shapes, no limits. It can absorb, and erode firmness. It can absorb and be powerful. This idea ties in so much to my life philosophy, and Water Style itself. Water can appear very gentle and beautiful, but so powerful, have so much strength and be so receptive."

"The Tao Te Ching also discusses that to have is to not have, not to have is to have. That kind of paradox I feel very linked to that. To be simple, really, if you can find the peace. Always bringing your peace with you. Simplicity. Harmony. Everything I talked about, eventually it's going towards harmony. With yourself, people around you, harmony with nature. I strive very hard for that. The ideas are so deep, and I feel I'm at the very beginning here. I feel it will take me a lifetime, to always learn from this.

I liken many things nowadays to Water style. There's speed in the form and slow parts. It's so much like human life. Sometimes you work, work, work and then you need to rest. Conserve your energy. Use it and apply it when it's the right time. When you don't need it, don't use it. That's how I see life as well."

"More and more I try to find something that is beneficial from the simplest thing, an everyday occurrence that's happening around me. I try to take that experience with me, make it something I can learn from. Innately that ability was always there, but I never had a chance to bring it out, to contemplate it fully. My experience with illness really magnified it. Now it's up to me to explore."

Looking Ahead Today Helen is a financial consultant at the bank, and continues to teach wushu at her father's school. "I think martial arts would always be an inseparable part of my life," she says. "Of course there's a lot more I need to explore and learn in martial arts. I want my children to learn martial arts. There are a lot of expectations for my family. Family is important to me. Family in harmony is important. I'd like to train, teach, and ever influence my children in the future. And students too. I'd really like to have my skill in martial art, and my experience, influence people in a positive way."

Helen teaches wushu forms and taiji, but not Water Style yet, though her video has introduced the form to many practitioners. But she hopes to use Water Style as an instrument that can contribute to contemporary culture and bring a profound understanding to more people.

"I think that this very ancient thing can link to modern society," she says, "and have a place in the modern world. Water Style combines theory and practice with a person. By understanding, and practicing Water Style, learning how that builds up strength, it may enable people to even reach enlightenment." And when asked about being a female role model doing this powerful and complex form, Helen smiles her characteristic humble smile, but remarks, "I think a girl doing Water Style can really bring a lot of positive things."

Acceptance Both the Buddhism and the Taoism that inspire the qigong that helped to vanquish Helen's illness place an emphasis on balance. Balance between acceptance and empowerment, between human will and the Tao of the universe.

"If I have a piece of advice," she says, "it would be to learn acceptance. If you have an illness, accept the fact that you are sick. I was in denial, but when I made the decision not to go for bone marrow I accepted the reality. Accept it as something normal, not sad or tragic. This is happening to me, what can I do? Accept different things, different people. Tolerance is very important. Become more adaptable. That way you never lose your center. "Events happen in life, one links to another, fate, chance. Everything happens for a reason. I can't say exactly what the reason is. But because of the things that happened to me I think I'm in a much deeper state now. Otherwise, it would take me another 30 years to realize. So I feel grateful. It puts things in so much more perspective."

Liu He Ba Fa (LHBF) is translated as *Six Unities/Harmonies and Eight Principles*, and was created by Taoist hermit Chen Tuan. LHBF is a unique 1000-year old internal martial art that incorporates the qualities and strengths of the three Internal Chinese martial art styles of Taichi, Xingyi, and Bagua.

Liu He (Six Unities):

1. Body unites with Heart-Mind (Tǐ hé yū xīn)
2. Heart-Mind unites with Intention (Xīn hé yū yì)
3. Intent unites with Qi (Yì hé yū qì)
4. Qi unites with Spirit (Qì hé yū shén)
5. Spirit unites with Action (Shén hé yū dòng)
6. Action unites with Emptiness (Dong he yu kong)

Ba Fa (Eight Principles):

1. Qi (氣; qì) – Energy (Vital Energy Circulation)
2. Bones (骨; gǔ) – Condensing the Power to the Bones
3. Shape (形; xíng) – Transcend the Forms through mimicking the Shapes
4, Follow (隨; suí) – Coherence coupled with Fluidity
5. Elevate (提; tí) – Head suspended in Emptiness
6. Return (還; huán) – Coming and Going in a Continuous Flow
7. Rein in (勒; lè) – Keep the Still and Guard the Empty
8. Conceal (伏; fú) – Illusive in Concealing Strategies

Benefits of Xin Yi Liu He Ba Fa (Water Style or Water Boxing) practice by Master Helen Liang:

- Move through life in a way that's harmonious, adaptable, and wise — for physical strength and flexibility, mental clarity, emotional balance, and spiritual growth to embody the Taoist teachings of water, Tao itself
- Create balance by integrating xin (your heart) and yi (your intention or will) — to cultivate a satisfied heart that's aligned with rational goals; "The intuitive mind is a sacred gift and the rational mind is a faithful servant. We have created a society that honors the servant and has forgotten the gift." - Albert Einstein
- Facilitate a deep connection between your internal Qi and the Qi of the natural world so you're in harmony with your surroundings and with the Universe — reducing stress and anxiety, enhancing focus, emotional stability, strength, and coordination; cultivate internal power (fa jin) for healing, martial art
- Focus on the integration of mind, body, and energy provides a powerful framework for cultivating Shen (which means spirit" or "mind" in Chinese thought) with Nourishing Shen with 5 Hearts Meditation
- For improving physical balance and stability by teaching you to root and ground into your body, and balance your left and right sides with natural unification of body, mind and spirit to achieve enlightenment.

The magic of manifestation happens when the Spirit (Shen), the Heart and the Mind join as ONE. - Dr Rulin Xiu

It utilizes the power of Xingyi as its center, utilizes the stepping patterns of Bagua for its turning and spinning, and utilizes the neutralizing power of Taiji for its variations. Its movements are sometimes high, sometimes low, sometimes fast, sometimes slow. These movements resemble that of floating clouds, and flowing water that is sometimes calm, sometimes surging. Therefore, it is also known as Water Style. The movements of Liu He Ba Fa are constantly fluctuating with clearly defined forward, backward, upward, downward, and lateral motions. Each and every movement is lead by the mind (xin yi). The mind initiates and the movements follow. It is therefore, also known as Xinyi Liu He Ba Fa. As an internal art, it not only serves as a system of self-defense; it also benefits health, strengthens the body, dispels sickness and increases longevity.

Experience the Way of Water for Inner Power and Flow via the internal martial art of Liu He Ba Fa

The Path from Effort to Effortlessness in Liu He Ba Fa by Helen Liang This union of movement and emptiness is only achievable through consistent practice and refinement. Mastery is built through understanding the cause-and-effect relationships that exist within each movement. This state of "doing without doing" embodies the emptiness in Liu He Ba Fa, where practiced effort gives way to graceful, unforced movement. Emptiness is not a state achieved by bypassing effort; rather, it is reached by thorough mastery of every detail. This parallels life itself, where accomplishments emerge only after dedication, blending effort and intention with a state of inner calm, openness.

Emptiness as Openness and Non-Attachment Beyond the physical practice, emptiness also fosters a way of seeing life and martial arts free from preconceptions. It encourages us to look beyond surface appearances and be open to the unique expression of each moment. Embracing emptiness means that, after mastering the form, one can practice and perform with individual expression, without deviating from the essence of the practice. Thus, the principle of *"Movement Unites with Emptiness"* is reflected not only in Liu He Ba Fa's physical flow but also in the mental and spiritual approach to both practice and life. Emptiness is a state of readiness and adaptability, allowing practitioners to navigate each moment with clarity and balance. It is a perspective that fosters wisdom, resilience, and compassion, helping us to embrace both movement and stillness with equal presence and composure.

Conclusion In Liu He Ba Fa, *"Movement Unites with Emptiness"* expresses the balance between effort and effortlessness, form and freedom. This union reflects the heart of the practice, where emptiness is both a mindset and a skillful application of movement. Emptiness here means that only through dedicated mastery of each element can one truly let go, allowing for movement that is both precise and natural. This is the essence of Liu He Ba Fa, a martial art and a path to deeper understanding, rooted in the harmony of movement and emptiness.

"Action unites with Kong. Kong is referring to a state of stillness. In Liu He Ba Fa practice, Kong acts as yin and action acts as yang. The movements heighten your concentration and unify your outer and inner Qi." – Master Helen Liang

The key to a long and healthy life is a combination of movement and stillness, cultivating life by guiding the Qi, the vital energy of the body, and moving the hands and feet through the practice of Kung Fu. – Lu Zijian (1893-2012)

To master the Tao is to unlearn the world's wisdom, for truth is not found in its illusions. – Chen Tuan

Sleep is a small death, and stillness is a small immortality. In both, the mind dissolves, and Tao arises. - Chen Tuan

What you call emptiness is the source of all things. In embracing the void, you embrace creation itself. - Chen Tuan

Do not fight the river's current. Instead, become the water that flows with it. - Chen Tuan

Chen Tuan 陳摶 (died August 25, 989[1]) was a Chinese Taoist credited with creation of the kung fu system Liu He Ba Fa ("*Six Harmonies and Eight Methods*"). Along with this internal art, he is also said to be associated with a method of qi (energy) cultivation known today as Taiji ruler and a 24-season Daoyin method (ershisi shi daoyin fa) using seated and standing exercises designed to prevent diseases that occur during seasonal changes throughout the year.

The character "Tuan" (摶) is sometimes confused with the very similar-looking character "Bo" (搏), thus the name is sometimes incorrectly romanized as Chen Bo or Chen Po. In Chinese, he is often respectfully referred to as "Aged Ancestor Chen Tuan" (陳摶老祖 Chén Tuán Lǎozǔ) and "Ancestral Teacher Xiyi" (希夷祖師 Xīyí Zǔshī).

Chen Tuan, styled Tunan, titled himself Fuyao Zi (one soaring upward in the high sky, from Nan Hua Jing written by Zhuangzi).

Known as the "Sleeping Immortal", he is credited with using and creating sleeping qigong methods of internal alchemical cultivation.

Little is certain about his life, including when and where he was born. He was born around the end of the Five Dynasties and Ten Kingdoms period (907 AD – 960 AD) and the start of the Song dynasty (960 AD – 1279 AD), possibly in what is now Luyi in Henan province. By another account, he was born in Zhenyuan of Haozhou (today's Anhui province).

Biography and legends Chen is said to have been astonishingly intelligent and erudite in his childhood.

According to certain Taoist schools who claim him as a founder, he lived two decades of a secluded life in the Nine Room Cave on Mount Wudang, though traveled frequently. In the first year of the Xiande period of the Later Zhou dynasty (954), he is known to have been living on the Mount Hua, one of the five sacred mountains of China.

The story goes that Chen Tuan had planned a career at the imperial court but flunked the state examination and became a hermit sage instead. Thus, as a student he was conversant with the Confucian classics, history, and the theories of various schools of thought. Among the classics, he was particularly fond of the Yi jing (Book of Changes), which he was unable to put down. Apart from the classics, he was said to be conversant with medical principles, astronomy and geography, and famous for his poems as well.

Chen Tuan had a good command of primordial Yi learning, taught the River Chart and Luo River Book as well as the Infinite and Taiji Charts. As an important teacher of Taoist doctrines who pioneered the Confucian school of idealist philosophy of the Song and Ming dynasties, he had a profound influence upon later generations.

Having rejected the emperor's orders and edicts, he was still conferred the title of "Master Xi Yi" (Master of the Inaudible and Invisible) by the emperor Taizong of the Song dynasty. During the first year of Duangong period (988), Chen appointed his disciples to cut a stone chamber in the Zhao Chao Valley (later renamed Xi Yi Valley); then Chen Tuan presented a report to the imperial court in which he wrote the following note: "I will die soon. I am about to leave, nowadays I'm transformed in the Zhang Chao Valley at the foot of Lotus Peak on the 22nd day of the tenth month of the lunar calendar." By the time he died when he cupped his cheek in his hand his facial features remained unchanged.

Many tales of Chen Tuan have been circulated around and it is said that "He wanders around and shows no concern for worldly benefits." However, despite many mystical and mysterious stories, Chen was known to care about and was compassionate to ordinary people. For this he is deeply respected by the common folk. This Taoist sage was considered the embodiment of the Supreme Lord Lao and received the nickname of "Aged Ancestor," a symbol of Taoism in Mount Hua. Chen Tuan is depicted in the Wu Shuang Pu (無雙譜, Table of Peerless Heroes) by Jin Guliang. Source: https://en.wikipedia.org/wiki/Chen_Tuan

Zhan Zhuang Qigong is practiced before commencing Liu He Ba Fa to circulate the Qi in the macrocosmic orbit, expand Wei Qi field, and build the lower dantien. The Liu He Ba Fa movements are very grounding building the Qi in leg meridians and arm meridians for healing and fajing (Qi emission) Kong power. – Master Ricardo B Serrano

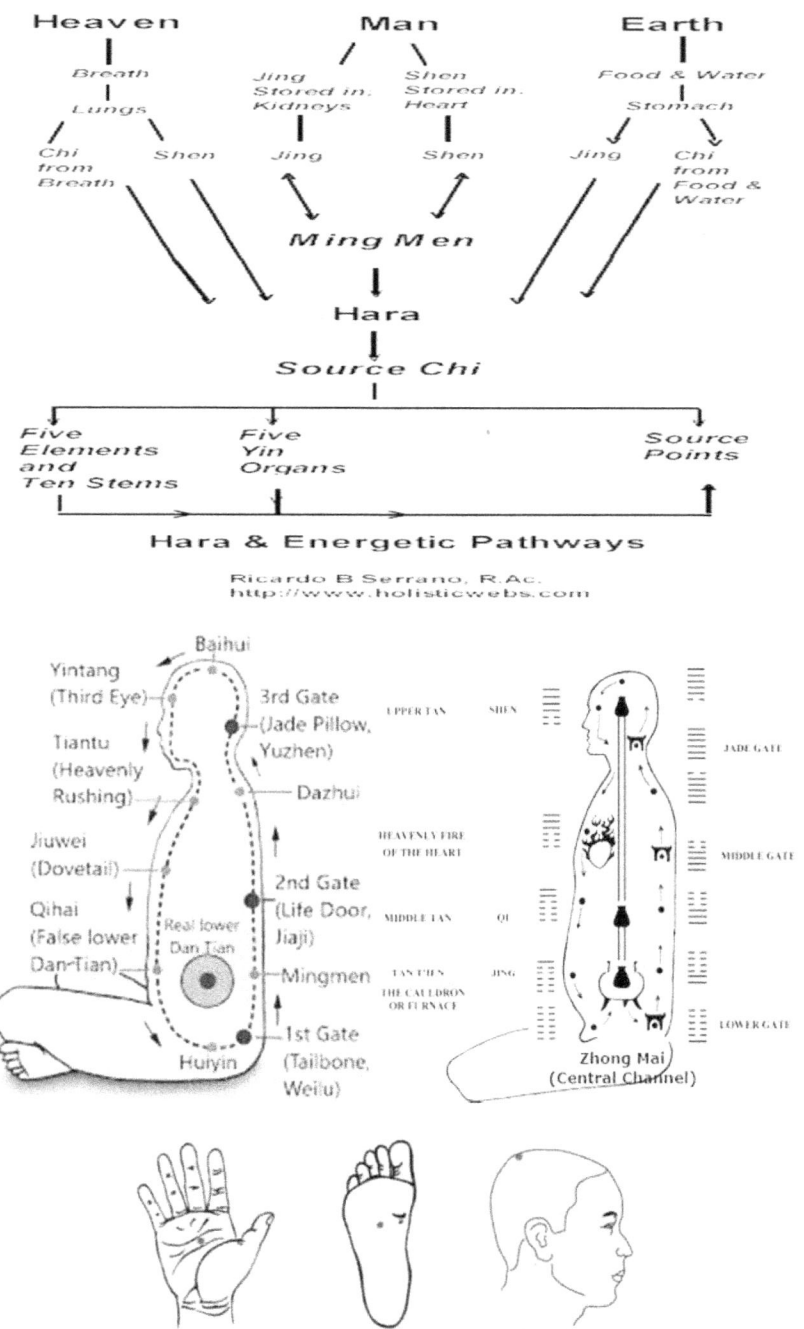

Small Heavenly Cycle (Microcosmic Orbit) with Zhong Mai (Central Channel)

The foundation of good health is regular, mindful activity.

This timeless saying comes from the Qing Dynasty scholar 颜元 (Yán Yuán, 1635–1704), a noted educator and reformer whose views on health were refreshingly practical. The phrase literally means: "*There's nothing better for nurturing the body than habitual movement.*" It reminds us that while rest, food, and medicine all play their roles, *the foundation of good health is regular, mindful activity*.

Yan Yuan's philosophy emerged during a period of scholarly introspection in late imperial China. Unlike many of his contemporaries who emphasized book learning over bodily discipline, Yan Yuan saw physical cultivation as equally vital. He urged his students not only to read Confucian classics but also to engage in physical practices such as *taijiquan* and traditional *martial arts*. For him, movement was not just a matter of staying fit—it was a moral practice, reinforcing discipline, focus, and inner balance. His teachings on the importance of movement influenced many scholars and practitioners, establishing a long-lasting legacy in the promotion of health through exercise in Chinese society.

The idea of nurturing life through movement (*yangsheng*) is deeply rooted in Chinese tradition. Daoist and Confucian texts alike promote regular, moderate activity as a way to harmonize the body's internal rhythms with the natural world. Whether through walking, breathing exercises, or gentle *qigong* routines, the principle is the same: *stagnation leads to decline; movement brings vitality*.

In a world where sedentary habits are increasingly the norm, this simple but profound idiom offers enduring wisdom. You don't need a gym membership or a strict regimen—just the daily habit of moving with awareness. As Yan Yuan might say: "*Let movement become your medicine*". "There is no better way to maintain health than regular movement."

***Wuji* Quan** is an ancient internal martial art form long veiled in mystery. A great number of people have long heard of; few, however, have ever seen it, and an even fewer have had a mastery over it. *Wuji* means *no extreme*. It is before *Tai Chi, the grand ultimate*. The entire form of *Wuji* depicts a vivid story that embodies profound Taoist and Buddhist philosophies; it is about how we cultivate our *'original spirit'* following the course of the cosmos and harmonizing with the myriad of changes of the universe. The physical movements and training express the ancient Taoist physical form and its many applications as well as having an in depth understanding of the theories and philosophies of this art. The movements develop Song, a relaxed state of fajing to build internal power and flow.

Caring for the Spirit: Everyday Nourishment

In traditional Chinese health philosophy, the body, mind, and spirit are not separate. Together, they form a complete picture of a person's well-being. Physical movement nourishes the body, stillness calms the mind—and attention nourishes the spirit.

The word for spirit in Chinese is *Shen* (神), and it refers not only to our consciousness, but also to our presence, clarity, and emotional harmony. A person with bright *shen* is said to have clear eyes, steady emotions, and a calm way of moving through the world. When the *Shen* is unsettled—due to stress, exhaustion, or emotional strain—we may feel anxious, forgetful, or emotionally reactive.

Caring for the *Shen* doesn't require any special rituals. In fact, the most important things are often the simplest: sleeping well, spending time in nature, keeping a regular routine, and maintaining meaningful connections with others. A quiet cup of tea in the morning, tending a garden, or taking a peaceful walk at dusk can all help restore and settle the spirit.

In Chinese medicine, the *Shen* is housed in the heart—not just the physical heart, but the center of emotional and spiritual life. When the heart is agitated, the *shen* becomes scattered. When the heart is at ease, the *shen* rests peacefully.

Practices like gentle breathing, *Qigong*, or even just watching the wind in the trees can help gather the spirit back into the body. These moments allow us to slow down and reconnect with something quieter than thought.

You don't need to believe anything. Just start by noticing: How does your spirit feel when you are rushed? How does it feel when you sit quietly, even for a minute? The more we care for the spirit, the more fully we can experience each moment—not just with our minds, but with our whole selves.

- *Shen* (神) – Often translated as "spirit" or "mind," *shen* reflects clarity, awareness, and emotional harmony. It is housed in the heart according to Chinese medicine.
- *Qigong* (气功) – A traditional practice combining gentle movement, breath, and focus to regulate the body's qi and calm the mind.
- *Qi* (气) – The body's vital energy, essential for health in Chinese thought. Balanced qi supports both physical function and emotional well-being. Source: Qi Journal https://chinesehealth.com

Liu He Ba Fa and **Wuji Quan** are rare and profound internal martial arts rooted in Taoist and Buddhist traditions. These practices blend flowing movement, meditative stillness, and deep internal awareness. They help calm the nervous system, enhance balance and coordination, build inner strength, and guide us toward clarity and peace - both physically and mentally.

Three Treasures Shen Qi Jing:

"All disease and suffering arise out of the imbalances of the Three Treasures, Jing, Qi and Shen." – Ron Teeguarden, M.H.

NOTE by Ricardo B Serrano, Master Herbalist: With thanks and acknowledgement to Dan-O Sun Sha Ron Teeguarden, Master Herbalist, whose knowledge on the Three Treasures, Chinese tonic herbs and Korean Mountain Taoism have assisted Oriental medicine practitioners including myself in my quest toward radiant health and happiness through his classic book, The Ancient Wisdom of Chinese Tonic Herbs, and herbal teachings. In the Orient it is called "*the Superior Herbalism.*" Six tonic or superior herbs revered by the great sages as the quintessential substances to cultivate the Three Treasures (*Qi, Shen, and Jing*) are Reishi mushrooms, Ginseng, Schizandra fruit (*Wu Wei Zi*), Asparagus Root (*Tian Men Dong*), Gynostemma Pentaphyllum (*Jiao Gu Lan*), and Rhodiola (*Hong Jing Tian*).

In the Daoist tradition, which forms the foundation of the traditional Oriental healing and health-promoting arts, there are said to be Three Treasures that in effect constitute our life. These are known as Jing, Qi and Shen. There are no exact translations for these terms in English, but they are generally translated as Essence, Vitality, and Spirit.

The ultimate goal of all of the Oriental healing and health-promoting arts is to cultivate, balance and expand the Three Treasures. At the highest level of the Oriental healing arts, the practitioner is attempting to harmonize all aspects of one's being. This is accomplished by focusing one's attention on the Three Treasures.

The author's great teacher, Master Sung Jin Park, used to describe the Three Treasures by comparing them to a burning candle. Jing is like the wax and wick, which are the substantial parts of the candle. They are made of material, which is essentially condensed energy. The flame of the lit candle is likened to Qi, for this is the energetic activity of the candle, which eventually results in the burning out of the candle. The radiance given off by the flaming candle is Shen. The larger the candle and the better the quality of the wax and wick, the steadier will be its flame and the longer the candle will last. The greater and steadier the flame, the steadier the light given off and the greater the light.

There are three treasures in the human body. These are known as *Jing, Qi and Shen*. Of these three, only Qi has received some recognition in the West so far. Qi is but one of the Three Treasures – the other two are equally wondrous.

Jing has been called the "superior ultimate" treasure, even though even in a healthy, radiant body, the quantity is small. Jing existed before the body existed, and this Jing enters the body tissues and becomes the root of our body. When we keep Jing within our body, our body can be vigorous. If a person cares for the Cavity of Jing [a space within the lower abdomen], and does not hurt it recklessly, it is very easy to enjoy a life of great longevity. Without Jing energy, we cannot live.

Qi is the invisible life force which enables the body to think and perform voluntary movement. The power of Qi can be seen in the power that enables a person to move and live. It can be seen in the movement of energy in the cosmos and in all other movements and changes. Coming from heaven into the body through the nose (Yang Gate), it circulates through the twelve meridians [the energy circuitry of the body] to nourish and preserve the inner organs.

Shen energy is similar to the English meaning of the words "mind" and "spirit." It is developed by the combination of Jing and Qi energy. When these two treasures are in balance, the mind is strong, the spirit is great, the emotions are under control, and the body is strong and healthy. But it is very difficult to expect a sound mind to be cultivated without sound Jing and Qi. An old proverb says that a sound mind lives in a sound body. When cultivated, Shen will bring peace of mind.

When we develop Jing, we get a large amount of Qi automatically. When we have a large amount of Qi, we will also have strong Shen, and we will become bright and glowing as a holy man.

Jing (Essence)

Jing is the first Treasure and is translated as "Regenerative Essence," or simply as "Essence." Jing is the refined energy of the body. It provides the foundation for all activity and is said to be the "root" of our vitality. Jing is the primal energy of life. It is closely associated with our genetic potential, and is associated with the aging process. Jing is stored energy and provides the reserves required to adapt to all the various stresses encountered in life. Since Jing is concentrated energy, it manifests materially. Jing also is said to control a number of primary human functions: the reproductive organs and their various substances and functions; the power and clarity of the mind; and the integrity of one's physical structure. Jing, which is a blend of Yin and Yang energy, is said to be stored in the "Kidney." Jing is generally associated these days with the hormones of the reproductive and adrenal glands, and Jing is the vital essence concentrated in the sperm and ova.

It is considered extremely difficult to enhance the original Jing after conception, although it is not at all difficult to deplete and weaken it, and thus to weaken and shorten one's life. The only way to strengthen the original Jing is through specific highly sophisticated yogic techniques such as those developed by the Taoists like Zhan Zhuang Qigong and by consuming certain potent tonic herbs known as Jing tonics. The purpose of taking Jing tonic herbs is to maintain healthy levels of postnatal Jing. If postnatal Jing is maintained at sufficient levels, prenatal Jing is used much more slowly and the aging process is slowed down.

When *Jing* is strong, vitality and youthfulness remain. Strong Jing energy in the Kidneys, so the Chinese say, will lead to a long and vigorous life, while a loss of Jing will result in physical and mental degeneration and a shortening of one's life. Jing is essential to life and when it runs low our life force is severely diminished and thus we lose all power to adapt. The quantity of Essence determines both our life span and the ultimate vitality of our life. Jing is burned up in the body by life itself, but most especially by chronic and acute stress and excessive behavior, including overwork, excessive emotionalism, substance abuse, chronic pain or illness, and marital excess (especially in men). Excessive menstrual patterns, pregnancy and childbirth can result in a dramatic drain on the Jing of a woman, especially in middle aged women. When Jing is depleted below a level required to survive, we die. Eventually everyone runs out of Jing and thus everyone dies (at least physically).

Qi (Vitality)

Qi, the second Treasure, is the energy that creates our vitality. Through the constant interaction of Yin and Yang change is brought into being. Qi is the activity of Yin and Yang. Movement, functioning and thought is the result of Qi. The nature of Qi is to move. In the Three Treasures system includes both Energy and Blood. It nourishes and protects us. Qi is said to be produced as a result of the functions of the Lungs and Spleen. Therefore, Qi tonics strengthen the digestive, assimilative and respiratory functions.

When Qi condenses, it becomes Jing. Fast moving Qi is considered to be Yang while slow moving Qi is Yin. In the system of the Three Treasures, blood is considered to be a part of the Qi component of our being. Blood is said to be produced from the food ingested after the Qi has been extracted through the action of the Spleen. The red blood cells are said to be nutritive and are thus associated with the Ying Qi (Yin), while the white blood cells are protective and are associated with Wei Qi (Yang). Qi tonics are generally believed to have potent immune modulating activity. Qi tonics, composed of Energy and/or Blood tonics, increase our ability to function fully and adaptively as human beings.

Shen (Spirit)

Shen is the third Treasure. *Shen* is the Holy Spirit which directs Qi. It may also be translated as our "higher consciousness." This is ultimately the most important of the Three Treasures because it reflects our higher nature as human beings. Chinese masters say that Shen is the all-embracing love that resides in our "Heart," a primary organ system. Shen is the spiritual radiance of a human being and is the ultimate and most refined level of energetics in the universe. Shen is not considered to be an emotion, or even a state of mind. It presides over the emotions and manifests as all-encompassing compassion, and non-discriminating, non-judgmental awareness. Shen is expressed as love, compassion, kindness, generosity, acceptance, forgiveness and tolerance. It manifests as our wisdom and our ability to see all sides of all issues, our ability to rise above the world of right and wrong, good and bad, yours and mine, high and low, and so on. *Shen* is our higher knowledge that everything is one, even though nature manifests dualistically and cyclically, often obscuring our vision and creating illusion. *When form is correct, spirit resides. When spirit resides, Qi flows.* – Neijing

Our true Spirit, which the Chinese call *Shen*, is the spark of divinity that resides within the heart of every human being and manifests as love, kindness, compassion, generosity, giving, tolerance, forgiveness, mercy, tenderness and the appreciation of beauty. It is the Spirit of a human being as the divine messenger, the channel of God's will and love. Shen is the purpose of all spiritual paths. It is the Buddha's desire to end suffering and it is Christ's love and compassion... Shen manifests only when the heart is open. Once the heart is open, Shen manifests as light that illuminates the path of a man or woman in life's journey toward the spiritual goal and along the spiritual path. *Source*: Radiant Health: The Ancient Wisdom of the Chinese Tonic Herbs by Ron Teeguarden, M.H., 1998

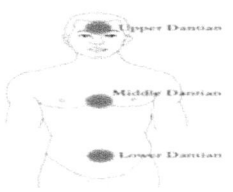

The Three Dantians: There are three major energy centers in the human body along the Taiji Pole (center channel) that store and emit energy. These Three energy centers in Ancient Daoist Energetic Anatomy and Physiology are called the three dantians. Located in the lower abdomen, chest, and head, each dantian has its own function and properties.

The Lower Dantian The Lower Dantian is the center of physical strength and stamina and is located in the center of a triangle formed in your pelvic bowel by drawing a line from your perineum, navel, and mingmen (lower back). The lower dantian is also responsible for kinesthetic feeling, awareness, and communication. Expert martial artists learn to become familiar with this important energy center to feel and anticipate an opponent s attack. This energy center houses the mind that gets subconscious feelings or gut feelings that the logical mind cannot process.

All Qigong training begins with focusing on the Lower Dantian in order to develop familiarity with remaining rooted by gathering the body s Qi and strengthening the foundation of the body's energy. The Lower Dantian is considered the most yin energy center of the three dantians. This Dantian is closest to the Earth (yin) and is associated with the Jing (essence) and the physical energy of the body. Because the lower dantian is closest to the Earth it naturally gathers and stores the Earth s yin energy which counter balances the great yang energy cultivated during Qigong practice. The first Wei Qi field (energy field) is associated with the lower dantian and is the closest to the physical tissue. Because the Lower Dantian represents Jing (essence) and matter, it is only natural that the first Wei Qi field only extends a few inches past the physical tissue.

The Middle Dantian The Middle Dantian is the center of emotional energies in the human body and is located in the chest area. This Dantian is capable of emotional communication through the empathy of the heart, which means that one can read the emotions of another.

Often times Qigong practitioners will focus on training the Middle Dantian to release psycho-emotional patterns. If enough emotions are brought to surface suppressed memories of traumas, which created certain daily behavior and emotional patterns, will manifest. In doing this a Qigong Practitioner will choose to address these issues by intercepting karma, taking responsibility, and projecting no blame. Then the healing occurs in the main organ related to the Middle Dantian, the heart. The heart is responsible for forgiveness and is the final stage of healing after addressing all emotions and boundaries created by traumas. This type of practice will often times bring about ego or spiritual deaths where a practitioner will completely change their life, change their energetic resonance and change friends, and increase energetic potential for it takes energy to suppress emotions. The Second Wei Qi field is associated with the Middle Dantian and manifests roughly two to three feet distance from the physical tissue. For people who see Auras, this is the Wei Qi field in which the colors of emotions are seen within.

The Upper Dantian The Upper Dantian is the center for intuitive awareness, psychic abilities, and spiritual Communications. Daoist Mystics and Alchemists have interest in the Upper Dantian for the Crystal Chamber in which is where psychic perceptions take place. Even though psychic abilities take place here, it is necessary to have all Three Dantians balanced for a more proper and effective perceptions. When peaceful, tranquil, and not disrupted by emotional troubles of the subconscious mind, a Qigong student can intuitively process information taken in by the universe. This ability is to know without knowing and is useful for observing the subconscious patterns of the practitioner and others.

Because the Upper Dantian is related to the Shen (spirit) as well as the 6th, 7th, and 8th chakras, it is used to spirit travel. The Third Wei qi Field is associated with the Upper Dantian and manifests from six feet to infinite space. The Upper Dantian is related to Shen (spirit) and thought. Do not practice Shen Gong exercises to open psychic abilities and intuitive awareness without first training the Lower Dantian to root to avoid self-induced energetic psychosis. *Sources*: Johnson, Jerry Alan. Chinese Medical Qigong Therapy. *Padmasambhava Mantra OM AH HUM* which is part of the Wing Chun Qi Gong lineage where the energetic fields are combined with mantra: *OM* = Upper Dantian (*Shen*), AH = Middle Dantian (*Qi*) and *HUM* = Lower Dantian (*Jing*). *OM AH HUM VAJRA GURU PADMA SIDDHI HUM*, Guru Mantra.

Soul Healing interview by Master Zhi Gang Sha

Heal the soul first, then, healing of the mind and body will follow. - Master Sha

When you say "soul healing," is it similar to qigong healing?

No. Qigong is energy healing. We go beyond energy. It's Divine Healing Hands or Divine Soul Healing. We can do one-to-one healing, group healing, and distance healing.

So you get good results from it.

Oh, phenomenal results.

So does this have anything to do with Chinese medicine or Taoism?

We have the Chinese saying, "*xiu xian cheng dao.*" "*Xiu*" means purify soul, mind, heart, and body. "*Xian*" means saint. In Buddhism, there are Boddisattvas and Buddhas. Taoism speaks of saints or sages. So, "*xiu xian*" is to purify the soul, mind, heart, and body to reach sainthood. "Cheng" means to reach.

What is Tao?

Tao is the creator and Source. Lao Zi, the ancient sage who wrote the classic Dao De Jing, explained that Tao is the blurred condition. Within the blurred condition, there are images. Within the blurred condition, there is matter and energy, which carry messages. This blurred condition is deep and profound. Thousands of years ago, beloved Lao Zi wrote that Tao cannot be seen, cannot be heard, and cannot be touched. Tao is the Wu World. "Wu" means emptiness and nothingness. Tao is emptiness and nothingness.

When you offer healing, does energy connect with Tao?

Tao is the Ultimate Creator. Tao carries the highest *jing qi shen*. Therefore, when I train soul healers, I teach them to invoke *jing qi shen* from the Source to offer blessing and healing. That is the sacred teaching and practice. Everyone can do it.

Is the healer the channel of Tao?

Tao creates a human being, Heaven, and Mother Earth. Tao is within everyone. Two sacred phrases from ancient wisdom are: *Tao bu yuan ren, ren zi yuan*. Tao is Source. "*Bu yuan*" means not far from. "*Ren*" means human being. "*Zi*" means self. *Tao bu yuan ren, ren zi yuan* means Tao is not far from a human being, but a human being is far from Tao.

Why are human beings far from Tao?

If a fish lives in polluted water, the fish is either sick or dies. This is a simple fact. Human beings are living in a polluted environment on Mother Earth. The air, water, land, food, and more are polluted. I think the most important pollution is *jing qi shen* pollution. Mother Earth is made of *jing qi shen*. Mother Earth is heavily polluted. Heaven is made *of jing qi shen*. Heaven is polluted also. A human being has so many systems, organs, and cells. They are all made of *jing qi shen*. They all can be polluted also. Therefore, there are all kinds of sickness in the physical, emotional, mental, and spiritual bodies. To save a fish in the polluted water, we must cleanse and purify the water. To save humanity, we must remove *jing qi shen* blockages. *Jing qi shen* blockages are the biggest pollution.

You said, "Soul leads mind. Mind leads energy. Energy leads matter." Can you explain?

There are four important ancient wisdoms contained in this one sentence. The first is *Qi Dao Xue Dao*. Qi means energy. Dao means arrive. Xue means blood. *Qi Dao Xue Dao* means when energy arrives, blood arrives. What does that mean? For example, if a person sprains an ankle, Qi is blocked there and the blood flow might be stagnant. Now if you focus your attention on the ankle and meditate, energy goes there. And if energy goes there, blood circulation will improve. Energy moves blood. So you can say energy is the boss of matter.

Yi Dao Qi Dao is the next wisdom. *Yi Dao Qi Dao* means when your mind arrives, energy arrives. So if you put your focus, meaning your mind or awareness, on your heart for example, energy will go there. And if energy goes there, blood will follow. So mind is the boss of energy, to put it very simply.

The third wisdom is *Xin Dao Yi Dao*. Xin means *heart*. This says the *heart is the boss of the mind*. That is why many ancient teachings don't talk about mind thinking; they actually talk about heart thinking. Because in our ancient understanding, the heart houses the mind and the soul.

The last important sentence is *Ling Dao Xin Dao*. Ling means *soul*. It means when the message of the soul arrives, the heart follows.

But we all suffer from negative emotions and mind-sets like grief or anger these days. What can we do against these emotions and how should we practice and purify.

The ancient teachings mentioned four techniques:

The first is *Shen Mi*. Shen means body and *Mi* means secret. Shen Mi means body secret. It means to use hand and body positions for healing. For example, a person might have a lot of anger. How can the person address that? Put one palm below the navel and the other palm over the liver and focus attention there. This is ancient wisdom of TCM (traditional Chinese medicine). The liver is a physical organ. Anger is related to the emotional body. The physical body and emotional body are interconnected. If the person has a liver sickness such as Hepatitis A, B or C, cirrhosis, or other issues, the person could be easily irritated and upset.

This is how the physical body affects the emotional body. If the person gets upset a lot, the emotional body can affect the physical body and could cause sickness in the physical body. This is how they influence each other.

The second ancient technique is named *Kou Mi*. *Kou* means *mouth*. Mi means secret. *Kou Mi* means *to chant a mantra*. Many Chinese, Indian, and many other ancient practices all chant. To chanting is to repeat certain sounds. These repetitive sounds carry invisible love, forgiveness, compassion, and light. Mantras can therefore remove *shen qi jing* blockages for healing. So you could place your hands on your body and chant a mantra to reduce your anger. Chanting healing mantras can remove blockages on any level.

The third ancient technique is *Yi Mi*. Yi means thinking. Mi means secret. *Yi Mi* means using *our consciousness for healing*. In our time, it refers to meditation. Yi Mi means creative visualization. Some people visualize the Divine or saints, heaven, sun, moon, ocean, etc. Meditation is creative visualization. You can visualize anything you wish that supports the healing function.

Where do these blockages occur and stem from?

Jing blockages are within the cells. Qi blockages are between the cells. Shen blockages include blockages of the soul, heart, and mind. Soul blockages stem from all kinds of negative karma including personal karma, ancestral karma, relationship karma, curses, voodoo, etc. Heart blockages include impurities such as selfishness, greed, etc. Mind blockages include negative mind-sets, negative beliefs, negative attitudes, ego, attachments, etc.

Can I also use these techniques for healing someone else?

Definitely you can use them for someone else. For example, when your child has health challenges, you can say, "Dear Divine, can I call you? My daughter has a health issue. Can you heal my daughter?" Then chant, "God's light." If your Third Eye is open, you may even see God appear shining gold, crystal, or other kinds of colors to your child's body. You can use the three techniques together for healing yourself, for healing your children, or anybody else. In the last eleven years my teaching has benefitted millions of people worldwide.

So everybody can be a healer for themselves and others?

Yes, definitely. The message of my teaching is:

I have the power to create soul healing miracles to transform all of my life.

You have the power to create soul healing miracles to transform all of your life. Together we have the power to create soul healing miracles to transform all life of humanity and all souls.

What is the cause for suffering and sickness?

In my teaching, I stress that karma is the root cause of success and failure in every aspect of life. Karma means the record of your services in all of your lives. There are two kinds of services. If a person serves others with love, care, compassion, generosity, kindness, grace, and integrity, Heaven will record this person as having good karma. If a person kills, harms, takes advantages of others, steals, cheats, and more, this person has a record of negative karma. According to karmic law, a person who offers good karma to others in all lifetimes, including past lifetimes and this lifetime, will receive rewards in health, relationships, finances, intelligence, success, and more. A person who has negative karma could learn lessons including sickness, challenges in relationships, finances, intelligence, and more. In 2003 the Divine gave me the authority to clear negative karma and this can create extremely good healing results.

Can you share a simple healing exercise with our readers that they can practice daily?

One of the most important fundamental and sacred practices is to put your mind on the *Ming Men* area. How can you find the Ming Men area? From your navel make a straight line to your back. That point is named the *Ming Men acupuncture point*. Ming means life. Men means gate. Ming Men literally means the life gate.

When the sun shines on the ocean, the water turns to steam. The steam rises. The steam is named the Qi of Mother Earth. Mother Earth's Qi rises to Heaven to form the clouds. The clouds will turn to rain and flow down.

In the same way, when you put your mind on the Ming Men area your mind acts like the sun. The Ming Men area is just like water. So the water will flow up automatically. The result is that you are producing liquid in your mouth. You need to swallow the liquid. This is one of the most powerful daily practices and is very healthy. There is no time limit. Put the tip of the tongue to the roof of the mouth. Put your mind on the lower back area of the Ming Men and you will receive benefits as soon as you do this. This is a powerful and practical technique.

My book, "Tao II: The Way of Healing, Rejuvenation, Longevity, and Immortality" explains two hundred twenty sacred phrases and sacred practices, but this is a simple and important one. I hope the readers benefit. Read *Love Peace Harmony*, page 135

How do we fix this or purify the blockages?

I teach Six Power Techniques™ to purify *jing qi shen*. They are Body Power, Soul Power, Mind Power, Sound Power, Breath Power and Tao Calligraphy Power. See Preface on *Six Power Techniques*. **Source:** *Empty Vessel Interview with Dr. Zhi Gang Sha, Spring 2016 Issue*

Soul leads Heart – Heart leads Mind – Mind leads Energy – Energy leads Matter

Tao Calligraphy Soul Light   Tao Grandmaster Zhi Gang Sha   Greatest Love

Tai Chi, Wuji Quan Master Chang San-feng   Ricardo B Serrano – Tao Soul Communicator

Wei Qi Field in Qigong

There are many names for the invisible auric field that surrounds the physical body in various mystical traditions such as torus, Lightbody, Electromagnetic Field (EMF), energy bubble, Merkaba or aura. The auric field is called Wei Qi Field in Medical Qigong which will be under discussion...

All living bodies generate an external field of energy called Wei Qi (pronounced *"whey chee"*), which translates as "protective energy." The definition of Wei Qi in Medical Qigong is slightly different than that of Traditional Chinese Medicine (TCM). In classical TCM texts, the Wei Qi field is seen to be limited to the surface of the body, circulating within the tendon and muscle tissues. In Medical Qigong, however, the Wei Qi field also includes the three external layers of the body's auric and subtle energy fields. This energy originates from each of the internal organs and radiates through the external tissues. There the Wei Qi forms an energy field that radiates from the entire physical body. This field of Qi protects the body from the invasion of external pathogens and communicates with, as well as interacts with, the surrounding universal and environmental energy fields.

Both internal and external pathogenic factors affect the structural formation of the Wei Qi. The internal factors include suppressed emotional influences (such as anger and grief from emotional traumas). The external factors include environmental influences when they are too severe or chronic, such as Cold, Damp, Heat or Wind, etc. Physical traumas also affect the Wei Qi field.

Any negative interchange affects the Wei Qi by literally creating holes within the matrix of the individual's external energetic fields. When left unattended, these holes leave the body vulnerable to penetration, and disease begins to take root in the body. Strong emotions, in the form of toxic energy, become trapped within the body's tissues when we hold back or do not integrate our feelings. These unprocessed emotions block the natural flow of Qi, thus creating stagnant pools of toxic energy within the body.

The body has an energy field that is composed of energetic lines called meridians and channels. Energetic blockages in these channels cause imbalances in the energy field, which can lead to dis-ease. A free flow of energy is needed in the body and energy system for good health and well-being.

Medical Qigong consists of specific techniques that uses the knowledge of the body's internal and external energy fields to purge, tonify, and balance these energies. Medical Qigong therapy offers patients a safe and effective way to rid themselves of toxic pathogens and years of painful emotions that otherwise, can cause mental and physical illness. This therapy combines breathing techniques with movement, creative visualization, mantras, Tao Calligraphy (see Greatest Love (Da Ai), page 127) and spiritual intent to improve health, personal power, and control over one's own life. *"Your Qi, the life force that flows through you, yearns to be harnessed. Qi and breath are never separate."* – Ricardo B Serrano. You experience deeper yin-yang balance, healing and self-cultivation with Liu He Ba Fa.

Merkaba is an interdimensional counterclockwise rotational vehicle of Light, Pranic or energy body and Soul. *Mer* - counterclockwise rotation of Light, *ka* - Pranic or energy body, *ba* - Soul. The mind directs, powers, and stabilises the *Merkaba* in unison with God. The higher your vibration of Cosmic Christ Consciousness embraced in Unconditional love, the stronger is your *Merkaba* field.

The *Merkaba* is the chosen interdimensional vehicle of the Masters. To truly extend ourselves into their conscious realms we must raise the vibration of Love within our personal *Merkaba*. The *Hologram of Love* is the ever continuous pattern of God's mind and thought because God only thinks and manifests in unconditional Love. The *Hologram of Love Merkaba* meditation accesses the unified field of consciousness through the galactic timing of the universe.

According to Master Thoth, "unconditional love is a powerful magnetic force which, once activated through the hologram of love, makes you truly magnetic within every cell of your body. As a result, you begin to attract all you need to become a cosmic vibration of higher wisdom. If we could understand time and love together, Thoth said, we would have the answer."

"The Hologram of Love Merkaba is our doorway home." - Alton Kamadon

Excerpts from page 25, *Meditation and Qigong Mastery*

What is the aim of sound in healing? According to Renee Brodie, "This is the aim of sound, for you to resonate with a piece of music, or the one you sound yourself, or a particular singing bowl so that it sound "*waves*" through you, touches you, touches where it is needed, and balances. Then you are healed, your auric field is "*in flow*" and you will radiate perfect health."

"Sound is an energy form generated by a vibrating body. Depending on its frequency, the human body will react to and perceive this energy in different ways. If the pitch is below the audible level and the amplitude is high, we may feel it although we do not hear it. If it is within the audible range, we will hear it and classify it according to our knowledge of sound. If the pitch is ultrasonic - above the audible range - we will not hear it but may experience unpleasant bodily reactions to what is known as White Sound."

Grounding (Earthing)

Grounding or *Earthing* is defined as placing one's bare feet on the ground whether it be dirt, grass, sand or concrete (especially when humid or wet). When you ground to the electron-enriched earth, an improved balance of the sympathetic and parasympathetic nervous system occurs.

The Earth is a natural source of electrons and subtle electrical fields, which are essential for proper functioning of immune systems, circulation, synchronization of biorhythms and other physiological processes and may actually be the most effective, essential, least expensive, and easiest to attain antioxidant.

Modern science has thoroughly documented the connection between inflammation and all of the chronic diseases, including the diseases of aging and the aging process itself. It is important to understand that *inflammation is a condition that can be reduced or prevented by grounding your body to the Earth*, the way virtually all of your ancestors have done for hundreds if not thousands of generations.

The most important health consequence of Earthing is providing your body abundant electrons from the Earth. The scientific research and hypotheses related to Earthing point to a major impact on the inflammatory process as a result of this electron transfer.

Your body has evolved a means to kill bacteria using reactive oxygen species (*ROS*) that are delivered to a site of injury by white blood cells. Although very effective at this task, ROS are also very reactive biochemically and can damage healthy tissues. *ROS* are usually positively charged molecules that need to be neutralized immediately to prevent them from diffusing into healthy tissues.

That is one of the major reasons why your body needs an abundant supply of *negative charges*. Food based antioxidants like *astaxanthin* are helpful but a regular supply of *electrons from the earth* can supply them as well.

Nature has solved this problem by providing conductive systems within your body that deliver electrons from your feet to all parts of your body. This has been the natural arrangement throughout most of human history. Negative charges have always been available, thanks to the Earth, to prevent the inflammatory process from damaging healthy tissues.

All of this changed when we began to wear shoes with rubber and plastic soles, and no longer slept in direct contact with the Earth. A variety of measures of physiological stress show that the person who is grounded is less stressed and more relaxed. These measures demonstrate a *shift from sympathetic to parasympathetic activation, reduction in muscle tension, and increased heart rate variability*.

Regardless whether or not grounding reduces exposure to environmental fields, these studies firmly demonstrate that Earthing does not stress the body; in fact, Earthing reduces every measure of stress used in studies.

Concerns about Earthing When I first became aware of Earthing in 2005, I was initially fascinated with the concept. But after reviewing it with some of my mentors in energy medicine there was a concern that Earthing may actually increase your exposure to so-called "*electromagnetic pollution*" or "*dirty electricity.*"

However, more careful analysis revealed that Earthing actually decreases your exposure to these potentially disruptive fields. To understand why this is so, it is crucial to look at the basic biophysics of electricity and magnetism.

Most of the confusion about this topic is due in part to the fact that research on Earthing the human body is opening up new perspectives, and requires a fresh examination of the basics of electricity and magnetism as applied to physiology and medicine. Another source of confusion arises from a belief that the unnatural frequencies referred to as "*electromagnetic pollution*" and "*dirty electricity*" flow through the wiring of homes and can be removed with filters. The reality is that these signals are present virtually everywhere in our environment as *electromagnetic* radiations, and cannot be completely removed with filters in the wiring.

Earthing actually decreases your exposure to these potentially disruptive *electromagnetic fields*, but we again emphasize that this is not the most important effect of Earthing.

Grounding May Be the Missing Link to Getting Healthy Earthing may be one of the most important overlooked factors in public health. When grounding is restored, many people report significant improvement in a wide range of ailments, including chronic fatigue.

These changes are rapid and often occur within 30 minutes.

To date all of the individuals who reported that they had inflammatory issues have benefited from Earthing. This includes people with various severe autoimmune diseases. It can be said without any equivocation that the human body evolved in contact with the Earth and needs to maintain this natural contact in order to function properly. When you provide your body a constant source of free electrons, through diet or grounding you help to radically reduce inflammation which is widely acknowledged as one of the primary factors contributing to premature aging and chronic disease. *Source: Ultimate Antioxidant* by Dr. Mercola

*I have used grounding mat with Qigong, LHBF, Wuji Quan to resolve my plantar fasciitis.

Earthing Mat An animal study published in the International Journal of Molecular Sciences revealed that earthing mats significantly reduce wake time and increase both REM (Rapid Eye Movement) and NREM (Non-Rapid Eye Movement) sleep in animal subjects.

Conducted by Korean researchers, the study demonstrated that when exposed to earthing mats, animal subjects showed considerable improvements in their sleep patterns, demonstrating a notable extension of total sleep duration as exposure time increased.

To test their theory, the researchers divided their test subjects into four groups — a control group (Nor), a group that used an earthing mat for seven days (A-7D), a group that used an earthing mat for 21 days (A-21D) and a group that used an electronic blanket for 21 days (EM).

These findings make earthing mats a compelling non-pharmacological alternative to traditional sleep aids, which often come with undesirable side effects. As noted by the study authors:

"Traditionally, pharmacological treatments such as benzodiazepines and barbiturates have been employed to manage sleep disorders or insomnia. However, these medications are associated with potential adverse effects, including dependency, cognitive impairment, and residual daytime sedation. We anticipated that this study would elucidate the effects of the earthing mat on sleep and provide insights into its influence on sleep-related mechanisms, thereby laying the groundwork for future research on the interactions between earthing and sleep regulation."

So how exactly do earthing mats impact your sleep? The study focused on two key areas that led to better sleep — orexin and superoxide dismutase (SOD) levels in your brain. When you sleep, your brain goes through a recovery and regeneration process that helps inhibit oxidative stress. But if you're sleep-deprived, your levels of superoxide dismutase (SOD), an antioxidant enzyme that reduces oxidative stress in the brain, decreases.

With the help of an *earthing mat*, your SOD levels increase, which then reduces oxidative stress and promotes relaxation and mental calmness. As explained by the authors:

"Previous studies have shown that antioxidant enzyme activity, including SOD, increases in animal models subjected to sleep deprivation. Consistent with these findings, the present study demonstrates that exposure to A-7D and A-21D significantly increased SOD levels in the LH. This result suggests that these treatments may reduce oxidative stress and improve the brain's oxidative defense system. The observed increase in SOD levels supports the hypothesis that interventions designed to maintain or restore antioxidant enzyme activity can mitigate oxidative damage associated with sleep deprivation and enhance overall brain health."

Grounding through *earthing mats* or direct contact with the Earth has shown promising results in various areas of health, such as:

- **Keeping your heart healthy** — An intriguing study investigated grounding's impact on blood viscosity post-exercise. According to the researchers, individuals who were grounded showed a noticeable reduction in both diastolic and systolic blood viscosity compared to those who were not. This finding is significant because lower blood viscosity is associated with improved circulation and cardiovascular health.
- **Improving sleep in Alzheimer's patients** — A 2022 randomized, double-blind study involving individuals with mild Alzheimer's disease also demonstrated its remarkable benefits on sleep quality. The participants, who were either grounded or sham-grounded for 30 minutes daily for over 12 weeks, reported significantly better sleep, as measured by the Pittsburgh Sleep Quality Index. This suggests that grounding helps enhance sleep for those suffering from cognitive impairments.
- **Easing chronic pain** — Another study published in the journal EXPLORE tells the story of an 85-year-old man suffering from chronic pain whose quality of life improved after grounding while sleeping. He had persistent low back pain and shoulder pain that interfered with his sleep, experiencing stiffness and soreness upon waking. After just two nights of grounded sleep, he reported having *"50% less pain, 80% reduction in pain interfering with sleep, and 75% reduction in waking stiff and sore."* He continued doing this, and after four weeks, reported that the pain was *"totally gone with only occasional mild stiffness."* This case exemplifies how grounding brings rapid and tangible relief for chronic pain sufferers.

In addition to using earthing mats during bedtime, I recommend spending time outdoors whenever possible. Exercising barefoot outdoors is a great way to incorporate earthing into your daily life and will also help speed up tissue repair and ease muscle pain associated with strenuous exercise.

The ideal location for walking barefoot is the beach, close to or in the water, as saltwater is a great conductor. (Your body is also somewhat conductive because it contains a large number of charged ions, called electrolytes, dissolved in water. Your blood and other body fluids are therefore good conductors.) A close second would be a grassy area, especially if it's covered with dew, and /or bare soil.

While any amount of grounding is better than none, research has demonstrated it takes about 80 minutes for the free electrons from the Earth to reach your blood stream and transform your blood, which is when you reap the greatest benefits. So, ideally, aim for 80 to 120 minutes of grounding each day. *Source: Using an Earthing Mat Helps You Get a Good Night's Sleep by Dr. Mercola*

Buteyko Breathing Method:

Buteyko breathing is the first strategy I use before and during meditation and exercise to achieve optimal healing in my physical, mental and spiritual bodies. – Ricardo B Serrano

The perfect man is breathing as if he is not breathing. – Lao Tzu

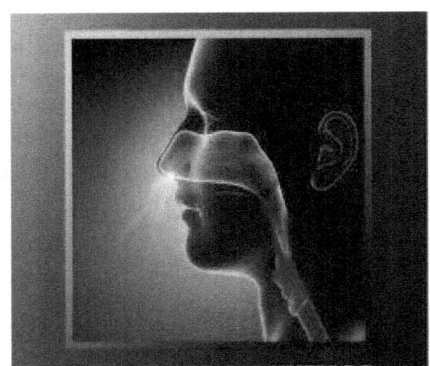

Three principles sum up the practice: (1) nasal breathing; (2) a return to normal breathing if there is a problem; and (3) a Control Pause of up to 15-25 seconds and a Maximum Pause of 40 seconds. The Control Pause measures how long the breath can be held after exhaling.

The Buteyko method includes seven exercises with slight variations. The goal of the practice is to breathe through the nose 24 hours a day with the tongue resting on the roof of the mouth. This helps to open the airways, improves blood circulation, and sends oxygen throughout the body. Because mouth breathing is so common, beginners may feel they are not getting enough air at first, but the feeling goes away with practice.

Exercise 1 clears nasal congestion and makes it easier to breathe through the nose.

Exercise 2 uses hand positions and blocked nostril breathing to increase the volume of inhaled air.

Exercise 3 engages belly breathing while walking.

Exercise 4 combines breath holds and walking to lengthen the time the breath can be held.

Exercise 5 makes breathing easier for adults and children with anxiety, asthma, or panic attacks.

Exercise 6 uses short, repetitive breath holds.

Exercise 7 induces relaxation with slow breathing.

Students of the Buteyko method learn to combine various exercises to meet specific needs. For example, someone with asthma or anxiety may practice exercises 5 and 7 to increase breathing capacity and calm the sympathetic nervous system and increase carbon dioxide (CO_2). Buteyko breathing normalizes stress related symptoms such as high blood pressure, high blood sugar, anxiety, asthma, insomnia or panic attacks.

Ricardo B Serrano, Certified Buteyko Breathing Instructor

Love Peace Harmony Song

Lyrics in Soul Language: *Lu La Lu La Li; Lu La Lu La La Li*

Lu La Lu La Li Lu La; Lu La Li Lu La; Lu La Li Lu La

The English translation of these lyrics is: *I love my heart and soul; I love all humanity;*

Join hearts and souls together; Love, peace and harmony, Love, peace and harmony

The Love Peace Harmony song carries a high frequency and vibration of greatest love, forgiveness, compassion and light. When we resonate with this elevated frequency, it can activate love, peace and harmony throughout our whole being. *Love melts all blockages*.

The Love Peace Harmony song has been credited with many deeply transformative experiences by many people around the world who have experienced it.

When we have billions of people singing the Love Peace Harmony song every day, we really can together create a more loving, peaceful and harmonious world!

Tao Calligraphy™ is a revolutionary healing art based on an ancient form of one-stroke calligraphy (Yi Bi Zi) that Master Sha learned from sole lineage holder, Professor Li Qiu Yun. The result is Tao Calligraphy™, which creates a powerful vibrational field, in this unique vibrational field, we can transform negative information and energy in our own vibrational field by absorbing the positive information and energy of the Tao Calligraphy. This can result in positive changes in our lives. The Tao Calligraphy Healing Field gives people access to a pure, positive field and the frequency and vibration of Source love and light. When we practice Tao Calligraphy through the act of writing, tracing or meditating within the Tao Calligraphy Healing Field, we align with the very essence of Oneness. – Master Sha

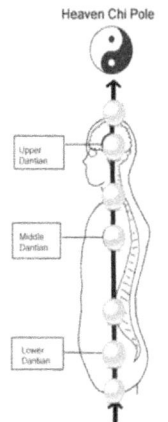

Soul Power Invocation: Dear Divine, Tao, Source, buddhas and saints

Dear Heaven and Mother Earth. Dear countless planets, stars, galaxies, and universes,

I love you, honor you, and appreciate you. Please purify and remove my soul mind body blockages of Enlightenment of my 7 Soul Houses and Ming Men. Please bless my spiritual practice, please bless me to achieve Enlightenment of my 7 Soul Houses and Ming Men. Please forgive my ancestors and me for all the mistakes we have made in all lifetimes. I am extremely sorry for all these mistakes. I am extremely honored and grateful. Love you. (3x) Thank you. Thank you. Thank you. Gong song. Read *Soul Healing*, page 123 *Heal the soul first; then healing of the mind and body will follow. - Zhi Gang Sha*

Mantras to reach oneness with the Tao

As a Traditional Chinese medical (TCM) practitioner, the following excerpt from the Vibrational Medicine book talks about sound healing in Chinese medicine, "The concept of a specific frequency of sound associated with each part of the *seven chakras* is not new. Various East Indian yoga teachings ascribe particular notes of music to each of the seven chakras. Another ancient system associating musical notes with subtle-energy systems of the body is the five Element Theory of acupuncture and Chinese medicine. The Chinese model views Earth and the human body in terms of the five elements of creation, which are fire, earth, metal, water, and wood. Each of the five elements is associated with particular acupuncture meridians and organ systems that energetically interact within the body according to the Law of the Five Elements and its cycles of energy flow. In addition to each element being linked to a particular organ system, it also has a particular musical note associated with it." *Wuji Quan* and *Liu He Ba Fa* are practiced to reach oneness with the Tao.

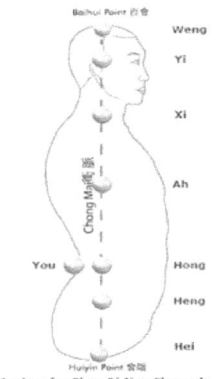
Mantras for Shen Qi Jing Channels

Mantras to purify and remove Shen Qi Jing blockages within the most important Shen Qi Jing channels in the body: The sacred mantra of the *Qi Channel* is: *Hei Heng Hong Ah Xi Yi Weng You* and *Guang Gan Qian Ai Fu Kuan Yuan Ci*. This mantra not only purifies and removes Shen Qi Jing blockages from the Qi Channel, it also further removes Shen Qi Jing blockages from and strengthens each Soul House, San Jiao, and Wai Jiao for healing all sickness.

The sacred mantra for the *Jing Channel* is: *You Weng Yi Xi Ah Hong Heng Hei* and *Ci Yuan Kuan Fu Ai Qian Gan Guang*. When you chant this mantra, you are cleansing the sacred pathways, and further remove Shen Qi Jing blockages and strengthen each Soul House, San Jiao and Wai Jiao for rejuvenation and longevity.

The sacred mantra of the *Shen Channel* (Tao Channel) is: *Weng Hei Hong You* and *Yuan Guang Qian Ci*. The mantra *Weng* connects with *Heaven*. The mantra *Hei* connects with *Mother Earth*. The mantra *Hong* connects with a *human being*. The mantra *You* connects with *Tao*. When you chant *Weng Hei Hong You* and *Yuan Guang Qian Ci*, the Shen Qi Jing of Heaven, Mother Earth, human being, and Tao will join as one to achieve immortality.

The 10 Da Tao Natures: *Guang* - greatest light; *Gan* - greatest gratitude; *Qian* - greatest humility; *Ai* - greatest love; *Fu* - greatest service; *Kuan* - greatest forgiveness; *Yuan* - greatest enlightenment; *Ci* - greatest compassion; *Chang Sheng* – greatest flourishing (*Ha*, lower dantian); *He Xie* – greatest harmony (tailbone) at Wei Lu, *Yu*. **Source**: Tao Classic of Longevity and Immortality: Sacred Wisdom and Practice Techniques by Master Sha, 2018

Conclusion

 I consider myself very fortunate to have started as a TCM practitioner over 40 years ago that assisted healing myself naturally without the use of prescription drugs except for my glaucoma eye drops. Not bad for a 75-year old who haven't used COVID vaccine since the start of the 2019 COVID pandemic solely relying in the meditation, Qigong, Liu He Ba Fa practices with herbs to strengthen my immune system.

I have included my teacher Master Helen Liang's story in this book as a dedication to her Liu He Ba Fa teachings *Six Unities* and *Eight Principles* and *Benefits in practicing Liu He Ba Fa, Wuji Quan* that assisted my understanding of TCM theory, and Fajin application of the forms.

Shen (spirit) manifests only when the heart is open. Once the heart is open, Shen manifests as light that illuminates the path of a man or woman in life's journey toward the spiritual goal and along the spiritual path. **The key is your open heart. Only when the heart is open can the Qi flow and make you truly happy and free.**

When form is correct, spirit resides. When spirit resides, Qi flows. - Neijing

"You found your teacher when you feel your teacher's Qi flow." - Master Ricardo B Serrano

When heaven, man and earth join as one we reach oneness with the Tao. Wuji Quan makes oneness with the Tao Source possible! - Ricardo B Serrano, certified Tao Soul Communicator

Tao is the Wu World. "Wu" means emptiness and nothingness. Tao is emptiness and nothingness. - Tao Te Ching, verse 11

1. Concentrating on the central stillness, All things work together.

2. From this I observe their returning.

3. All things under heaven flourish in their vitality,

Yet each returns to its own root. This is stillness. Stillness means returning to its destiny.

Returning to its destiny is steadfastness. To know steadfastness means enlightenment.

Not to know steadfastness is to act forcefully.

Acting forcefully brings disaster. Knowing the steadfast implies acceptance.

Acceptance is impartial. Impartial is regal. Regal is heaven. Heaven is Tao.

Tao is beyond danger even when the body perishes. - Chapter 16 (Tao Te Ching)

Form is emptiness, Emptiness is form. – Heart Sutra

Tao is called the Great Mother: empty yet inexhaustible, it gives birth to infinite worlds. It is always present within you. You can use it any way you want. - Tao Te Ching, verse 6

Prajñāpāramitā-Hṛdayam (Heart Sutra in Sanskrit)

Oṁ! Namo Bhagavatyai Ārya-Prajñāpāramitāyai!

Hail! Reverence to the Fortunate and Noble Perfection of Wisdom

Ārya-Avalokiteśvaro Bodhisattvo,

The Noble Buddha-to-be Avalokiteśvara,

gambhīrāṁ prajñāpāramitā caryāṁ caramāṇo,

while dwelling deep in the practice of the perfection of wisdom,

vyavalokayati sma panca-skandhāṁs

beheld these five constituent groups (of mind and body)

tāṁś ca svabhāvaśūnyān paśyati sma.

and saw them empty of self-nature.

Iha, Śāriputra, rūpaṁ śūnyatā, śūnyataiva rūpaṁ;

Here, Śāriputra, form is emptiness, emptiness is surely form;

rūpān na pṛthak śūnyatā, śunyatāyā na pṛthag rūpaṁ;

emptiness is not different from form, form is not different from emptiness;

yad rūpaṁ, sā śūnyatā; ya śūnyatā, tad rūpaṁ;

whatever form there is, that is emptiness; whatever emptiness there is, that is form.

evam eva vedanā-saṁjñā-saṁskāra-vijñānaṁ.

the same for feelings, perceptions, volitional processes and consciousness.

Iha, Śāriputra, sarva-dharmāḥ śūnyatā-lakṣaṇā,

Here, Śāriputra, all things have the characteristic of emptiness,

anutpannā, aniruddhā; amalā, avimalā; anūnā, aparipūrṇāḥ.

no arising, no ceasing; no purity, no impurity; no deficiency, no completeness.

Tasmāc Śāriputra, śūnyatāyāṁ *Therefore, Śāriputra, in emptiness*

na rūpaṁ, na vedanā, na saṁjñā, na saṁskārāḥ, na vijñānam;

there is no form, no feeling, no perception, no volitional processes, no consciousness;

na cakṣuḥ-śrotra-ghrāna-jihvā-kāya-manāṁsi;

there are no eye, ear, nose, tongue, body or mind;

na rūpa-śabda-gandha-rasa-spraṣṭavya-dharmāḥ;

no forms, sounds, smells, tastes, touches, thoughts;

na cakṣūr-dhātur yāvan na manovijñāna-dhātuḥ;

no eye-element (and so on) up to no mind-consciousness element;

na avidyā, na avidyā-kṣayo yāvan na jarā-maraṇam, na jarā-maraṇa-kṣayo;

no ignorance, no destruction of ignorance (and so on) up to no old age and death, no destruction of old age and death;

na duḥkha-samudaya-nirodha-mārgā;

no suffering, arising, cessation, path;

na jñānam, na prāptir na aprāptiḥ.

no knowledge, no attainment, no non-attainment.

Tasmāc Śāriputra, aprāptitvād Bodhisattvasya

Therefore, Śāriputra, because of the Buddha-to-be's non-attainments

Prajñāpāramitām āśritya, viharaty acittāvaraṇaḥ,

he relies on the Perfection of Wisdom, and dwells with his mind unobstructed,

cittāvaraṇa-nāstitvād atrastro,

having an unobstructed mind he does not tremble,

viparyāsa-atikrānto, niṣṭhā-Nirvāṇa-prāptaḥ.

overcoming opposition, he attains the state of Nirvāṇa.

Tryadhva-vyavasthitāḥ sarva-Buddhāḥ

All the Buddhas abiding in the three times

Prajñāpāramitām āśritya *through relying on the Perfection of Wisdom*

anuttarāṁ Samyaksambodhim abhisambuddhāḥ.

fully awaken to the unsurpassed Perfect and Complete Awakening.

Tasmāj jñātavyam Prajñāpāramitā mahā-mantro,

Therefore one should know the Perfection of Wisdom is a great mantra,

mahā-vidyā mantro, 'nuttara-mantro, samasama-mantraḥ,

a great scientific mantra, an unsurpassed mantra, an unmatched mantra,

sarva duḥkha praśamanaḥ, satyam, amithyatvāt.

the subduer of all suffering, the truth, not falsehood.

Prajñāpāramitāyām ukto mantraḥ tad-yathā:

In the Perfection of Wisdom the mantra has been uttered in this way:

gate, gate, pāragate, pārasaṁgate, Bodhi, svāhā!

gone, gone, gone beyond, gone completely beyond, Awakening, blessings!

Iti Prajñāpāramitā-Hṛdayam Samāptam

Thus the Heart of the Perfection of Wisdom is Complete

Source: Prajnaparamita-Hyrdayam, Edited by Edward Conze Translated by Anandajoti Bhikku

The Heart Sutra teachings help us empty the heart. The heart is the key in all of Master Sha's teachings. The heart must become empty of all the human thinking and emotions. It must become qing jing—clean, light, quiet, still, and peaceful. **The heart must be filled with love. A heart that is filled only with love is the most powerful way to help heal and transform humanity. The Heart Sutra helps us do exactly that**. It teaches us to empty the heart so we can reach the state of stillness. In this state we are one with Tao. We are one with our true self. We are one with humanity. This is the state that millions are searching for and we not only have the possibility to learn these teachings, but also put them into practice, and be with our teacher. To be present in the field that Master Sha will create at the Heart Sutra Retreat is to receive one of the greatest opportunities to clear blockages affecting our soul journey. I feel in my heart the power of the heart sutra is:

- To uplift our soul so that we can be empowered in a greater way to serve humanity
- To help us transform our negative thoughts so we can more easily reach a qing jing xin. To help us open and purify our heart deeper so we can embody the Ten Da to a higher level

- To cleanse our negative information, energy, and matter so we can uplift our soul journey
- To bless our journey to stop reincarnation. To prepare our soul, heart, mind, and body to become a higher level Tao Hands Practitioner, higher level Kuan Yin Lineage Holder and Ten Da Lineage Holder.
- To bless our total soul enlightenment journey. The path to reach Buddhahood and reach highest enlightenment which is to reach "the other side of the shore" and truly understand to reach Buddhahood and become immortal are the same.

The Heart Sutra is the most transformative and essential mantra to reach the Kong (Tao, Buddha) state. It is necessary to purify the heart (soul) to awaken the true heart (xin) by chanting the Heart Sutra. – Ricardo B Serrano, certified Soul Communicator

Neuroscience of chanting Sanskrit mantras

Many of us have heard the Gyuto Monks of Tibet. With their extraordinary chanting and the low throaty drone of ancient sacred texts, they have kept audiences in the West spellbound with their long, careful and accurate recitations of potent Tibetan Buddhist texts. Sitting in their presence, you feel clarity and a potent spiritual transference of energy and healing. The Buddhist tradition stems from India and the sacred language of *Sanskrit*. While Tibetan Buddhists have a rich chanting tradition, in India, this age-old tradition goes back even further.

Sanskrit scholars in India learn to chant ancient texts from a tender age. They chant simple mantras, *Sanskrit* poetry, and prose, along with memorizing and chanting the most ancient Sanskrit texts, including the Shukla Yajurveda, which takes six hours to chant. While those listening to these chanting receive the gift of the sacred texts they are sharing with us, the chanting of long texts does, in fact, have an amazing effect on the brain.

Neuroscience shows how rigorous memorizing can help the brain. The term the '*Sanskrit Effect*' was coined by neuroscientist James Hartzell, who studied 21 professionally qualified *Sanskrit* pandits. He discovered that memorizing Vedic mantras increases the size of brain regions associated with cognitive function, including short and long-term memory. This finding corroborates the beliefs of the Indian tradition which holds that memorizing and reciting mantras enhances memory and thinking...

Dr Hartzell's recent study raises the question whether this kind of memorization of ancient texts could be helpful in reducing the devastating illness of Alzheimer's and other memory affecting diseases. Apparently, Ayurvedic doctors from India suggest it is the case and future studies will be conducted, along with more research into Sanskrit. While we all know the benefits of mindfulness and meditation practices, the findings of Dr Hartzell are truly dramatic. In a world of shrinking attention spans, where we are flooded with information daily, and children display a range of attention deficit disorders, ancient Indian wisdom has much to teach the West. Even introducing small amounts of chanting and recitation could have an amazing effect on all of our brains. **Source**: Azriel ReShel, Science proves the power of chanting

Comment by Ricardo B Serrano: The Sanskrit effect of chanting *Sri Vidya beej mantras* together with *Heart* Sutra *in Sanskrit* is kundalini activation with balancing and normalizing the *Default Mode Network* in the brain and the chakras along the spine resulting in healing, energizing and blissful Turiya state of transformation. - *Meditation and Qigong Mastery*

Herbs for Eyes in Chinese Medicine that work *Goji berries* and *Chrysanthemum Flowers* are two Chinese herbs together with green tea I **personally use for my Glaucoma** combined with eye drops prescribed by my eye doctor. **T**hese herbs also control high blood pressure.

Chrysanthemum (*Ju Hua*) and goji berries (*Gou Qi Zi*) are a classic combination in Chinese medicine for treating eye conditions - including dry, itchy, red eyes, eye infections, styes, poor vision, tired eyes - an imbalance of Qi and blood stasis in the liver/ kidney meridians.

Like many classic herbal combinations, the herbs work in different but complimentary ways. The chrysanthemum is cooling and clears heat from the eyes, while the goji berries are nourishing to the Liver and Kidney systems which support eye health.

Goji berries (*Lycium barbarum*), also known as wolfberries, have a long history of use in Traditional Chinese Medicine (TCM), where they are believed to nourish the liver and kidneys and benefit eye health, including conditions like glaucoma. In TCM, glaucoma is often attributed to deficiencies or imbalances that Goji is thought to address. The traditional use of goji berries for eye health underpins their application in cases of glaucoma, although this is based primarily on historical and anecdotal reports rather than rigorous scientific evidence. Goji berries moisturize the eyes, enhance liver health, vitality and longevity.

There is, however, some emerging laboratory and animal research suggesting potential neuroprotective and antioxidative effects of *goji berry* constituents, such as *polysaccharides* and *zeaxanthin*, which could theoretically be relevant to glaucoma, a disease characterized by retinal ganglion cell death and oxidative stress. Nonetheless, direct clinical studies in humans specifically investigating goji berry supplementation for glaucoma are lacking as of 2024. Therefore, while traditional use is well documented, scientific validation for this specific indication remains limited, and goji berries should not be considered a proven or primary therapy for glaucoma to lower intraocular pressure.

Chrysanthemum flower tastes both sweet and bitter. This tea has been used in Chinese Medicine for over a thousand years and it said to prevent aging. This herb is known to clear heat from the Liver. Chrysanthemum has a long history of being used to treat blurred or spotty vision. It also contains beta-carotene and is a good source of vitamin Bs like choline, folacin, niacin, as well as riboflavin. In China, it is common to sip on a cup of chrysanthemum tea for dry or sore eyes after long hours of visual focus. The flowers have anti- inflammatory properties and their natural vitamin C content fights germs and infections. A little tea made from chrysanthemums will make an eye wash that can combat infections.

This simple Chinese herbal tea is traditionally used to treat eyestrain and dizziness, and can soothe and nourish the eyes. Both chrysanthemum flowers and goji berries can be found in Asian grocery stores. 1 tb chrysanthemum flowers; 1 tb goji berries. Combine with 2 cups of boiling water and steep for 5 minutes. Add honey to if you like and enjoy up to 3 cups a day.

Mantra of Avalokiteshvara – Namo Ratna Trayaya *Sanskrit Lyrics with English translation*:

- **Namo Ratna Trayāya** (Homage to the Triple Gem)
- **Namo Ārya Jñāna Sāgara** (Homage to the ocean of noble wisdom)
- **Vairocana** (The Luminous One or The Illuminator)
- **Vyūharā jāra** (To the King of the Manifestations.)
- **Tathāgatāya** (To the Tathāgata)
- **Arhate** (To the Arhat)
- **Samyaksam Buddhāya** (To the perfectly awakened one)
- **Namo Sarwa Tathāgatebhyaḥ** (Homage to all Tathāgatas)
- **Arahatabhyah** (To the Arhats)
- **Samyaksam Buddhebhyaḥ** (To the fully and perfectly awakened ones)
- **Namo Arya Avalokiteśvarāya** (Homage to Noble Avalokiteśvara)
- **Shoraya Bodhisattvāya** (To the Bodhisattva)
- **Mahasattvāya** (To the Great)
- **Mahakarunikāya** (To the Greatly Compassionate one)
- **Tadyathā. Ōṃ** (Thus. Om)
- **Dhara Dhara**, **Dhiri Dhiri, Dhuru Dhuru** (Sustain us, Sustain us, Sustain us)
- **Iṭṭe we, itte** (May we have the strength)
- **Cale Cale** (or Itte cale) (To move forward, to move forward)
- **Puracale Puracale** (To move forward further, to move further along the path)
- **Kusumē, Kusuma ware** (Where to pick the fruits.)
- **Ili Milli Chiti jvalam Apanāye. Svāhā**. (Who bring the blazing understanding. Hail!).
- **Om Mani Padme Hum** (Jewel in the lotus)

Eleven main benefits:

1. **One's body will be free from illness.**

2. One will be constantly remembered by the Buddhas of the ten directions.
3. All wealth, clothing, and food will naturally be abundant without lack.
4. One will be able to defeat all enemies.
5. One will instill compassion in all sentient beings.
6. No poison or fever will be able to harm one.
7. No weapons will be able to injure one.
8. One will not be swept away by water-related disasters.
9. One will not be burned by fire-related disasters.
10. One will not experience untimely death.
11. After death, one will be reborn in the Land of Infinite Life (Amitābha's Pure Land).

OM MANI PADME HUM By His Holiness the Dalai Lama

We have within us the seed of purity, the essence of a One Gone Thus (Tathagatagarbha), that is to be transformed and fully developed into Buddhahood. - Dalai Lama

It is very good to recite the mantra *Om mani padme hum*, but while you are doing it, you should be thinking on its meaning, for the meaning of the six syllables is great and vast. The first, *Om* is composed of three letters, A, U, and M. These symbolize the practitioner's impure body, speech, and mind; they also symbolize the pure exalted body, speech, and mind of a Buddha..........

Can impure body, speech, and mind be transformed into pure body, speech, and mind, or are they entirely separate? All Buddhas are cases of beings who were like ourselves and then in dependence on the path became enlightened; Buddhism does not assert that there is anyone who from the beginning is free from faults and possesses all good qualities.

The development of pure body, speech, and mind comes from gradually leaving the impure states arid their being transformed into the pure.......... How is this done? The path is indicated by the next four syllables. *Mani*, meaning jewel, symbolizes the factors of method- the altruistic intention to become enlightened, compassion, and love. Just as a jewel is capable of removing poverty, so the altruistic mind of enlightenment is capable of removing the poverty, or difficulties, of cyclic existence and of solitary peace. Similarly, just as a jewel fulfills the wishes of sentient beings, so the altruistic intention to become enlightened fulfills the wishes of sentient beings..........

The two syllables, *padme*, meaning lotus, symbolize wisdom. Just as a lotus grows forth from mud but is not sullied by the faults of mud, so wisdom is capable of putting you in a situation of non-contradiction whereas there would be contradiction if you did not have wisdom. There is wisdom realizing impermanence, wisdom realizing that persons are empty, of being self-sufficient or substantially existent, wisdom that realizes the emptiness of duality-that is to say, of difference of entity between subject an object-and wisdom that realizes the emptiness of inherent existence. Though there are many different types of wisdom, the main of all these is the wisdom realizing emptiness..........

Purity must be achieved by an indivisible unity of method and wisdom, symbolized by the final syllable hum, which indicates indivisibility. According to the sutra system, this indivisibility of method and wisdom refers to wisdom affected by method and method affected by wisdom. In the mantra, or tantric, vehicle, it refers to one consciousness in which there is the full form of both wisdom and method as one undifferentiable entity. In terms of the seed syllables of the five Conqueror Buddhas, *hum* is the seed syllable of Akshobhya - the immovable, the unfluctuating, that which cannot be disturbed by anything..........

Thus the six syllables, *om mani padme hum*, mean that in dependence on the practice of a path which is an indivisible union of method and wisdom, you can transform your impure body, speech, and mind into the pure exalted body, speech, and mind of a Buddha. It is said that you should not seek for Buddhahood outside of yourself; the substances for the achievement of Buddhahood are within. As Maitreya says in his Sublime Continuum of the Great Vehicle (Uttaratantra), all beings naturally have the Buddha nature in their own continuum. We have within us the seed of purity, the essence of a *One Gone Thus* (*Tathagatagarbha*), that is to be transformed and fully developed into Buddhahood.

The Six-Syllable Mantra *'OM MANI PADME HUM'* is the heart mantra of Bodhisattva Avalokiteshvara as well as all the Buddhas. Avalokiteshvara is the compassionate embodiment of all the Buddhas and Bodhisattvas; the mantra is the essence of the 84,000 (literally means uncountable methods) of Buddha's teachings.

Reciting "*OM MANI PADME HUM*" is all-powerful and brings blessings to all sentient beings in the six realms of existence. The benefits of reciting the "OM MANI PADME HUM" are:

- Purifying our negative karma, removing obstruction, bad habits and ignorance.
- Closing the door to the six realms of reincarnation.
- Removing physical and mental sickness.
- Repelling demonic forces.
- Liberating us from samsara and thus allowing us to be reborn in Pure Land.

Taking refuge doesn't protect us from problems in the world. It doesn't shield us from war, famine, illness, accidents, and other difficulties. Rather, it provides tools to transform obstacles into opportunities. We learn how to relate to difficulties in a new way, and this protects us from confusion and despair. Traffic jams do not disappear, but we might not respond by leaning on our horns or swearing. Illnesses may afflict us, but we might still greet the day with a joyful appreciation for being alive. Eventually we rely on the best parts of our being in order to protect ourselves from those neurotic tendencies that create dissatisfaction. This allows for living in the world with greater ease and without needing to withdraw into untrustworthy circumstances in order to feel protected. - Mingyur Rinpoche

Tara, mother of Tibetan Buddhism

Tara (Sanskrit: Tara; Tib. Drolma), the female Buddha, is considered the other most revered Bodhisattva in Tibetan Buddhism, next only to Chenrezig (Avalokiteshvara).

In Tibetan Buddhism it is believed that Tara practice was given by Buddha Sakyamuni together with the Vajrayana teachings about the Nature of the Mind and Buddhist tantra. It became very popular in India and later with Guru Rinpoche was brought to Tibet.

There are a few accounts about the origin of Tara:

According to the most popular story Tara was a young princess who was living millions of years in the past. Her name was Yeshe Dawa, which means "Moon of Primordial Awareness".

After doing this practice for a long time, the monks were suggesting Tara that because of her high attainment, to progress further towards enlightenment, she should pray to be reborn as a male:

To what Tara answered, that from the point of view of Enlightenment there is no separation between male or female, it belongs to the conditioned world only. Therefore she vowed to be always reborn as a female bodhisattva until samsara ends.

After this Tara went into deep state of meditation for 10 million years and released tens of millions of beings with the power of her meditation. Seeing this, Tonyo Drupa told her she will henceforth manifest supreme Buddhahood as the Goddess Tara in many world systems in the future.

Another story depicts Tara as being born from the tears of Chenrezig (Avalokiteshvara):

Once, when the great Bodhisattva Chenrezig out of deep compassion was looking to the sentient beings a tears flow from his eyes and formed lakes with lotus flowers. When the lotus flowers opened, it revealed Tara inside.

This way from the teardrop from Chenrezig's left eye White Tara was emanated and Green Tara from his right eye.

When Guru Rinpoche brought Buddhism to Tibet, he was also giving many teachings regarding Tara practice to his consort, the Daikini of wisdom Yeshe Tsogyal and the first Tibetan King who was Buddhist – Trisong Detsen.

People believed an incarnation of White Tara was born in China, who became a princess and mother of Tibet, the wife of King Trisong Detsen, and the Green Tara incarnation was born as a princess of Nepal. In the next centuries the Tara practice became very popular in Tibetan Buddhism.

The Green Tara is known as Buddha of enlightened activity, who provides protection from fears, she is prayed for a good luck and fortune, and it is said Green Tara protects from 8 obscurations:

1. lions (pride)
2. wild elephants (delusion and ignorance)
3. fires (hatred and anger)
4. snakes (jealousy)
5. bandits and thieves (wrong views, including fanatical views)
6. bondage (avarice and miserliness)
7. floods (desire and attachment)
8. evil spirits and demons (deluded doubts)

White Tara is known for compassion, long life, healing and serenity:

White Tara counteracts illness and helps to have a long life. She embodies compassion and motivation and is said to be as white and radiant as the moon. She provides relief from bad karma as experienced by ordinary beings in cyclic existence.

Tara meditation is often recommended for small kids who haven't started yet the general practice. Tara is associated with all qualities of the mother and mother's love.

The most widely popular Tara forms are the White Tara and Green Tara as discussed above. But there can be many more:

One of the main Tara practices in Tibetan Buddhism is Praises to 21 Tara or Homage to 21 Tara, which is practiced in all 4 traditions of Tibetan Buddhism, usually in mornings.

As the name suggests there are considered 21 forms of Tara, each with a slightly different set of enlightened qualities. But the most popular forms are:

1. Green Tara, known as the Buddha of enlightened activity;
2. White Tara, also known for compassion, long life, healing and serenity; also known as The Wish-fulfilling Wheel, or Cinta-chakra;

3. Red Tara, of fierce aspect associated with magnetizing all good things;
4. Black Tara, associated with power;
5. Yellow Tara, associated with wealth and prosperity;
6. Blue Tara, associated with transmutation of anger, also known as patroness of Nyingma tradition.
7. Cintamani Tara, a form of Tara widely practiced at the level of Highest Yoga Tantra in the Gelug School, portrayed as green and often conflated with Green Tara.
8. Khadiravani Tara (Tara of the acacia forest), who appeared to Nagarjuna in the Khadiravani forest of South India and who is sometimes referred to as the "22nd Tara"

The mantra of Tara is: **Om Tare Tuttare Ture Soha**

Source: Buddhism: Red Zambala

Namo Amituofo

"There is a renowned spiritual teaching in Buddhism. Millions of people throughout history have chanted *'Na Mo A Mi Tuo Fo'*. They chant only this one mantra. If you are upset, sick, weak, emotional chant *'Na Mo A Mi Tuo Fo'* (pronounced 'nah maw ah mee twaw faw'). If you have relationship challenges, chant *'Na Mo A Mi Tuo Fo'*. If you have financial challenges, chant *'Na Mo A Mi Tuo Fo'*. To transform life takes time. You must understand this spiritual wisdom so that you will practice chanting and meditation more and more. The more you practice, the more healing and life transformation you could receive." - Master Zhi Gang Sha, Book: Tao Song and Tao Dance

Suffering is not holding you, You are holding suffering. – Buddha. (Let go of the past, learn from it and move on!) Chant '*Na Mo A Mi Tuo Fo*' Mantra.

Benefits of Namo Amituofo Recitation: The recitation of Namo Amitoufo, Amitabha Buddha will safeguard the reciter on the top of one's head and emit His light for protection. People who feel a sense of chaos or confusion would experience a stabilized calmness afterward. There is a warming peaceful harmonious body and soul tranquility throughout the whole being. Amituofo could help to ride through the waves of adversity.

Namo Amitoufo's six-character is a powerful fortunate positive energetic great name of the Buddha. It could abolish evil calamity and negative matters. Generating the magnetic field of illuminating light, warmth, gentle harmony, peace, and joy. It enables the focus of the mind, eradicates karmic offenses, increases blessings wisdom.

Reciting *Namo Amitoufo* draws in the blessings to the mind and soul. Further, it brings in the flows of luck and fortune. Most directly, *Amituofo* brings forth tranquility in feeling great satisfaction and a sense of abundance. Regardless of being wealthy in possessions or the poorest of the poor, the first request is to have the greatest satisfaction. When the heart and soul are completely satisfied, it is the true happiness and joy. Reciting *Namo Amitoufo* will broaden the magnanimity. The opening one's heart and soul, the sense of compassion, and love will lead to embracing the differences in people's opinions and ideas.

Amitabha (Amituofo) is a manifestation of Primordial Buddha, or Adi Buddha, embodying void and ultimate emptiness. Shakyamuni Buddha described 15 benefits in chanting Namo Amituofo: 1. Guided by Amitabha, 2. Bathed in Buddha's light. 3. Supported by all Buddhas. 4. Joined by Bodhisattvas. 5. Guarded by spirits. 6. Clearing bad karma. 7. Gathering wisdom. 8. Avoiding disasters. 9. Ensuring health. 10. Peaceful passing. 11. Karma assurance. 12. End reincarnation. 13. Rebirth in the Pure Land. 14. Attain Buddhahood. 15. Deliverance of others.

May Guru Rinpoche's blessing through his Vajra Guru Mantra grant enlightenment and healing to yourself and others. – Ricardo B Serrano, *Guru Rinpoche's devotee*

Vajra Guru Mantra – Om Ah Hum Vajra Guru Padma Siddhi Hum

The Vajra Guru mantra, OM AH HUM VAJRA GURU PADMA SIDDHI HUM, is pronounced by Tibetans: Om Ah Hung Benza Guru Pema Siddhi Hung. This explanation of its meaning is based on explanations by *Dudjorn Rinpoche* and *Dilgo Khyentse Rinpoche*.

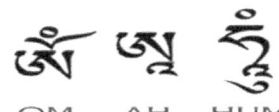

OM AH HUM The syllable OM AH HUM have outer, inner, and "secret" meanings. At each of these levels, however, OM stands for the body, AH for the speech, and HUM for the mind. They represent the transformative blessings of the body, speech, and mind of all the buddhas.

Externally OM purifies all the negative actions committed through your body, AH through your speech, and HUM through your mind. By purifying your body, speech, and mind, OM AH HUM grants the blessing of the body, speech, and mind of the buddhas.

OM is also the essence of the form, AH the essence of sound, and HUM the essence of mind. So by reciting this mantra, you are also purifying the environment, as well as yourself and all the other beings within it. OM purifies all perceptions, AH all sounds, and HUM the mind, its thoughts and emotions.

Internally OM purifies the subtle channels, AH the wind, inner air or flow of energy, and HUM the creative essence.

On a deeper level, **OM AH HUM** represent the three kayas of the Lotus family of the buddhas: OM is the *Dharmakaya*: the *Buddha Amitabha*, Buddha of Limitless Light; AH is the *Sambhogakaya*: Avalokiteshvara, the Buddha of Compassion; and HUM is the *Nirmanakaya*:

Padmasambhava. This signifies, in the case of this mantra, that all three kayas are embodied in the person of Padmasambhava. The Buddha says in one of the Tantras: "*Of all the buddhas who have ever attained enlightenment, not a single one accomplished this without relying upon a master, and of all the thousand buddhas that will appear in this eon, none of them will attain enlightenment without relying on a master.*" *To blend your mind with the teacher's mind is the most profound of all practices, and the shortest path to realization.* – Dilgo Khyentse Rinpoche

At the innermost level, OM AH HUM bring the realization of the three aspects of the nature of mind: OM brings the realization of its unceasing Energy and Compassion, AH brings the realization of its radiant nature, and HUM brings the realization of its skylike Essence.

VAJRA GURU PADMA

VAJRA is compared to the diamond, the strongest and most precious of stones. Just as a diamond can cut through anything but is itself completely indestructible, so the unchanging, nondual wisdom of the buddhas can never be harmed or destroyed by ignorance, and can cut through all delusions and obscurations. The qualities and activities of the body, speech, and wisdom mind of the buddhas are able to benefit beings with the piercing, unhindered power of the diamond. And like the diamond, the Vajra is free of defects; its brilliant strength comes from the realization of the Dharmakaya nature of reality, the nature of the Buddha Amitabha.

GURU means "weighty"; someone replete with every wonderful quality, who embodies wisdom, knowledge, compassion, and skilled means. Just as gold is the weightiest and most precious of metals, so the inconceivable, flawless qualities of the Guru -- the master -- make him unsurpassable, and above all things in excellence. GURU corresponds to the Sambhogakaya, and to Avalokiteshvara, the Buddha of Compassion. Also, since Padmasambhava teaches the path of Tantra, which is symbolized by the Vajra, and through the practice of Tantra he attained supreme realization, so he is known as "*the VAJRA GURU.*"

PADMA means lotus, and signifies the Lotus family of the buddhas, and specifically their aspect of enlightened speech. The Lotus family is the buddha family to which human beings belong. As Padmasambhava is the direct emanation, the Nirmanakaya, of Buddha Amitabha, who is the primordial buddha of the Lotus family, he is known as "PADMA." His name Padmasambhava, the "*Lotus-born,*" in fact refers to the story of his birth on a blossoming lotus flower.

When the syllables **VAJRA GURU PADMA** are taken together, they also signify the essence and the blessing of the View, Meditation and Action. VAJRA means the unchanging, diamantine, indestructible Essence of the truth, which we pray to realize in our View. GURU represents the luminosity Nature and noble qualities of enlightenment, which we pray to perfect in our Meditation. **PADMA** stands for Compassion, which we pray to accomplish in our Action. Through reciting the mantra, then, we receive the blessing of the wisdom mind, the noble qualities and the compassion of Padmasambhava and all the buddhas.

SIDDHI HUM SIDDHI means "real accomplishment," "attainment," "blessing," and "realization." There are two kinds of siddhis: ordinary and supreme. Through receiving the blessing of ordinary siddhis, all obstacles in our lives, such as ill-health, are removed, all our good aspirations are fulfilled, benefits like wealth and prosperity and long life accrue to us, and all of life's various circumstances become auspicious and conducive to spiritual practice, and the realization of enlightenment.

The blessing of the supreme siddhi brings about enlightenment itself, the state of complete realization of Padmasambhava, that benefits both ourselves and all other sentient beings. So by remembering and praying to the body, speech, mind, qualities, and activity of Padmasambhava, we will come to attain both ordinary and supreme siddhis.

SIDDHI HUM is said to draw in all the siddhis like a magnet that attracts iron filings. HUM represents the wisdom mind of the buddhas, and is the sacred catalyst of the mantra. It is like proclaiming its power and truth: "So be it!" The essential meaning of the mantra is: "I invoke you, the *Vajra Guru*, *Padmasambhava*, by your blessing may you grant us ordinary and supreme siddhis."

Dilgo Khyentse Rinpoche explains: It is said that the twelve syllables **OM AH HUM VAJRA GURU PADMA SIDDHI HUM** carry the entire blessing of the twelve types of teaching taught by the Buddha, which are the essence of his eighty-four thousand Dharmas. Therefore, to recite the Vajra Guru mantra once is equivalent to the blessing of reciting ... or practicing the whole teaching of the Buddha. These twelve branches of the teachings are the antidotes to free us from the "Twelve Links of Interdependent Origination," which keep us bound to samsara: ignorance, karmic formations, discursive consciousness, name and form, senses, contact, sensation, craving, grasping, existence, birth, old age and death. These twelve links are the mechanism of samsara, by which samsara is kept alive. Through reciting the twelve syllables of the Vajra Guru mantra, these twelve links are purified, and you are able to remove and purify completely the layer of karmic emotional defilements, and so be liberated from samsara.

Although we are not able to see Padmasambhava in person, his wisdom mind has manifested in the form of the mantra; these twelve syllables are actually the emanation of his wisdom mind, and they are endowed with his entire blessing. The Vajra Guru mantra is

Padmasambhava in the form of sound. So when you invoke him with the recitation of the twelve syllables, the blessing and merit you obtain is tremendous. In these difficult times, just as there is no buddha or refuge we can call upon who is more powerful than Padmasambhava, so there is no mantra that is more fitting than the Vajra Guru mantra. *ADDITIONAL NOTE* by Ricardo B. Serrano, Dipl.Ac.: *White OM* is focused at the forehead, *Ruby red AH* is focused at the throat, and *sky blue HUM* is focused at the heart of the practitioner while visualizing light rays radiating from Padmasambhava's forehead, throat and heart. Guru Padmasambhava is visualized above the practitioner's head. **SOURCE**: The above two most famous Sanskrit Mantras in Tibet - mantra of Avalokiteshvara, the Buddha of Compassion, *OM MANI PADME HUM* and the mantra of Padmasambhava, called the *Vajra Guru Mantra* – articles are excerpts from Sogyal Rinpoche's Tibetan Book of Living and Dying, pages 393-398.

GURU YOGA (*Deity Yoga*) All the buddhas, bodhisattvas, and enlightened beings are present at all moments to help us, and it is through the presence of the master that all their blessings are focused directly at us. Those who know Bodhisattva Padmasambhava know the living truth of the promise he made over a thousand years ago: "*I am never far from those with faith, or even from those without it, though they do not see me. My children will always, always, be protected by my compassion.*"

H.H. Penor Rinpoche said: "The most important qualities to ensure the success of the (Guru Yoga) practice in the students' mind are faith, devotion, trust and pure view. If a student is truly bent upon benefiting from his or her practice and his or her association with the dharma, those qualities are indispensable."

Dilgo Khyentse Rinpoche said: "*There have been many incredible and incomparable masters from the noble land of India and Tibet, the Land of Snows, yet of them all, the one who has the greatest compassion and blessing toward beings in this difficult age is Padmasambhava, who embodies the compassion and wisdom of all the buddhas. One of his qualities is that he has the power to give his blessing instantly to whoever prays to him, and whatever we may pray for, he has the power to grant our wish immediately.*"

According to Dilgo Khyentse Rinpoche: Devotion is the essence of the path, and if we have in mind nothing but the guru and feel nothing but fervent devotion, whatever occurs is perceived as his blessing. If we simply practice with this constantly present devotion, this is prayer itself. When all thoughts are imbued with devotion to the guru, there is a natural confidence that this will take care of whatever may happen. All forms are the guru, all sounds are prayer, and all gross and subtle thoughts arise as devotion. Everything is spontaneously liberated in the absolute nature, like knots untied in the sky. Through the guru yoga practice, all obstacles can be removed and all blessings received. And through merging our mind with the mind of the guru and remaining in that state of inseparable union, the absolute nature will be realized. This why we should always treasure guru yoga and keep it as our foremost practice.

According to Shechen Rabjam Rinpoche: Guru Yoga should be at the heart of every practice we do. It gives our practice strength and depth, and prevents us from straying into all the side-tracks dreamed up by our wild thoughts. The very essence of Buddhist practice is to destroy ego-clinging, totally -- and the most inspiring way to do that is the through the practice of Guru Yoga.

The essence of Guru Yoga is simply to remember the guru at all times: when you are happy, think of the guru; when you are sad, think of the guru; when you meet favorable circumstances, be grateful to the guru; and when you meet obstacles, pray to the guru, and rely on him alone. When you are sitting, think of the guru above your head. When you are walking, imagine that he is above your right shoulder, as if you were circumambulating him. When you are eating food, visualize the guru at your throat center and offer him the first portion. Whenever you wear new clothes, first offer them to the guru, and then wear them as if he had given them back to you.

At night, when you are about to fall asleep, *visualize Guru Rinpoche in your heart center, the size of the first joint of your thumb, sitting on a four-petalled red lotus. He is emanating countless rays of light, which fill your whole environment, melting the room and the entire universe into light, and then returning to absorb into your heart. Then the guru himself dissolves into light. This is the luminous state in which you should fall asleep.* **Note by Ricardo B Serrano**: *To realize our Buddha Nature is Guru Yoga's goal and purpose.*

WHAT BUDDHA NATURE IS The Spiritual fetus is a symbolic term for Buddha Nature or the "*incarnated Soul*" that is lodged above the head. This illustration was taken from a Taoist book "Cultivating the Energy of Life" written by Liu Hua-yang and translated by Eva Wong. It is based on the book "Hui-ming ching." The text Hui-ming ching is part of the book "Wu-Liu, Hsien- Tsung" (Techniques of Immortality by Wu and Liu) by Taoist masters Wu Chung-hsiu and Liu Hua-yang.

"The Buddha Nature is lodged above the head which radiates outward, forming the aura. Through the divine cord, the three silver cords and the three permanent seeds, the different bodies (the physical body, the energy body, the astral body and the mental body) are infused with the essence of the Buddha Nature. Just as the etheric body interpenetrates the physical body, likewise the essence of the Buddha nature interpenetrates the physical body; at the same time, it is beyond the physical body. That is why the physical body is actually within the Buddha nature, and not the Buddha nature within the physical body. The physical body is like a sponge. If you put the sponge in a bathtub filled with water, the water is inside and outside the sponge. In other words, the sponge is inside the water. The physical body, energy body, astral body and lower mental body are all inside the incarnated Buddha nature. Therefore, it would be accurate to define a person as a Buddha nature with a physical body, rather than a physical body with a Buddha nature. To express this more accurately, a person is a Buddha nature with a physical body and other subtle bodies. The Buddha nature, as seen from the point of lower clairvoyance, is spiritual energy which is fluidic in nature. But from the perspective of higher spiritual clairvoyance, the Buddha nature is radiatory and is omnipresent within a certain "radius of space." - Master Choa Kok Sui's OM MANI PADME HUM book

"You don't have a soul. You are a soul. You have a body. Quiet the mind and the soul will speak. Your body is precious. It is our vehicle for awakening. Treat it with care. Your purpose in life is to find your purpose and give your whole heart and soul to it." – Buddha

Guru Yoga: Merging with the Wisdom Mind of the Master

Hum!

In the northwest of the land of Oddiyana,

In the heart of a lotus flower,

Endowed with the most marvelous attainments,

You are renowned as the "Lotus-born,"

Surrounded by hosts of dakinis.

Following in your footsteps,

I pray to you: Come, inspire me with your blessing! *GURU PADMA SIDDHI HUM*

O Guru Rinpoche, Precious One,

You are the embodiment of

The compassion and blessings of all the buddhas,

The only protector of beings,

My body, my possessions, my heart and soul,

Without hesitation, I surrender to you!

From now until I attain enlightenment,

In happiness or sorrow, in circumstances good or bad, in situations high or low:

I rely on you completely, O Padmasambhava, you who know me:

think of me, inspire me, guide me, make me one with you!

OM AH HUM VAJRA GURU PADMA SIDDHI HUM

I have no one else to turn to; In these evil times, the beings of the Kaliyuga

Are sinking in a swamp of intense and unbearable suffering. Free us from all this, O Great guru!

Grant us the four empowerments, O blessed one! Direct your realization into our minds,

O compassionate one! Purify our emotional and cognitive obscurations, O powerful one!

OM AH HUM VAJRA GURU PADMA SIDDHI HUM

I pray to you from the bottom of my heart, It's not just words or empty mouthings: Grant your blessings from the depth of your wisdom mind, And cause all my good aspirations to be fulfilled, I pray!

OM AH HUM VAJRA GURU PADMA SIDDHI HUM

Just as if you put your finger into water, it will get wet, and if you put it into fire, it will burn, so if you invest your mind in the wisdom mind of the buddhas, it will transform into their wisdom nature.

According to *Dzongsar Jamyang Khyentse Rinpoche*: The purpose of Dharma practice is to attain enlightenment. Actually, attaining enlightenment is exactly the same as ridding ourselves of ignorance, and the root of ignorance is the ego. Whichever path we take, whether it's the long and disciplined route, or the short and wild one, at the end of it the essential point is that we eliminate the ego...

This is the reason why, in the Vajrayana, guru devotion, or Guru Yoga, is taught as a vital and essential practice. As the guru is a living, breathing human being, he or she is able to deal directly with your ego. Reading a book about how to eliminate ego may be interesting, but you will never be in awe of that book, and anyway, books are entirely open to your own interpretation. A book cannot talk or react to you, whereas the guru can and will stir up your ego so that eventually it will be eliminated altogether. Whether this is achieved wrathfully or gently doesn't matter, but in the end, this is what the guru is there to do, and this is why guru devotion is so important.

 The following article and quotes by Yongey Mingyur Rinpoche on natural mind, also called *tathagatagarbha*, *Buddha nature*, *enlightened essence* or *true nature*, compares it to an inexhaustible treasure that when recognized as our essential nature we become free from suffering since the mind is the source of all experience, and that by changing the direction of the mind, we can change the quality of everything we experience.

The Buddha often compared natural mind to water, which in its essence is always clear and clean. Mud, sediment, and other impurities may temporarily darken or pollute the water, but we can filter away such impurities and restore its natural clarity. If water wasn't naturally clear, no matter how many filters you used, it would not become clear.

"If an inexhaustible treasure were buried in the ground beneath a poor man's house, the man would not know of it, and the treasure would not speak and tell him, "I am here!" - Maitreya, the Mahayana Uttaratantra Shastra

Now let me ask a question. Who is wealthier - someone who lives in an old house surrounded by jewels he doesn't recognize, or someone who understands the value of what he has and lives in total comfort? It's the same for all of us. As long as we don't recognize our real nature, we suffer. When we recognize our nature, we become free from suffering. Whether you recognize it or not, though, its qualities remain unchanged. But when you begin to recognize it in yourself, you change, and the quality of your life changes as well. Things you never dreamed possible begin to happen. – Excerpts from The Joy of Living: Unlocking the Secret and Science of Happiness, 2007

"Ultimately, happiness comes down to choosing between the discomfort of becoming aware of your mental afflictions and the discomfort of being ruled by them."

"A disciplined mind invites true joy."

"The essence of Buddhist practice is not so much an effort at changing your thoughts or your behavior so that you can become a better person, but in realizing that no matter what you might think about the circumstances that define your life, you're already good, whole, and complete. It's about recognizing the inherent potential of your mind. In other words, Buddhism is not so much concerned with getting well as with recognizing that you are, right here, right now, as whole, as good, as essentially well as you could ever hope to be."

"The teachings of the Buddha—and the lesson inherent in this exercise in non-meditation—is that if we allow ourselves to relax and take a mental step back, we can begin to recognize that all these different thoughts are simply coming and going within the context of an unlimited mind, which, like space, remains fundamentally unperturbed by whatever occurs within it."

"Let your own experience serve as your guide and inspiration. Let yourself enjoy the view as you travel along the path. The view is your own mind, and because your mind is already enlightened, if you take the opportunity to rest awhile along the journey, eventually you'll realize that the place you want to reach is the place you already are."

"All phenomena are expressions of the mind."

"For example, children who were regularly humiliated and criticized by their parents or other adults may experience inappropriately strong feelings of fear, resentment, or other unpleasant emotions when dealing with authority figures in adult life."

"if, as the Buddha proposed in the first teachings he gave upon attaining enlightenment, the essence of ordinary life is suffering, then one of the most effective antidotes is laughter—particularly laughter at oneself. Every aspect of experience assumes a certain kind of brightness once you learn to laugh at yourself."

"Non-conceptuality is an experience of the total openness of your mind. Your awareness is direct and unclouded by conceptual distinction such as "I" or "other," subjects and objects, or any other form of limitation. It's an experience of pure consciousness as infinite as space, without beginning, middle, or end. It's like becoming awake within a dream and recognizing that everything experienced in the dream isn't separate from the mind of the dreamer."

"Whatever passes through your mind, don't focus on it and don't try to suppress it. Just observe it as it comes and goes."

"One of the earliest lessons I was taught by my father was that Buddhists don't see the mind as a discrete entity, but rather as a perpetually unfolding experience."

"The opportunity to receive these transmissions also taught me, in an indirect way, the extremely valuable lesson that to whatever degree a person commits himself or herself to the welfare of others, he or she is repaid a thousandfold by opportunities for learning and advancement. Every kind word, every smile you offer someone who might be having a bad day, comes back to you in ways you'd never expect."

"The habit of thinking that things exist "out there" in the world or "in here" is hard to give up, though. It means letting go of all the illusions you cherish, and recognizing that everything you project, everything you think of as "other," is in fact a spontaneous expression of your own mind."

"As in other exercises my father taught me, the way to begin is to sit up straight, breathe normally, and gradually allow your mind to relax. "With your mind at rest," he instructed those of us in his little teaching room in Nepal, "just allow yourself to become aware of all the thoughts, feelings, and sensations passing through it. And as you watch them pass, simply ask yourself, 'Is there a difference between the mind and the thoughts that pass through it? Is there any difference between the thinker and the thoughts perceived by the thinker?' Continue watching your thoughts with these questions in mind for about three minutes or so, and then stop."

"Compassion is reciprocal. As you develop your own mental and emotional stability and extend that stability through a compassionate understanding of others and dealing with them in a kind, empathetic way, your own intentions or aspirations will be fulfilled more quickly and easily. Why? Because if you treat others compassionately—with the understanding that they have the same desire for happiness and the same desire to avoid unhappiness that you do—then the people around you feel a sense of attraction, a sense of wanting to help you as much as you help them.

"Compassion is reciprocal. As you develop your own mental and emotional stability and extend that stability through a compassionate understanding of others and dealing with them in a kind, empathetic way, your own intentions or aspirations will be fulfilled more quickly and easily. Why? Because if you treat others compassionately—with the understanding that they have the same desire for happiness and the same desire to avoid unhappiness that you do—then the people around you feel a sense of attraction, a sense of wanting to help you as much as you help them.

...In a sense, compassion practice demonstrates the truth of interdependence in action. The more openhearted you become toward others, the more openhearted they become toward you."

"Don't criticize or condemn yourself when you find yourself following after thoughts. The fact that you've caught yourself reliving a past event or projecting into the future is enough to bring you back to the present moment and strengthens your intention to meditate. Your intention to meditate as you engage in practice is the crucial factor.

It's also important to proceed slowly. My father was very careful to tell all his new students, including me, that the most effective approach in the beginning is to rest the mind for very short periods many times a day. Otherwise, he said, you run the risk of growing bored or becoming disappointed with your progress and eventually give up trying altogether. "Drip by drip," the old texts say, "a cup gets filled."

(...) there is one very practical guideline, which my father emphasized again and again to all of his students in a way that would make it easy for us to remember: Short periods, many times.

(...) Meditation is about learning to work with the mind as it is, not about trying to force it into some sort of Buddhist straitjacket."

Guru Padmasambhava also widely known as *Gugu Rinpoche* was the important figure in *Tibetan Buddhism* and in *Vajrayana Buddhism*. Guru Rinpoche is depicted perfectly, he sits on a moon disc on a lotus on a royal posture with the piercing gaze. *Guru Padmasambhava* wears a beautiful crafted colorful robe and a tantric hat. His right hand holds a *Vajra*, and his left-hand holds a skull vase filled with immortality nectar. In the curve of his left hand, he holds the Khatvang trident.

For most Himalayan Buddhists, Guru Rinpoche is *the second Buddha*, the Buddha of all enlightenment forms and teachings, with a focus on the tantras. Tantra teaches us to first see our teachers as Guru Rinpoche, just as the Great Way leads us to see and name our enlightened nature as *Buddha-nature*. Then we see everything through the eyes of Guru Rinpoche, right down to our atoms, all beings equally, and every scrap of every blade of grass, every grain of sand. Finally, when we recognize our natural, timeless awareness, we recognize Guru Rinpoche.

We are all buddhas by *Yongey Mingyur Rinpoche, my teacher* https://vajrayana.tergar.org/

We're all buddhas. We just don't recognize it. We are confined in many ways to a limited view of ourselves and the world around us through cultural conditioning, family upbringing, personal experience, and the basic biological predisposition toward making distinctions and measuring present experience and future hopes and fears against a neuronal warehouse of memories.

Once you commit yourself to developing an awareness of your buddha nature, you'll inevitably start to see changes in your day-to- day experience. Things that used to trouble you gradually lose their power to upset you. You'll become intuitively wiser, more relaxed, and more openhearted. You'll begin to recognize obstacles as opportunities for further growth. And as your illusory sense of limitation and vulnerability gradually fades away, you'll discover deep within yourself the true grandeur of who and what you are.

Best of all, as you start to see your own potential, you'll also begin to recognize it in everyone around you. Buddha nature is not a special quality available to a privileged few. The true mark of recognizing your buddha nature is to realize how ordinary it really is—the ability to see that every living creature shares it, though not everyone recognizes it in him- or herself. So instead of closing your heart to people who yell at you or act in some other harmful way, you find yourself becoming more open. You recognize that they aren't "jerks," but are people who, like you, want to be happy and peaceful. They're only acting like jerks because they haven't recognized their true nature and are overwhelmed by sensations of vulnerability and fear. https://justdharma.org/we-are-all-buddhas-mingyur-rinpoche/

Guru Rinpoche with Vajra, Bell, Damaru and Mantras

In Tibetan Buddhism, the vajra (*dorje*) and bell (*ghanta*) are essential ritual instruments, representing the inseparable union of method (compassion) and wisdom (emptiness). Guru Rinpoche (Padmasambhava) is frequently depicted holding these items, symbolizing his mastery over the indestructible nature of reality and enlightenment.

Symbolism and Use:

- Vajra (Method): Represents compassion and skillful means, functioning as a "diamond scepter" that represents indestructible awareness-energy.
- Bell (Wisdom): Represents the clear, space-like nature of wisdom, with its sound symbolizing the impermanence of phenomena arising from and returning to silence.
- Combined: Used together, they signify the union of the male (vajra) and female (bell) aspects, representing the ultimate realization of emptiness and bliss.
- Usage: They are employed in rituals to invoke deities, remove obstacles, and remind practitioners to connect with their own inherent enlightened nature.

Guru Rinpoche's Connection: *Guru Rinpoche*, or *Padmasambhava*, is the founder of Tibetan Buddhism and is often associated with the Vajra Guru mantra ("*OM AH HUNG VAJRA GURU PADMA SIDDHI HUM*"), which encapsulates the blessing of his enlightened mind, acting as a "*vajra*" in the form of sound. In his manifestation as Orgyen Dorje Chang, he is depicted holding these items, emphasizing his role as the ultimate holder of Vajrayana teachings.

Mantras (8 Offerings) done with Hand Mudras and/or Vajra and Bell by Thupten Donyo

- **Om Argham Ah Hum** Water for Drinking; **Om Padyam Ah Hum** Water for Washing;
- **Om Pupe Ah Hum** Flower; **Om Dhupe Ah Hum** Incense; **Om Aloke Ah Hum** Light; **Om Ghande Ah Hum** Perfume; **Om Neude Ah Hum** Food; **Om Shapta Ah Hum** Music

The Damaru (Hand Drum) The damaru is a small, double-sided hourglass drum. It represents the "sound of Sunyata" (emptiness) and the rhythm of the cosmic heartbeat. In tantric practice, its sound is used to summon enlightened wrathful deities and cut through mental delusions. Chöd Damaru, a larger version is used specifically in the Chöd practice to symbolize the impermanence of the body and the ego. The Chod Damaru is considered to be the dwelling place of the divine feminine, Dakini, a Tantric princess and muse for spiritual practice, therefore, playing the Chod Damaru summons the *kundalini* of a Tantric princess. Damaru's particular rhythm calms the mind, activates the chakras.

In Vajrayana Buddhism, the **damaru** (hand drum), bell (ghanta), and vajra (dorje) are essential ritual instruments that symbolize the path to enlightenment through the union of dualities. Practitioners often use these tools during sadhana (daily practice) or communal pujas to increase devotion and receive blessings from deities.

This mantra cultivates a sense of connection and alignment with the enlightened qualities and blessings of Vajrayogini. Mantra: **Oṃ Vajrayoginī Hūṃ Phaṭ Svāhā**

The primary reasons for practicing with the vajra and bell:

Symbolism of Inseparable Principles

- Vajra (Right Hand - Male): Represents skillful means (upaya), compassion, and the indestructibility of enlightenment, often likened to a diamond.
- Bell (Left Hand - Female): Represents wisdom (prajna), which understands the nature of emptiness (sunyata).
- The Union: The two are rarely separated because enlightenment requires the combination of both compassion (acting in the world) and wisdom (understanding the true nature of reality).

Tools for Meditation and Visualization

- Creating Sacred Space: The sound of the bell is believed to cleanse the environment, drive away negative energies, and invite blessings.
- Symbolizing Emptiness: The hollow of the bell represents the void from which all phenomena arise, while the sound represents the voice of the Buddha dharma.
- Focus and Energy: The rhythmic, intentional use of these tools helps to focus the mind, channel energy (prana), and deepen concentration, often used to bridge the gap between the practitioner and the enlightened state of a deity.

Transformation of the Mind

- Destroying Ignorance: The vajra symbolizes the power to break through ignorance, selfish ego, and delusions.
- Purification: Rituals involving these tools (like in tsok offerings or sadhana) help purify negative karma of body, speech, and mind.
- Generating Bliss: The combination of sound and symbolic action is intended to evoke the "*great bliss*" of non-dual awareness.

Representation of Buddha-Nature

- The Five Wisdoms: A five-pronged vajra represents the transformation of the five "poisons" (anger, greed, ignorance, pride, jealousy) into the five wisdoms of an enlightened mind.
- Body, Speech, and Mind: The items represent the body (bell), speech (sound), and mind (vajra) of the Buddha. In summary, the practice is a physical, auditory, and mental ritual used to constantly remind practitioners of their goal: to unite compassion and wisdom, transforming ordinary, ego-driven existence into the enlightened state of a Buddha.

Reference Books:

- *Daikini Teachings*: Padmasambhava's Oral Instructions to Yeshe Tsogyal; Revealed by Nyang Ral Nyima Oser and Sangye Lingpa, 1999.
- *The Lotus-Born: The Life Story of Padmasambhava*, Composed by Yeshe Tsogyal; Revealed by Nyang Ral Nyima Oser, 2004.
- *The Tibetan Book of the Dead*, Composed by Padmasambhava; Revealed by Terton Karma Lingpa; Translated by Gyurme Dorje, 2005.
- *The Tibetan Book of Living and Dying* by Sogyal Rinpoche, 1994.
- *The Joy of Living*: Unlocking the Secret and Science of Happiness by Mingyur Rinpoche, 2007.

The *Tibetan Book of the Dead* (Bardo Thödol) describes deities appearing in the intermediate state (bardo) between death and rebirth, which are actually projections of the mind, guiding the consciousness through visions of peaceful and wrathful figures (like Green Dzambhala, Ucchusma Vajra, Palden Lhamo, Vajrayogini, Mahakala, Vajrapani) representing aspects of our own consciousness to achieve liberation. These deities, often depicted in detailed mandalas, are not external gods but manifestations of the mind's luminous nature, meant to be recognized as such to avoid clinging and attain enlightenment, guiding the deceased (or living) through life's difficult moments and the final transition.

Key Deities & Concepts:

- Peaceful Deities: Represent pure, enlightened qualities, like Buddhas and Bodhisattvas, often appearing as manifestations of wisdom.
- Wrathful Deities: Fierce, often terrifying figures (like Dharmapalas) that embody powerful energies and negative emotions, meant to be seen as projections of inner fears, not external demons, to overcome attachment.

- The Great Liberation (Zab chos zhi khro dgongs pa rang grol): The larger text from which the Bardo Thödol comes, focusing on these peaceful and wrathful manifestations.
- Bardo States: The text details several "bardos," or intermediate states, including the bardo of dying, the bardo of ultimate reality, and the bardo of becoming (rebirth).

Purpose:

- *Guide for the Deceased*: To help consciousness navigate the confusion of the after-death state, recognize the true nature of mind, and achieve liberation from the cycle of rebirth (samsara). *Guide for the Living*: To prepare for death, overcome fear, and recognize the "deities" (inner experiences) of life and death as projections of the mind, fostering deeper self-awareness. *Practice Guru Yoga (Deity Yoga), page 154*

Origins: A Terma (hidden treasure) text revealed by Karma Lingpa (1326–1386). In essence, the deities in the *Tibetan Book of the Dead* are profound psychological and spiritual symbols, not anthropomorphic gods, serving as a map for the consciousness to find its way home to enlightenment.

Remember the pure clear white light from which everything in the universe comes, to which everything in the universe returns; the original nature of your own mind. The natural state of the universe unmanifest. Let go into the clear light, trust it, merge with it. It is your own true nature, it is home. – Tibetan Book of the Dead

The Tibetan Book of Living and Dying says that death is the graduation ceremony, while living is just a long course in learning and preparing for the next journey. If we acknowledge death as the beginning, then how can we fear it? – Nikki Sixx

Quotes by Guru Rinpoche and other Rinpoches: "*Only those who honor the guru, treasure the dharma and practice diligently shall attain enlightenment.*" - Guru Rinpoche

Do not investigate the root of things, investigate the root of Mind. Once the root of Mind is found, you will know the one thing that liberates all. – Guru Rinpoche

May all sentient beings be endowed with happiness. May they all be separated from suffering and its causes. May they be endowed with joy, free from suffering. May they abide in equanimity, free from attachment and aversion. – Guru Rinpoche

I am present in front of anyone who has faith in me, just as the moon casts its reflection, effortlessly, in any vessel filled with water. – Guru Rinpoche; Padmasambhava said: When a disciple calls upon me with yearning devotion, and with the melodious song of the Seven-line *prayer, I shall come straightaway from Zangdokpalri, like a mother who cannot resist the call of her child. – Dongse Garab Rinpoche*

The one who has the greatest compassion and blessing towards beings in this difficult age is Padmasambhava, who embodies the compassion and wisdom of all the buddhas. One of his qualities is that he has the power to give his blessing instantly to whoever prays to him, and whatever we may pray for, he has the power to grant our wish immediately. – Dilgo Khyentse Rinpoche

When realization occurs you should definitely be free from samsara, so that your disturbing emotions naturally subside and become original wakefulness. What is the use of realization that fails to reduce your disturbing emotions? – Guru Rinpoche

Buddha was asked, "*What have you gained from meditation?*" He replied, "*Nothing! However, let me tell you what I lost: Anger, Anxiety, Depression, Insecurity, Fear of old age and death.*"

In the Path of Liberation, all the Vajrayana teachings are given step by step. There are five levels, all of which explore the unity of awareness, love and compassion, and wisdom, which is within you and is what we call the "nature of mind." By doing that, if you really practice again and again, then it becomes a deeper spiritual journey. And in the end, it can lead you to full enlightenment. - Mingyur Rinpoche, Ricardo B Serano's Vajrayana teacher

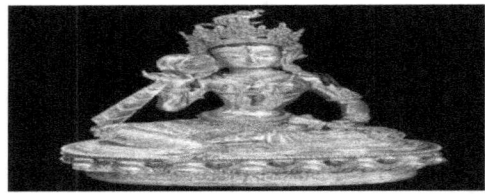 

Vajrayogini practicing ChodDamaru ,Bell **Chod practitioners at Boudhanath stupa,** page 160

Red Vajrayogini *oṃ oṃ oṃ sarvabuddhaḍākiṇīye vajra varṇanīye vajra vairocanīye hūṃ hūṃ hūṃ phaṭ phaṭ phaṭ svāhā* **Om Vajrayogini Hum Phat Svaha**

Om Kroma Dakini Namo Hum Phat, Om Tadyata Gate Gate Paragate Parasamgate Bodhi Svaha - Troma Nagmo and Prajna Paramita Mantras accompany Vajrayogini Mantra
White beams of light are visualized to support well-being, purify all sickness and negative karma. The main role of Vajrayogini is to aid us to recognize our buddha nature.

Understanding the Vajrayogini Mantra Meaning The *Vajrayogini* is a tantric deity in Tibetan Buddhism who represents the path that leads to Buddhahood. She is regarded as the goddess of grace as well as destruction as she destroys the illusions of the ego. *Vajrayogini* is a 16-year-old female dakini embodying divine wisdom. She is a feisty manifestation of the divine feminine.

There are several representations of *Vajrayogini*, but she is mostly depicted as a young and naked tantric deity, blood red (representing her inner fire), wearing ornaments of the human skeleton, a necklace of skulls (representing 16 vowels and 32 consonants that symbolizes purity of speech).

This *Vajrayogini* mantra holds immense significance in Tibetan Buddhism. It comes from Anuttara Yoga tantra and should be recited with proper guidance and instructions. Like any other Tibetan Buddhist mantra; this *Vajrayogini* mantra can be a powerful tool for self-transformation, healing and liberation from samsara. See *photo of Chod Damaru and bell practitioner chanting Vajrayogini mantra.*

om om om sarva buddha dakiniyé vajra varnaniye vajra vairocaniyé hum hum hum phat phat phat soha; oṃ va jra yo gi nī hūṃ phaṭ svā hā oṃ vajrayoginī hūṃ phaṭ svāhā

According to the Vajrayarahi tantra, after understanding this mantra, if one recites it 36 times every day, they can benefit from this not only in this lifetime but at the bardo state and lifetimes after that as well. Chant with Wrathful Black Mother *Om Khrodha Kali Troma Nagmo Ram Svaha*

Each syllable and word in this mantra holds meaning and significance.

- **OM**- *Om is a sacred syllable regarded as the universal sound. Om is indicative of the nature of the consciousness or the ultimate reality.*
- ***Vajrayogini***: *Vajrayogini is a fierce goddess embodying divine wisdom.*
- ***Hum-Hum*** *is a seed syllable that is associated with Vajrayogini. This syllable is indicative of essence and her power. This is used to invoke her presence, blessings.*
- ***Phat-Phat*** *is a dynamic syllable used as a shield against negative forces and dispels obstacles along the way.*
- ***Svaha***: *This is a commonly used syllable in Buddhism and Hinduism. This is used to seal the mantra and make an offering towards the deity while expressing one's dedication and surrender.*

Awakening Energy: Vajrayogini practices are deeply connected to the awakening of spiritual energy, often referred to as Kundalini Shakti in tantric contexts.

The Subtle Body (Vajra Nadi): Vajrayogini practices activate and direct this energy through the central channel of the body, known as the sushumna in Kundalini yoga or the vajra nadi in Tantric Buddhism.

As a Vajrayana practitioner, I practice daily Vajrayogini mantra as Guru (Deity) Yoga with Chod Damaru and Bell for efficacious healing and transformation. – Ricardo B Serrano

"Therefore, a method such as this, which has the wisdom to transform delusions, is of the utmost need, especially as it has the profound property of becoming more powerful as delusions get more stronger." - Lama Yeshe

Embodiment of Cognitive functions Vajrayogini is also known as Vajravarahi in Vajrayana or Tantric Buddhism. And who is Vajrayogini? To put the answer simply, the female embodiment of the cognitive functions that lead to Buddhahood is in fact Vajrayogini herself. Vajrayogini practice has always emphasized experience over speculation. *Red Form and Bliss*: She is commonly depicted in a vibrant red color, which symbolizes the transformation of desire into enlightened awareness, and she is often surrounded by fire, symbolizing the fire of wisdom consuming ignorance. Vajrayogini is often considered an "*enlightened Dakini*" or a "*Female Buddha*" rather than just a deity, representing the ultimate, non-dual wisdom of the Buddhas.

Vajrayogini in this Dissipated Times Of all the Vajrayana meditative deities, Vajrayogini is credited with being the one practice for our busy, hectic, terrifying times, among all the other Vajrayana meditative deities. It can ultimately lead us, in one lifetime, to Enlightenment. Her visualization, appearance, mantra and sadhana are all intrinsically designed to combat our modern obstacles. More precisely, the obstacles of our dissipated times. In our modern age, life is very hectic, we have no time.

Life is always in the way of practice, and we struggle with many fears, including but not limited to, terrorism, global warming, wars, capitalism, paying the bills, healing our sickness, etc. Her practice will not only free us from the prisons of our minds but will actually help us look into and understand the inherent flaws of our socio-political superstructure and to actively resist its ideological submission. By not adhering to the norms or confirming this ideology, we will have separated ourselves from its illusions and will finally get rid of our delusions.

The source Tantra, in the condensed Root Tantra of Heruka, explains there are **ten key spiritual benefits** to practice, many not available from other practices:
1. Easy to practice: although a Highest Yoga Tantric practice, the visualizations of the mandala is relatively easy, the sadhanas are relatively short, and the mantra is relatively easy.

2. Ideal for this degenerate age: Unlike other practices, Vajrayogini brings fast benefits, since Heruka and her mandalas are closer to us than other deities.
3. Vajrayogini's mantra is supreme for attainments. Although somewhat long, it is easy to memorize. It is said that Vajrayogini's mantra alone is all a practitioner would ever need, provided they have faith.
4. Powerful blessings: not just blessings, but quick blessings.
5. Can accomplish all attainments: many of the great mahasiddhas accomplished enlightenment and other realizations from her practice.
6. Can practice both generation and completion stage together: if you don't know what this means, teacher guidance is best.
7. Overcome attachments: sensous nature and red color signify she is suitable for overcoming desires and cutting attachments, hence her flaying knife.
8. Vajrayogini practice contains the essence of all practices even though it is short in nature.
9. Uncommon Yoga of Inconceivability. Pure Land Rebirth: It offers the benefit of being born in a pure land (like Khechara) without needing to leave one's body, which is a powerful incentive for dedicated practitioners.
10. Special body mandala practice. Inner Wisdom and Bliss: Vajrayogini symbolizes the union of profound emptiness and great bliss, promoting mental clarity and deep spiritual experience.

Practicing Vajrayogini Vajrayogini practice and Vajrayogini mantra is one of the Highest Yoga Tantra that requires both permission and empowerment. It is not exclusive, and anyone can honor, pray to and meditate on her as an external deity. However, without initiation, one is not permitted to visualize the self as Vajrayogini and probably not chant the mantra. Still. one can come closer to Vajrayogini enlightened qualities through praise, offerings and prayers, but it goes without empowerments.

Unlike other meditations, the nature of Vajrayogini practice is very energetic. And even though it is designed to deal with the high pace of degenerate times, it does require some guidance from a qualified teacher with proven lineage is the best path to Vajrayogini. *Source*: LamaYeshe.com and Tharpa.com

Mahasthamaprapta, Amitabha, Avalokiteshvara - Prajnaparamita - Om Ah Hum Vajra Guru Padma Siddhi Hum

About Author As a seeker of enlightenment and healing, my path includes Liu He Ba Fa, Wuji Quan, Shaktipat meditation, Merkaba meditation, chanting So Ham, Om Namah Shivaya, Da Bei Zhou, Heart Sutra, Om Mani Padme Hum, Vajrayogini mantra, Hanuman Qigong, Wuji Qigong.

- I would also like to thank my teachers Alton Kamadon, Master Li Jun Feng, Master Faye Li Yip, Master Zhi Gang Sha, Michael Winn and Guruji Amritananda Natha with Bhagawan Nityananda. I would also like to thank Master Chenhan Yang for his Wuji Quan instruction and Master Helen Liang for her Liu He Ba Fa.
- Alton Kamadon taught me Merkaba meditation which activates the hologram of love Merkaba expanding it to connect with Cosmic Consciousness all around the universe so I can facilitate Merkaba meditation for healing and transformation. *Om Tare Tuttare Ture Soha*
- Master Li Jun Feng taught me Hanuman Qigong, Kuan Yin Qigong, Jesus Qigong and Taoist Qigong which opened my heart to the unconditional love of the universe for healing and enlightenment. Michael Winn's Wuji Qigong (Tai Chi for enlightenment) by Chang San-feng is practiced also. Chang San-feng's Wuji Quan is passed down by Vancouver's Shouyu Liang. The 5 Tibetan rites was taught to me by Master Nona Castro.
- Master Faye Li Yip taught me Six healing Qigong and Ba Duan Jin Qigong for healing and transformation. Master Zhi Gang Sha and his certified teachers taught me Taoist meditation and Buddhist meditation that included chanting Da Bei Zhou, Om mani Padme Hum and Heart Sutra mantras, Tao songs, Soul Healing, Love Peace Harmony song, Tao Healing Hands Mantra of Avalokiteshvara, Amituofo and Soul Communication for healing & transformation.
- Lastly, I was taught Sri Devi, Om Namah Shivaya mantras by my Guruji Amritananda Natha, Baba Muktananda together with Nityananda's grace bestowing power for Shaktipat meditation by Om Namah Shivaya mantra. Mingyur Rinpoche together with Lama Tantrapa, my Qi Dao teacher, taught me about Guru Rinpoche, Guru (Deity) Yoga.

This book together with my other nine books are a result of my healing and spiritual enlightenment experiences because of my meditation, 5 Tibetan rites, Qigong, Tai Chi and Vajrayana practices taught by my teachers and are dedicated to my teachers and students.
– Master Ricardo B. Serrano, Dipl.Ac., Liu He Ba Fa, Wuji Quan and Qigong teacher/soul healer

www.ingramcontent.com/pod-product-compliance
Lightning Source LLC
Chambersburg PA
CBHW082204230426
43672CB00015B/2898